# PSYCHOANALYSIS AND
# THE CHALLENGE OF ISLAM

# PSYCHOANALYSIS
# AND THE CHALLENGE
# OF ISLAM

Fethi Benslama

*Translated by Robert Bononno*

University of Minnesota Press
Minneapolis • London

Poetry by Rainer Maria Rilke in chapter 1 is quoted from Rainer Maria Rilke, *Duino Elegies,* translated by Robert Hunter (Eugene, Ore.: Hulogosi Communications, Inc., 1987).

Postscript to chapter 1 was originally published as "Islam: What Humiliation?" in *Le Monde,* November 27, 2001.

*Psychoanalysis and the Challenge of Islam* was originally published in French as *La psychanalyse à l'épreuve de l'Islam.* Copyright Editions Aubier Montaigne, 2002.

English translation copyright 2009 by Robert Bononno

Published by the University of Minnesota Press
111 Third Avenue South, Suite 290
Minneapolis, MN 55401-2520
http://www.upress.umn.edu

Library of Congress Cataloging-in-Publication Data

Benslama, Fethi.
 [La psychanalyse à l'epreuve de l'Islam]
 Psychoanalysis and the challenge of Islam / Fethi Benslama ; translated by Robert Bononno.
  p.   cm.
 Includes bibliographical references and index.
 ISBN 978-0-8166-4888-7 (hc : alk. paper) — ISBN 978-0-8166-4889-4 (pb : alk. paper)
  1. Islam — Psychology.   I. Title.
 BP175.B46    2009
 297.2'61 — dc22                                      2009006987


Printed in the United States of America on acid-free paper

The University of Minnesota is an equal-opportunity educator and employer.

16 15 14 13 12 11 10 09      10 9 8 7 6 5 4 3 2 1

# Contents

# Preface

Sigmund Freud, throughout an extensive body of work in which religion is omnipresent, refers to Islam directly only in his discussion of monotheism. The reference occurs in his last book, *Moses and Monotheism*, but he quickly dismisses Islam as a subject for further investigation. Yet Freud's theory of religion, aside from the study of purely religious phenomena, raises questions about the foundation of human society, the genesis of the law, and the chronic crisis of civilization. What would happen if, a century after Freud, we were to integrate into this vast scaffolding the primal fictions of Islam and the workings of its symbolic systems? How has the monotheistic memory embodied in the oral and written histories of its foundation been reworked? Do they reveal a different way of looking at the role of the father and questions of origin, which have remained undecipherable when viewed from the perspectives of Judaism and Christianity alone?

This book extends to Islam Freud's project of exposing the repression on which religious institutions are based and undertakes to translate their metaphysics into metapsychology. It takes a psychoanalytic approach to texts and events that have assumed pride of place for this religion, in correlation with the origin of the two other monotheistic religions.

Clearly, this type of research would have been inconceivable if Islam (which for years fell outside the scope of modern investigation, assigned, as it was, to the backwaters of orientalism) hadn't erupted onto the world stage, forcing us to explain ourselves along with it, spurred on by the senses of urgency and necessity that are closely related to Islam's access to the modern condition. Far from just beginning, this access has entered a decisive phase: the emergence in Islamic societies of a subject that differs from the subject of tradition, one that has precipitated into a form of historical action that overflows the field of consciousness. It is this circumstance, and the disruptions and contradictions of which it is the result, that prompted my investigation.

That is why this book, although it involves an exploration of the structure of the origins of Islam, must confront the heart of its tormented present. The first chapter, "The Torment of Origin," is devoted to the contemporary crisis of Islam, an approach to its genesis and most symptomatic manifestation (the Islamist movement), whose interpretation as I present it differs from that customarily found in political sociology.

Islam's ongoing importance during the past fifteen years reveals, in a thousand different ways, the break with the subject of tradition and the release of destructive forces that flow directly from that break. The process is one of historical mutation, wherein the transition of man from the psyche of god to the psyche of the unconscious must be conceptualized. This movement justifies the title of this book, *Psychoanalysis and the Challenge of Islam.* I wanted this title to refer to a challenge, to a responsibility that I have recognized as my own for many years, during the course of which I have written a number of essays that are here assembled into a coherent whole. Of course, I could also have titled my book *Islam and the Challenge of Psychoanalysis,* but I began to investigate Islam as a psychoanalyst and through psychoanalysis. In doing so, I have attempted to identify certain problems associated with contemporary Islam and its origins, examining them through the eyes of our universal psychoanalytic knowledge concerning the relationship between psyche and civilization.

To examine the transition from the psyche of god to that of the unconscious does not imply the abolition of the past, which it is not in our power to ordain, but consists in investigating a relationship to the past, an interpretive relationship that assumes that we can access the older interpretations and the assumptions on which they are based. Given that symbolic systems and, more particularly, religion are under scrutiny, the psychoanalyst considers that the power of the fundamental apriority is a function of repression. It is what resides in the unconscious that forces mankind to bend to its empire.

Although unintentional, my research gradually and irresistibly led me toward the role of women, the feminine, and femininity in the repressive processes that underlie the symbolic and institutional structure of Islam. The majority of the book is devoted to this question, which is examined more fully in chapter 2, "The Repudiation of Origin," and chapter 3, "Destinies of the Other Woman." In exposing the question of the feminine coincident with the origin of Islam, and in examining the continuity of its syntax at a given moment, a moment here referred to as "*The Arabian Nights* as Clinic," a shift occurs. This shift is examined in chapter 4, "Within Himself," where my analysis concentrates on the problematic of masculine narcissism and the attempt to resolve its dead ends and violence — the central issue in the elaboration of monotheistic culture.

Naturally, the issues covered by this research are not all specific to Islam. The intersections between European culture and Islamic culture are manifold, assuming we understand them in both senses of the Latin *intersectio,* that is, as a point that is simultaneously encounter and division. Were I to limit myself to the specificity of Islam, I would fall into the trap of a differentialist essentialism; conversely, if the universal were not confronted by concrete actualities, the reverberations of alterity, I would risk the fallacy of an abstract universalism.

This challenge is important to psychoanalysis to the extent that its transmission throughout the Islamic world — which is beginning to assume importance on the individual and group level and, in some cases, through the establishment of specific institutions[1] — will raise new questions and problems, because the shift of psychoanalytic interest is occurring outside its traditional historical and anthropological domains, in Europe and America.

This challenge is important, as well, to the women and men of the Islamic world. They are now confronted with a mutation of critical subjectivity for which a knowledge and experience of psychoanalysis are going to provide possibilities and opportunities within the long process of the formation of the modern subject and what Freud called the "cultural work" *(Kulturarbeit)* of which the modern subject is a corollary. This importance is based, in my understanding, on the axiom that the metapsychological translation that Freud took to be one of the tasks of psychoanalysis is not a simple application of theory. Freud radically reconceptualized theory as a form of *deconstruction,* given that he employs terms such as *auflösen* (to dissolve, to untie, to undo mythological conceptions of the world) and *umsetzen* (to convert, transpose, shift).[2] These operations, which affect the architecture of mythotheologic structures, are used to comprehend the workings of their invisible foundations and to discover, in the face of such formations, the kernel of the impossible around which language forms an imaginary shell, a projection of the psyche toward the external world. If this book is able to contribute to this conjunction of interests and expectations, it will have achieved its goal.

# 1

# The Torment of Origin

## Transgression

Islam has never been a major concern for me or my generation. It was because Islam began to take an interest in us that I decided to take an interest in it. This generation, which finally opened its eyes with the end of colonialism and the establishment of national governments, thought it had seen the end of religion and that religion would no longer be an element in the organization of political life. Although it had helped mobilize the uprising against the occupier, we saw it as responsible for having dragged our world into darkness for centuries on end, a torpor from which we were awakened by the hubbub of the European armies of occupation. The cry of the poet Aboul Kacem Chebbi informed us of the cause of our misfortunes: "Oh people, you are like a small child / who plays with sand in the darkness / a force chained by shadows since the dawn of time."[1] From Chebbi we learned that our shadowy chains were those of religion, the oppressive guardian of a destiny that was deaf to the appeal of the living, for it understood only the language of the grave. In the face of fanaticism ("Take this wretched heretic from the temple"), the political response consisted in taking the temple from us. By the early 1960s, the Tunisian Habib Bourguiba had begun the process: he closed the large theological university of Zitouna, nearly three thousand years old, scattered its teachers across the country, and, most humiliating of all, transferred them to secondary schools.[2] At the same time, he initiated the revolution in women's rights: equality of legal and political status with men, the abolition of repudiation and polygamy, and the removal of the obligation to wear the veil. He completely restructured the Islamic law of filiation, by introducing the possibility of full adoption, including the modification of the adopted child's civil status.[3] In the middle of the month of Ramadan, before the television cameras, he drank to the health of his people.

1

Today it may be difficult to estimate the audacity of Bourguiba's gesture. His image circulated for years throughout the Arab world, still impregnated by religious law. He was bitterly criticized and cursed, and the imams were shocked. Bourguiba's gesture assumed the value of a radical transgression, one that produced a split in people's way of thinking, a point at which the possible and the impossible suddenly came together. With their appearance in the 1970s, the so-called Islamist movements considered Bourguiba's gesture to be a prime example of the absolute impiety whose elimination justified their presence. This was not the act of someone who violated a religious proscription by transgressing its rules and its sanctions for his own benefit. Rather, this was a political affirmation that publicly interrupted sacred temporality, which had been regulated by immutable rite. It declared that the people were now free from theological subjection and introduced the arrival of a new era within the very center of the fracture. Bourguiba's theatrical thirst, slaked during the torpor of the fast, was far more significant than all the speeches about freedom and all the promises of liberation. It was the kind of transgressive act that Georges Bataille might have referred to as "sovereign," to the extent that it was focused not on a particular object but on a time within which all objects move.

It is clear that this transgression created an event that affected my entire generation, in spite of disagreements with certain aspects of Bourguiba's government. We were far from comprehending the full implications of this decision: the replacement of a normative system, Islam and its subject, with other underpinnings and a new legality. We were unable to understand that the interruption of tradition brought with it an element of danger, a period during which a range of passions and forces was to be unleashed.

At the time, the transgression succeeded in stirring up, primarily among adolescents, who were discovering the irreverence of the modern world, what constitutes in my sense the most powerful desire that modernity has managed to create: the desire to be an other, sustained by the effectiveness of technology and its discourse. Who was this other? Marx's revolutionary? Freud's unconscious subject? Sade's libertine? Ségalen's "exote"? Rimbaud's verbal alchemist? A universalist? A citizen of the world? He was all of them at the same time, assembled of bits and pieces gleaned from secondhand information, for we were unfamiliar with the texts to which these concepts and names referred. But their atoms were present in the very air we breathed.

It was only later, much later, that the full import of Bourguiba's act was understood. Understanding did not occur with the awareness of the danger represented by Islamist extremism, an awareness that was slow to form globally. It was only when we were forced to acknowledge what was happening to us, while the world was being asked to combat a phenomenon whose nature and foundations it misunderstood, that the full impact of his gesture was felt. I recall that in the speech Bourguiba gave at the time of his televised transgression, he justified his act not in the name of secularism, human rights, or the great principles of the Enlightenment but rather in the name of Islam itself! He said, in substance, that it was necessary to make the transition from a time of holy war (*jihad*) against colonialism, which was a secondary battle, to the more important struggle, the one directed inward (*ijtihad*), which involves meditation, a reassessment of the real, interpretation, and work. He wanted to convince the people that the month-long fasting ritual clashed with an effort that would last for the duration of the twentieth century. By adding two letters to the term *jihad,* the operation resulted not in legitimizing the break through an explicit reference to Western values but in creating an internal contradiction wherein Islam confronted Islam; where a form of Islam whose meaning is enclosed, which has no future (since the lack of a future assigns mankind a finite meaning), confronted another Islam, where nothing is accomplished because it demands an interminable internal effort, and where thought is directed toward the unknown. In the early 1980s, while reflecting upon my own intellectual responsibilities during a critical historical period marked by the growth of fanaticism and the extended resonance its demands provoked, I felt that I would do best to commit myself to considering the difference between a "finite Islam" and an "infinite Islam."

There is little doubt that the politician who undertook this internal subversion was inspired by the principles of the European struggle for freedom and had in mind their implementation at the beginning of the century in Kemal Atatürk's Turkey. Educated in a French university, Bourguiba was quite familiar with the language of universalist consciousness, but as a man of the people, with a political intelligence that had been acquired in concrete situations, he felt it necessary to employ his own language and its symbolic referents. That is why he inscribed his transgression within a process of *translation* rather than through a massive injection of European discourse. Through the interplay of letters, he called to mind an entire swath of the enlightened history of Islam, opening the way toward a conceivable future articulated in a language that all could understand, even if, here and there, there was resistance to his ideas.

Later, the task of transhistorical and transcultural translation, an essential condition of a politics of modernity, needed for "continuity in the mental life of successive generations," as Freud put it (*Totem and Taboo* [1912–1913], *SE*, 13:158), would disappear beneath the twofold burden of the rapid extension of technology and the mechanics of "expropriation" of global capitalism. It was as if the peoples who had emerged into the modern world were unable to live out their present experience through an accessible language; they no longer had the ability to make meaningful connections through their idioms but were forced to undergo the physical transformations of their world and the harassment of so-called Western discourse without alteration. From within and without there arose a class of fearsome "experts" claiming to operate directly on the real in all areas of knowledge, mouthing collectivist or liberal platitudes; experts who gave lessons, issued orders, dismantled. The prosaism of their jargon, which claimed to be both scientific and universal, asserted that it contained an intangible truth providing immediate access to a radiant tomorrow. In the name of development, the transition to the modern involved aimless wandering in the unthinkable.

This effort toward the widespread liquidation of speech and political meaning went on for two decades and produced a state of generalized ignorance. Falsehoods became commonplace. The field was ready for Islamist speech and its extreme representations. Having come on the scene with a moralizing language that implicated the body and our anxieties about existence, Islamists erected a monolithic Islam free of internal contradiction; they polarized the opposition between Islam and the West and announced their intent to restore what was proper (in both senses: the exclusive and the immaculate) through another form of immediacy, that of access to the "originary plenitude of politics." This was the promise of a return to the golden age of the founding of Islam, when the beginning and the commandment were united in a single principle in the hands of, first, the Prophet-founder-legislator, then his four successors. This period was assumed to have been one of ideal justice on Earth, before the fall into the division and internal sedition (*fitna*) that the community would later experience.[4]

One of the causes of Islamist extremism is the catastrophic collapse of language: language was no longer able to translate for people a particularly intense historical experience, that of the modern era, which entails not only the scientific and industrial transformation of the world but also the conjunction between this furious power of transformation and the desire to be an other. Yet "Islamist" extremism is driven by an impulse, and this impulse is simply the inverse of the desire to be an other: "the despair that wills to be Itself," as Kierkegaard expressed it.[5] What is this Self? Its identity is defined by its origin, and its origin is bound by a framework of unique features: one religion (Islam), one language (Arabic), and one text (the Koran), to which is often added the national anthem here and there. The modern era replaced the desire to be an other with the despair that wills to be itself, enclosing us in a confrontation each of whose terms represents the impossible.

## Return and Detours

### Islam and Islams

Awareness of an "Islamist" presence was very slow to take shape. A great deal of time was needed to abandon belief in a linear path toward progress, to acknowledge that this was not a passing phenomenon, and to begin to realize what was taking place. It is important to bear in mind the human factor underlying these events. Behind the words *Islam* and *Islamism* exists a multiform reality of a billion people on several continents, made up of societies that are extremely different and that crisscross heterogeneous cultural regions which sometimes do not communicate with one another. In this sense, one can speak of various Islams behind Islam, given that the diversity of languages, traditions, and histories has created significant regional and local specificities. Whether in Asia with its Indian, Pakistani, Afghan, and Indonesian components; Africa with the Maghreb in the north and the "Black Continent" south of the Sahara; Europe with Turkey and its Slavic extensions and the peoples of the former Soviet Union; or the Middle East, along with Iran and the Arab world — which constitutes only a minor part of this vast whole — everywhere it exists Islam has been grafted onto existing cultures that it has not sought to eradicate but to which it has attempted to acclimatize itself, allowing itself to be transformed by them, except for an invariable theological and judicial core.

And yet, in spite of this diversity and the vast size of the geopolitical and cultural spaces involved, all were affected by a movement that seriously disturbed a significant part of tradition and its conservative adepts, pushing a number of them toward what has been variously called

"Islamism," "Islamist movements," "fundamentalism," "Islamic radical-ism," or "religious extremism." The proliferation of names in this context, under the impulse of a new political sociology of Islam that was often in a hurry to keep pace with current events, at least superficially, has not helped to clarify the situation. On the contrary, it has strengthened what I refer to as the resistance to the intelligibility of Islam. This arises from an old repulsive force in the history of western Europe, against which the insights of Islamic scholars, in spite of their accumulated knowledge, have proved powerless. In the recent past, the ignorance has even increased, finding new pretexts in our tortured present. Psychoanalysts are no less culpable, Freud first of all.

We cannot overcome such resistance to intelligibility by arbitrarily establishing the meaning of terms whose usage has been unregulated along several dimensions. This problem of naming, with the confusion of thought it implies, is too serious a symptom of the internal upheavals within Islam and the chronic crisis of its relationship to what is referred to as "the West" to simply dismiss it as a bad habit or a misuse of lan-guage. In this chapter I want to gradually establish my arguments by considering the scope of meaning of the obstacle. For now it is sufficient to recall four aspects of the signifier *Islam* that we need to keep in mind when we encounter the word. Two of them are fundamental elements: the Muslim religion as faith, dogma, and rite, anchored in the phenome-non of revelation found in the Koran and the tradition of the Prophet's words and deeds; and Muslims in their diversity, considering their ways of life, their cultures, and their differences of sensibility and opinion. To these fundamental elements must be added two forces that are particu-larly relevant at this time. One is the fundamentalist current, which has always existed and which mandates the strict application of Islamic di-rectives, with reference to the original message. This is the conservative and harsh face of Islam, which claims to be timeless and rejects literature, music, and poetry, and which does not seek to control the state apparatus but, on the contrary, maintains its distance, sometimes its complete sepa-ration, from the state. The other force is political movements that want to control the state, considering Islam to be not only a religion but also an ideology and a system of government. Their project aims at the complete Islamicization of society and the creation of an Islamic state. It is such move-ments, of varying degrees of radicality and violence, that forced them-selves into public view during the 1970s. Obviously, other forces exist, such as traditionalists, reformists, and secularists, but none of them has reflected the despair of the masses as much as Islamist political militants.

Interferences exist among these four aspects of the term *Islam,* and they must be analyzed with considerable caution. But we cannot merge these four different elements into the concept of Islamism without losing our ability to make fine distinctions. It is because Muslims, at least in most countries, have not confused the religious institution of Islam with its heterogeneous human reality, or fundamentalism with political militancy, that despair and terror have not swept everything away in their path.

Of course, not every country experienced the transformations and public displays established by Bourguiba; far from it. Similarly, the virulence and extent of the phenomenon vary with context, being a function of the scope of economic and political violence, social reform, and the "plastic force" of each people, as Nietzsche put it. But the fact that similar protests broke out across the extent of the Muslim world implies that a single shock wave made its way through a single substructure.

When one has witnessed the furious dislocation of a world that has been illuminated by the promise of freedom; when every day brings with it a whirlwind of anger and violence in the name of faith; when one witnesses previously stable men and women burst into imprecations that express a crushing feeling of guilt and fear before their god, as if they had been charged with capital crimes, the idea arises that something vital has been affected, something capable of bringing into being a sense of political despair that will manifest itself in mass outbreaks or exhaust itself in revenge and murder. How can we conceptualize this disturbance and its devastating effects?

## *The Psychoanalytic Angle*

Caught up in the turmoil of events that have brought their share of drama and disillusionment, my interest in psychoanalysis has been entirely transformed. From psychoanalysis as a personal adventure, a form of research limited to "individual psychology," I have adopted a much broader perspective. I have been led to place my ideas within a political context, in the fundamental sense of the word, and to establish a close and continuous relationship with Freud's writings on civilization and its discontents, and on group psychology, religion, and the origins of society. In the face of the unparalleled drama of events, the day-to-day relevance of Islam demanded a continuous effort of analysis and interpretation. One need only recall some of the major crises experienced during the last ten years: the Rushdie affair; the first Gulf War; Bosnia; Algeria; the chronic Israeli-Palestinian conflict; the logic of intimidation and terror that fanaticism has brought about, including the wearing of the veil; fatwas; the murder of intellectuals; and the massacre of civilians.

The current reality of Islam forced me — forced us, I should say, namely the editorial staff of *Cahiers Intersignes*[6] — to recognize an extraordinary experience melding the unconscious and politics during a period of accelerated global transformation. This took place within a civilizational buffer where everyone encountered the other both in reality and in imagination, against a background of historical contest that had been reactualized by relations of interdependence whose logic and focus were diverse. It is an understatement to claim that this situation created a series of contradictions and paradoxes, forcing us to continuously shift and reverse our position and to anticipate multiple points of view, sometimes culminating in the undecidable, a possible temptation — whether misfortune or lucidity — for the psychic being in the era of globalization.

Simultaneously, in my clinical practice and in daily life, I was forced to acknowledge that, for subjects who had been raised in the Islamic tradition, one could not avoid the reference to Islam in the approach to the unconscious, especially given the painful reality of fundamentalist activism and political militancy. This does not imply that Islam was in any way complicit with the culturalism I had previously criticized and whose shortcomings I had discussed. I simply realized that, for many people, Islam was still implicated in subjective and transindividual structures. The distance between politics and religion was inconsistent, even illusory, because it lacked the effort of separation that would have introduced the possibility of release, as well as repression, just as it had in Europe over the course of several centuries. At best, there was a demarcation that did not result in any new imprinting. The "revolution in modern interpreting," to borrow an expression from Pierre Legendre, had not taken place. Religion was not making a return, because it had never gone away. Worse yet, like someone who has been artificially put to sleep, Islam awoke with a start and glared at the world from the depths of its somnambulism.

In fact, while an elite thought it had full access to modernity, that it had traced the outlines of free thought, the minarets were rising and their shadows growing. Modernization was no more than an imitation (not mimesis) of the modern through which a trompe l'oeil decor was constructed.

This cruel and suffocating fact (although we will need to refine our analysis of it) took shape only five years before the Rushdie affair (1989), certainly one of the most symptomatic events of the contemporary world and one of its most serious challenges. It came as a kind of rude awakening, and its consequences had to be faced. These were theoretical and practical, political and psychoanalytic, particularly with regard to the commitment of an intellectual project that led to an investigation of the question of origins in Islam, where psychoanalysis was challenged, both clinically and theoretically, when it found itself transported to a cultural context different from the one in which it had taken shape.

Transport of psychoanalysis, transport with psychoanalysis — I found myself returning to the mythic site of origins even while, through my geographic and cultural move to Europe, I thought I could escape it, drawn by the desire for a different kind of knowledge. Have I ever gotten over this quirk of history, or my astonishment in the face of what had returned or of that to which I was returning? It was a return that never materialized, however, because the Islam I plan to investigate here will never again be the Islam of my heritage but an Islam interpreted through the problematic of the unconscious. The event that signaled its appearance on the public scene was the conference "La psychanalyse aux abords de l'Islam," organized at the Collège international de philosophie in May 1987.[7]

## The Torment of Origin

Why this shift *toward* an origin, which is also a shift *of* origin? I want to rapidly review the reasons for my personal involvement. A subject cannot sidestep the order of "historical truth" (which is how Freud referred to the "truth quotient" in religion) that has determined his childhood without its coming back to haunt him in one way or another. The challenge is to transform this truth of origin into a truth of provenance; in other words, to welcome it and recognize its imaginary and symbolic genesis so as to be able to conceptualize the field of actualizations it delineates.

As soon as I began to pay attention to the language of Islamist speech, I realized it was haunted by the question of origins. Its proponents gradually succeeded in attracting the masses through a promise that did not hold any expectations for the future but, rather, incorporated a regression to some distant past, when time was an identical repetition of what had already taken place during Islam's foundation.

This attempt to attract the masses to a point of origin was sometimes received with shock and incredulity, but it produced a hypnotic state that subjugated many members of the working and middle classes. It justified an infantile disposition of memory, an anachronism in which the archaic and the ideal noisily shared the public stage. Manifestations of the abject were multiplied — physically, in modes of dress, and in forms of group behavior — as if mildew were a guarantee of authenticity. Language became the tireless repetition of ancestral bromides. Some even felt it was unfair that they had been born into the modern world. They adopted what they assumed were the words, gestures, and attitudes of those who had lived "at the dawn of Islam." The present was constantly compared to a distant past and perceived as a palimpsest of that past, which, in floating back to the surface of lived time, submerged the present.

One may be tempted to laugh off this ridiculous "remake of the real," except that the observer is soon reminded of the danger inherent in this quest for origin, for it brings with it feelings of injustice, humiliation, and hatred — a growing howl of resentments. The urge to return to one's origins is accompanied by a terrifying wish for vengeance in the present. Social and mental poverty were signs of having deserted one's origin, which suffered from having been cut off from the sweep of a history it had made possible. People were told that, separated from the source, they were participating in its pollution, and that their present misfortunes were simply the well-deserved penalty for the crime of distancing themselves from their beginnings. Their being found its rationale exclusively in the reappropriation of the essence, or "proper" *(propre)*, of what they had been. This conjunction between the immaculate and the exclusive, between possession and cleanliness, between belonging and purity that the concept harbors is indicative of the salvation this ideology promised and, consequently, of the threat it posed.

What do this political desire for origin and the terror that accompanies it signify? What is the meaning of this return to primal scenes and the death match surrounding them, conducted in their name? How do we interpret this desire for exile from the present, a future reduced to a concluded past about which nothing new can be said, so that the present is no more than a shadow of what has already occurred? Isn't this withdrawal of becoming the zero point of messianism, its reversal or possibly the collapse of perspective, something religion has always tried to maintain?

I felt that the psychoanalytic position I had been trying to sustain would make sense in this critical situation only if it were directed at the "torment of origin" that we had begun to experience and that continues even today.[8] Of course, it was necessary to approach this situation as the symptomatic expression of a disturbance that had to be identified, but it was also a question of survival in the face of the threat of the destruction of language and civilization that this adhesion to origin spread around itself.

## Abduction in Freud

Within this context Freud's *Moses and Monotheism*, written during a period of grave danger (1939), assumes a special place in my analysis. I am not interested in comparing the rise of Islamism to that of National Socialism, something that has been done, at least superficially, in recent years. Such analogies are not very useful and reproduce the shortcomings of those who wish to experience the present as a form of "iconic fidelity" to the past, as Nietzsche put it.[9] Rather, it is Freud's struggle with the demon of origin that I want to focus on.

Readers may recall the opening lines of the book: "To deprive a people of the man whom they take pride in as the greatest of their sons..." By engaging in this primal abduction, by attempting to demonstrate that Moses was a stranger to the Hebrew people, Freud in his final work gave us a construction that juxtaposed the autofoundation of the proper, its closure, with the originary hospitality of the "great foreigner" (as he referred to Moses) as a condition of civilization. Every religion, every culture, every community bound by language or memory cannot be Itself at its beginning, cannot learn to be Itself before being challenged by the Other and the Foreign. That is why the essence of the Self is a remainder whose condition is an original impropriety.

Thus, in 1939, the darkest period in the ideology of origin and purity in Europe, Freud deconstructed originary uniqueness, proposing a multiple and repetitive understanding of origin, one that was always heterogeneous and outside the totality it had been used to justify. Its disparity, he tells us, is temporal, geographic, material, and linguistic. This extends to the founder himself, who cannot escape the composite nature of his identity, because, for Freud, there were at least two Moses. This is the notion of infinite origin, which seems capable of expressing the deconstructive gesture of *Moses and Monotheism,* an infinite origin that is the *incompleteness* of origin.

This gesture, the most radical in monotheistic culture in terms of an "ethnic ideal" (the expression is Freud's), comes from a man who, at the very moment when he was threatened because of his origins, chose to trace or expose what Pierre Fédida has called the "vanishing point of origin." In *Le site de l'étranger,* Fédida sees *Moses and Monotheism* as the culminating moment of the disengagement of the father, considered as renunciation, as withdrawal, as the silence of the neutral that provides language with its site (the vanishing point of origin), threatened by "the monstrous return of the mass."[10] In fact, my initial approach to the question of origins in Islam involved a consideration of Freud's gesture in *Moses and Monotheism.*

## The Opening of Origin

Given the representation of originary plenitude that extremism was beginning to promote, the goal of my first book was to follow the traces of the founder's experience and show at what point it became dangerous.[11] The reinvention of another monotheism was not an act of self-sufficiency; it was based not on the logic of narcissistic assurance and the self-conception of the prophetic subject but on an experience of anxiety, uncertainty, and exposure to an obliteration when nearly nothing took place. The difference (one of the names of the Koran) with respect to other monotheisms was not written in indelible letters on crystalline tablets but involved the initial challenge of the withdrawal and agony of the Self, paralyzed by a separation where place took place.

Even in the earliest biographical narratives of the Prophet, this experience appears to be marked by an initial withdrawal, which established a void in the heart of the child Muhammad. At four years of age, orphaned by his father before being orphaned by his mother and left with a wet nurse, he had a terrifying vision of three men clothed in white, who opened his chest and tore out his heart, thereby bringing about the removal of the dark flesh, where the letter would subsequently find its place as a border, or edge, in the infantile body — in Arabic a letter is literally an "edge" *(harf).* It is this operation which marks the event of openness *(fath)* as a gift of withdrawal. *Openness* is the originary signifier of the Muhammadan religion *(al-fath al-muhammadi)* and its spirituality. Yet it is true that institutionalized theology and, even more so, extremism are based on forgetting the truth of this experience and on the reversal of its meaning as "victory," for the same signifier later came to mean "military conquest." In this way a lack became fulfillment.

The operation of opening continued through a succession of challenges, wherein whatever assumed the status of "Islam" acquired its essentiality only from its provenance in the "Foreign," which had lodged in this recess of infantile narcissism. Here, provenance is not passive reception, it is the effect of a transposition in language, given that Koranic revelation is considered to be a reception, in Arabic, of the hyperoriginary text of the Other, known as the "mother of the book."[12] "Read" was the inaugural injunction of the Islamic text, transmitted as ordered by the angel Gabriel, because it had already been written: everything is already written on the "guarded tablet." Origin would then be merely an operation of deciphering an ancient text that the Prophet embraced in the cut in the Self, from which a future text would come into being. To read is to bring the text of the Other to gestation. It is the first operation of the Law. The Law in Islam does not offer redemption from any original sin, and yields to universal reason and law only as a secondary matter; its initial action is to *open* to internal difference and the field of the possible through a separation in the flesh. The intruder in the heart of man is language.[13] It follows that man is never entirely man. He is intimately foreign to his species.[14]

The second dimension of the "challenge of the foreign" resides in the relationship to earlier versions of monotheism, especially the biblical text in which the origin of Islam is presaged through the story of Hagar and Ishmael, before the beginning of Islam proper. Recall that the book of Genesis presents us with the drama of the sterility of Abraham and Sarah, and the use of the servant Hagar, who is inseminated by the patriarch to obtain a child. After Isaac's miraculous birth, Ishmael, Abraham's older son, is chased away along with his mother at the instigation of Sarah so that he cannot inherit from his father (Genesis 21:12–14). But the biblical god previously promised Hagar and her son that they would give rise to a great nation. Ishmael has been considered by biblical tradition as the eponymous ancestor of the twelve Arabic tribes of Transjordan and northern Arabia (Genesis 12:25). In chapter 2 I will examine this key sequence in the narrative of the origins of Islam. For its founder established the Arabic monotheism of early Islam as a genealogical connection to Abraham through Ishmael, and as an emanation of a primary mono-theistic filiation through the older son, which was prefigured in the scrolls of the Father *(shuhuf ibrahim)*. In short, Islam was a biblical promise. Its founder read it, remembered it, and caused it to endure.

As a result, the concept of origin in Islam was split between a cut *(entame)* and a beginning *(commencement)*. The cut precedes the beginning; it is always an opening and a trace in the memory of the Other and can, therefore, wait a considerable time for reading to begin. In this sense, there is never any beginning. When the opening bell is struck, the cut is not minimized; it continues to operate on history unconsciously, beyond the beginning that derives from and envelops it.

This plunge into the language and ancient texts of Islam gave me an opportunity to closely familiarize myself with a religious history that was not transmitted to me along traditional lines by the previous gener-ation, or else was transmitted in a spiritualized and secular fashion, that is, with theological gaps. Therefore, it was through separation that I came to discover the language that underlies the Islamic order of discourse and its institution. It is true, as Freud pointed out in *Moses and Mono-theism,* that "there is an element of grandeur about everything to do with the origin of a religion," just as Islam, because of the richness of its archive, took shape in the sixth century, "before the eye of history," as Ernest Renan put it. Working from a discontinuity in the transmission allows for a free-dom of interpretation of these materials and the ability to maintain one's distance from a sensitive area of repression, which a shared heritage forces the subject to comply with continuously. The deep split that manifests itself risks being transformed into a violent break with tradition, both subjec-tively and politically.

### The Satanic Verses

This line divides not only moderates from fanatics, rationalists from be-lievers, and the logic of science from the logic of faith, but also those who claim to have found a truth of origin in traditional texts — which could be accomplished through rational procedures, accompanied by advanta-geous use of the historical method — from those who consider those same texts to be a fiction or fable. The opposition hardened once the fictive was seen as something that was not true, not real, and that, therefore, had no being or did not exist. On the one hand, we have the claim that the discourse of origin is transparent to what it signifies: truth, being, the absolute. On the other hand, it is accused of being counterfeit, and we are reminded that the truth of an event is always compromised by the necessary transition of that event to a text, a work of writing and authorship, and that even if the event is true, its exposition in language pulls it into the realm of fiction, that is, what we today refer to as literature.

This conflict was present from the start in the text of the Koran, where the word of god claims it has no relationship with that of the poets, referred to as raving liars who cause men to go astray.[15] In other words, from the beginnings of Islam, the difference between divine-true and poetic-false disturbed Koranic speech and shaped the discourse of the law within it. By the sixth century, the period of treating biblical writing as the veridical receptacle of the divine logos concerning the origin and fate of the world was behind us. In the interim, monotheistic writings had grown in number, and Islam's texts were wrapped in controversy. From the outset, the Koranic utterance harbored an internal war, a violent conflict between the word of truth and the claims of fiction, whose most extreme manifestation is found in an episode of the Satanic Verses.

This episode is known to Islam, and commentary is found in a number of scriptural sources,[16] but it was repressed in the ordinary believer. What was this episode? In the midst of the revelation of a sura affirming the absolute uniqueness of god, Satan is said to have assumed the identity of the angel of revelation, the archangel Gabriel, to praise the female goddesses of the pre-Islamic Arab pantheon. The Prophet then says that the (male) ONE would share his kingdom, accepting the intercession of (female) OTHERS! The incident occurred at the moment when the Prophet was looking for a political arrangement with his polytheistic adversaries, who worshipped these goddesses. In this sense, Satan would have profited from the temptation of compromise to falsify the true word, without the Prophet's perceiving it at the time. Although he quickly realized the error, nonetheless the lie was able to manifest itself as the word of truth, if only for a brief period of time.

The belief in origin would not exist if the Prophet's story had not been credited with a fundamental truth, one that lies in the balance between being and speech. Without the originary revelation of truth, there is no transcendence, no origin; everything becomes a fable, a simulacrum, a delusion. And it is along this fault line between truth and fiction that Salman Rushdie's work opens. The terror that accompanies intellectuals in the Muslim world who touch upon the question of origin and the actual violence that has taken place would be pointless if our contemporary world weren't tragically exposed to the defeat of this division.

When the Rushdie affair broke out, the defense of the author and the secondary quarrels overshadowed the work itself: *The Satanic Verses*.[17] Yet the novel was the literary realization of a return to origin, designed to destroy its theological truth and reduce it to various elements that could be freely assembled, as in those children's toys with movable parts. The author structures his text around the episode in the Satanic Verses where falsehood has momentarily assumed the appearance of truth, subsequently hijacking the text: what if Satan had continued to dictate revelation without anyone's noticing, what if truth were only a lie in disguise, and what if everything were only fiction? The book begins with the hidden assumption that the truth of origin might have been infiltrated by the murmurings of evil and become a history of going astray, of confusion, an inextricable mixture of true and false, of real and fictional.

The novel begins with the fall of the two principal characters, Muslims of Indian origin, from a plane that explodes over London. This fall draws in its wake the entire narrative of the origins of Islam in a story filled with humor and intrigue, in which individuals and events from the beginnings of Islam are disguised but nevertheless remain recognizable for anyone raised in the religion. Everything falls: people, their identity, their originary speech, their holiness in exile, and numberless distractions. An attentive reading of the novel shows that it is a dissection of the "textual body of the Father" in Islamic tradition, carried out with premeditation, with the manifest intent of confronting Islamists with the inanity of their return.[18] Where there were originary truth, saintliness, and salvation, there is nothing but wild laughter, a childish game subservient to an imagination without faith or destination. I coined the expression "vertical exile" to refer to this fall of the myth of the father, coextensive with his entrance into the modern world. This fall results in the dispersion of the unity of his narrative in literature, which is, in one sense, simply the diaspora of his signifier, the result of a pulverized origin.

We are all familiar with what happened next: the accusation of blasphemy, the condemnation to death, the demonstrations and violence seen throughout the Muslim world. To this the author responded that blasphemy exists only where there is belief. Raised in a Muslim environment, he had the right to believe that this story had no truth value and to propose to everyone, in the name of literature, a new pact whose terms are as follows:

> Maybe they'll [Muslims] agree, too, that the row over *The Satanic Verses* was at bottom an argument about who should have power over the grand narrative, the Story of Islam, and that that power must belong equally to everyone. That even if my novel were incompetent, its attempt to retell the story would still be important. That if I've failed, others must succeed, because those who do not have power over the story that dominates their lives, power to retell it, rethink it, deconstruct it, joke about it, and change it as times change, truly are powerless, because they cannot think new thoughts.[19]

What Rushdie advocates is literature as an act of justice with respect to origin, so that it ceases to be the reserved domain of an exclusive authority. The narrative must no longer be consigned to a shared but untouchable archive, or one touchable only by those who are authorized. The phrase "power must belong equally to everyone" clearly indicates the nature of the pact proposed, one that involves a form of free use ("deconstruct . . . joke . . . change") in which everyone shares. The ark in which is preserved the memory of origin is transferred from the jurisdiction of divine right to that of the common law of subjects. Its truth becomes truly subjective. Something akin to a right to literature is created in this transition.

Throughout this period of turmoil involving *The Satanic Verses* and its author, I felt as if the transition had intensely mobilized the figure of Oedipus and reactualized his tragic consequences for the subject and for truth in the face of religious power. To the act of tearing from the Sphinx the possibility of answering the riddle of destiny by oneself corresponds, in the case of Rushdie, the snatching of origin from the pious guardianship of tradition. To the self-reflexive Oedipal position that consists in the gesture of designating oneself as the center of the riddle — a gesture in which self-consciousness and Apollonian-Socratic egocentrism ("Know thyself") are affirmed — corresponds the assumption underlying the pact proposed by Rushdie, namely, that every man is an "author," that anyone can grab hold of what was once a divine prerogative: writing the meaning of the world, beginning with oneself as a resource. In other words, the truth of origin is determined by the subject, and the subject responds, Everything is literature. In that sense, Rushdie enacted on the world stage a new version of the tragic conflict between the freedom of the subject (to write) and the power of the *fatum* (the religious writing of truth). Every element of the Oedipal tragedy was incorporated in this real theater: the theme of the "guilty innocent" at the center of the debate between the writer's supporters and detractors; and the writer's prescience in antici- pating his own condemnation, for, in the next-to-last page of *The Satanic Verses*, Rushdie has his principal character "thinking, too, . . . about how he was going to die for his verses, but could not find it in himself to call the death-sentence unjust."

We could call this new version of the tragedy "Oedipus the Writer" or, better yet, "Oedipus the Autobiographer," to designate another dimen- sion of Oedipal transgression. What is in play is not only a matter of the relationship between the subject of desire and knowledge as we have learned to interpret it ever since Freud, nor merely the subject of science and philosophy, but literature to the extent that its subject is based on the writing of the self as the very aim of the act of writing. The essential turn in this writing of the self, which encompasses everything, consists in giv- ing truth the structure of fiction and in presenting, behind the absolute of the book, the proliferation of the ego in history.

Let's take this one step further. Salman Rushdie has shown us that it is only when truth is given a fictive structure that the identification of the subject of literature with the Father can be assumed. Although for five hundred-odd pages the author tears apart the myth of origin, sometimes brutally, suddenly he presents his principal character, Saladin Chamcha, before the deathbed of his father, Changez. In the last twenty pages, the novel shifts to an unveiling of what it really is from beginning to end: a plot within the orbit of the question of the father, of his physical myth and his mythical body, and the literary rewriting of his metaphor. Simul- taneously, the terrible cruelty so present in fiction writing — once we are willing to admit that hatred consists in denying to the other or his speech knowledge of the good — falls away and changes into love for the father and his signifiers. Rushdie writes:

> To fall in love with one's father after the long angry decades was a serene and beautiful feeling; a renewing, life-giving thing, Saladin wanted to say, but did not, because it sounded vampirish: as if by sucking this new life out of his father he was making room, in Changez's body, for death. Although he kept it quiet, however, Saladin felt hourly closer to many old, rejected selves, many alter-

native Saladins — or rather Salahuddins — which had split off from
himself as he made various life choices, but which had apparently
continued to exist, perhaps in the parallel universes of quantum
theory.

At the same time, the voice is revealed so that the subject welcomes
the return of the letter in his name: "If only he could have been this person
all his life, Saladin (who had begun to find the sound of his full, unEng-
lished name pleasing for the first time in twenty years) found himself
wishing. How hard it was to find one's father just when one had no choice
but to say good bye."

Yet the return of the letter leads the subject toward a symbolic connection between the individual dead father and the founding Father of
Islam, Muhammad, whose biographical story he has just unraveled: "'Now
you can stop acting at last.' Yes, this looked like the start of a new phase,
in which the world would be solid and real, and in which there was no
longer the broad figure of a parent standing between himself and the in-
evitability of the grave. An orphaned life, like Muhammad's; like everyone's. A life illuminated by a strangely radiant death, which continued to
glow, in his mind's eye, like a sort of magic lamp."

Not only does the fictionalization of religious truth result in wild
profanation but also, by passing through the letter and the dead body of
the father (the last comment is made by the side of his corpse), it exposes
the subject's consciousness to the name of the father as a determiner of
his existence. Indeed, the word *orphan* is one of the major signifiers of the
founding of Islam, for it designates the struggle of the man Muhammad,
who, abandoned by all — first by his dead father and mother, then by his
dead substitute fathers — believed, after an initial period of waning divine inspiration, that god had also abandoned him. It is because of this
test of being orphaned, in the form of abandonment by the fathers, that
the word *Islam* would come to designate the religion of the god who saves
even within abandonment, or who turns abandonment into the refuge of
being. And if we recall that the god of Islam addressed the Prophet by
calling him the "orphan" *(al-yatim)*, we see, following Jacques Lacan, that
this is one of the Names-of-the-Father in Islam.[20]

All the same, isn't it strange that a novel that was denounced as blas-
phemous and considered to have harmed the figure of the Prophet should
end up identifying with the founder of the religion and the assumption
of his name? This shows, quite clearly, that what we consider literature

makes use of diversion to enact, outside religious truth, what the existence of the subject owes to the naming that established him in language —
unless literature is itself a form of religion, the cult of the holiness of the
letter when it promotes truth in a shared fictional structure.

So, aside from the global violence and the ensuing din it triggered,
the Rushdie affair reveals the nature of the torment of origin: the disruption of the relationship between truth, language, and subjectivity in Islam.
Not only are we living in a time when we see a major subversion of the
traditional structure of Islam, but we are also witnessing the emergence
of new alternatives in the creation of foundational metaphors.

That it is through the literary subject and not the subject of science
that this subversion is bursting into public view is not without significance. During the years leading up to the Rushdie affair, many of us believed that a major confrontation with religious forces was about to take
place. But we believed that it would come through philosophical or scientific speech. We had in mind the model of the Enlightenment and the
great historical demystifications, such as that through which the Bible lost
its immemorial prerogative as the oldest book written by god himself, after
the archaeologist G. Smith deciphered the Mesopotamian tablets in 1872.[21]

The shock, in the case of Islam, came from where it was least expected:
the literary fiction that presented the truth of origin as an artifice. But we
need to ask why. Is it because Islamic theology, made rigid by centuries
of immobility, had ended up convincing its followers that origin was a
reality that resisted any significant unmasking? The slightest hint of imagination placed that theology in the position of the offended individual
who suddenly sees his most intimate defect exposed. The possibility of
evil at the heart of the sanctity of the verb, the vibrant core of the mystery
of creation, becomes a threat to its credibility. Doesn't the uproar over
*The Satanic Verses* illustrate that perversion is something primal in the
discourse of truth and its revelation? But even though the Prophet bore
witness to the fact that sanctity was neither given once and for all nor
immunized against evil, the institution of Islam attempted to seal this
crack and, over the years, constructed its sovereignty as the sovereignty
of the true and the good, whose protection was absolute. In this sense,
Rushdie's *The Satanic Verses* is the return of the repressed of Islam at the
cruelest point possible, the point where the "impossible immunity" has
been signified but set aside.[22]

However, if this impossible immunity recurs in writing, it is because
circumstances have allowed it. Of course, Rushdie is the author of the act

that propelled the return of the repressed, but the action of the literature he is a part of surpasses his individual case. It is part of the historical process of modernity, which attains in its development the point that Nietzsche suggested in the well-known expression "Parmenides said: 'one cannot think what is not'; we take hold of the other end of the stick, and say: 'what cannot be thought, must be a fiction.'"[23] If our modern condition culminates in the idea, the belief, the ideology that being can be thought only because it is a fiction, then literature will have been and will be, for a long time to come, the experiment responsible for this claim and its ultimate consequences.[24]

These developments are a sufficient indication that the crisis of the Rushdie affair is not a matter of blasphemy, as Islam has so abundantly experienced for fourteen centuries, but reflects a mutation in civilization, which has upset the nature of the relation between truth and subjectivity by affecting collective scenes of origin. Rushdie has been the *agent* of an act and, at the same time, has been *acted upon* by a historical process that introduces the possibility that someone produces this act. This position of the agent or actor acted upon calls to mind that of the guilty innocent.

Consequently, I have modified my working position to reflect the following analysis. With respect to the actor: I support the unconditional defense of the author, his life, and his right to free expression.[25] There is no doubt that, without these, no further intellectual work is possible. Moreover, the simple fact of condemning a writer to death opens the possibility of killing others, anywhere in the Muslim world, especially in Algeria.

With respect to the historical process: There is a need to revisit the question. Where religious texts are concerned, is it enough to decide that they are fictions for the problem to be resolved? If Salman Rushdie did not believe in their truth, why did he want to eliminate that truth, turn it into its opposite, and propose its distribution? Aren't the reversal of a truth and the subjective sharing of its text still this truth, if not its fulfillment? Doesn't the opposition between truth and fiction itself belong to the language of metaphysics? This is exactly what Philippe Lacoue-Labarthe wrote, when commenting on the Nietzsche quotation cited earlier: "But we see that fiction is not something that can maintain itself, something that can be said and affirmed other than by reference to the truth. To invoke fiction as Nietzsche constantly does, especially after *Human, All Too Human,* is to continue to speak the language of truth, to acknowledge that there is no other."[26]

## The Actuality of Religion

You may recall how Freud, in *The Future of an Illusion* (1927), rails against what he called "the philosophy of as if" and compares it to the *credo quia absurdum* (I believe it because it is absurd) of the theologians. Freud believed that we cannot be satisfied simply with considering religious beliefs as fictions: "We must ask where the inner force of those doctrines lies and to what it is that they owe their efficacy, independent as it is of recognition by reason" (*SE*, 18:169). And we must provide an explanation of that inner force through the problematic of desire and the actuality *(Wirchlichkeit)* of imaginary formations.

Freud's hypothesis is that one of the sources of the actuality of religion lies in its capacity for illusion. Illusion, he says, is not an error; it is not false like delusion, although it is similar; nor does it necessarily contradict reality; nor is it a falsification or even something unrealizable. Illusion is a force, a force tied to a very ancient desire that aims at its fulfillment by renouncing any endorsement from reality. This force originates in the infantile despair of abandonment that each of us experiences at a given moment of our existence, and in the desire to protect ourselves from it by inventing a tutelary power, comparable to the one we attribute to the father, that can watch over us and prevent despair. That is why, although it corresponds to a real threat in the past, illusion is its energetic denial, to such an extent that it becomes irrefutable. Only the slow process of demobilizing the barrier of illusion allows us, over time, to overcome infantile fear and escape the "encounter with hostile life," as Schiller wrote. Illusion finds its root in a lived despair whose return it wishes to avert.

Freud's irreligious convictions did not prevent him from recognizing that religious illusion is constructed around a real, namely, infantile distress, and that it is, consequently, closer to the historical truth of that distress than the secondary rationalization that denies it. Nonetheless, by fulfilling a protective function in the face of this real, by trying to avoid despair, religious representation travesties truth and transforms it. In other words, the Freudian category of illusion, which is neither an error nor the opposite of reality, neither truth nor even its contrary, aims for the impossible. It does this in two ways: first, in the sense that human distress is impossible to eliminate, because it arises from an essential loss that cannot be filled; and second (given that the religious response is an impossible response to this impossible), to the extent that it promises a resolution of the loss and makes god its fulfillment. With the Freudian concept of illusion, we leave behind us the opposition between truth and fiction and approach the problematic of a new relationship: the impossible and the actuality of the imaginary. Note that this is a relationship, not an opposition. The actuality of religious formations is based on the imaginary structure it produces around the impossible, a structure through which it becomes authoritative.

This is one of the conclusions I draw from the Rushdie affair and, in its light, a rereading of *The Future of an Illusion:* fictions of origin are not based on the question of truth and are not antagonistic to it but must be considered in terms of the impossible. How does the imaginary of origin in Islam accommodate the impossible? Around what fictional structures does it recognize its sovereignty? What relation does it maintain with the question of the father? This book tries to address these questions. It presents my detour of origin in Islam, in every sense of the term: to draw apart and separate from, to alter a trace, to change an intent, to follow a difficult path....

## Abrogation

Presenting the problem of the fiction of origin in terms of the impossible also alters the perception of torment and its causality. In the following pages I would like to try to clarify Islamist ideology using the following hypothesis as a background. The truth this ideology seeks to restore, making use of Koranic law to ensure its earlier status, serves to mask the impossible, with which the modern world confronts the system of tradition. In other words, the torment of origin is a symptom of the undoing of the traditional solidarity between truth and law (*haqiqa* and *sharia*), leaving the subject with an excess of the real and of *jouissance,* which horrifies him because he cannot find anything within his imaginary universe and antique symbolism to block its release. The appeal to origin reflects the hope of restoring the shield of religious illusion. However, because the shield has been damaged in its encounter with the challenge of the contemporary scientific and historical world, it must be repaired by incorporating the new materials of this world. As we will see later on, the Islamist movement is not the vector of a simple return of religion, as has been claimed, but a new and heterogeneous ideological composition. More specifically, this Islamist ideological composition came into being only because there was a breakdown of the religion it intensifies in the very gesture that seeks to preserve its truth.

But where does this return to origin come from, what topos of Islamic tradition is it associated with, and how is it inscribed in the internal logic of Islamist ideology? In the wake of the Rushdie affair, these questions lead us to inquire into the rise of Islamist movements and the historical conditions of their discourse. The result of that inquiry will reveal how collective delusion comes into being.

## Return and Interpretation

The traditional concept of return is the heart of Islamic hermeneutics, for which origin is attained only to the extent that it has been lost and veiled in the very act of its representation. This principle establishes the general function of all interpretation. I would like to quickly sketch the framework. It is characterized by two key concepts: *tafsir* and *tawil*.

*Tafsir* literally means "to explain and comment upon." The word is an anagram of *tasfir* — an unveiling. The science of exegesis, which corresponds to it, associates its origin with the period of the Prophet, who explained to his companions the meaning of the revealed text. In the following centuries it became a method that was used by traditional commentators and was characterized by respect for the letter of the text, by a reliance on the authority of the first generation of exegetes, and by the rejection of personal interpretation. It is presented as an impersonal compilation, where the author juxtaposes the various traditions that might help explicate a Koranic text. It follows these verse by verse and word by word, takes the precaution of indicating the sequence of authorities, and rarely promotes a personal opinion, and then only with great caution.

*Tawil*, which literally signifies "the return to what is first," refers to interpretation to the extent that it attempts to surpass the limits of exegesis and avoid literalness. Ever since Avicenna and the flowering of mysticism and philosophy, *tawil* has been a creative spiritual process that makes use of the cosmology, anthropology, and theology of antiquity and assumes there is a hidden meaning beneath the obvious meaning. It is a hermeneutic process that is presented as a developing investigation that communicates, on the one hand, an attempt at internal research and, on the other, a revelation of new horizons, which are exposed as knowledge of the self and understanding of the external world approach one another. Allegorical interpretation plays an important role in this, as it does in the work of the great mystical philosopher Ibn Arabi. I will give an example of *tawil* in "Sacrifice and Interpretation" (in chapter 4).

The philosopher Al-Jurjani (fourteenth century) provided the following definition of *tawil:* "It is the relationship, within a word, between an apparent meaning and an assumed meaning, if the assumed meaning agrees with the Book and tradition, as when God says that he 'extracts the living from the dead.'"[27] Interpretation is, therefore, an operation of displacement in language, which finds its adequacy (or inadequacy) in an act of procreation from death. It is this relationship which constitutes a return to an initial meaning, a meaning oriented by death to the extent that it is the starting point for meaning.[28] Consequently, among Islamic philosophers, origin is defined by its inaccessibility, precisely as indicated by Ibn Manzūr, author of the encyclopedic dictionary the *Lisān al-'Arab* (thirteenth century): "To originate something is to kill it through knowing it, in that way you will know its origin." Origin, therefore, is the killing of the thing.[29] In other words, interpretation is the activity of connecting speech with death, whose creative act consists in imposing finitude, thus exposing infinite meaning. With Islamist ideology we are a long way from such activities, for it is *accessibility* to origin that it claims to bring about, the presence and not the representation of origin that it seeks to stipulate.

## Return, Theory, and Delusion

The history of the Islamist movement reveals something that the discourse of political science mentions only in passing, without going into detail, as if it were a minor issue. This is the unprecedented event that I refer to as the abrogation of origin,[30] which occurred when the theoretical foundations of Islamism were established in Egypt, by Hassan Al-Banna (1906–1949), and in Afghanistan, by Abu Ala Mawdudi (1903–1976), at the beginning of the twentieth century. The Egyptian Sayyid Qutb continued their work and shaped it into a doctrine whose central idea is that Muslims have returned to the time of the *jahiliyyah,* that is, the period before the foundation of Islam, or the preoriginary period.

Sayyid Qutb arrived at this astonishing conclusion through the following argument: He first makes a logical distinction between Islam and Islamic societies, then finds that those societies are no longer governed by Islamic law *(sharia)* to the extent that they have adopted a modern form of government and a corresponding legal system, which were invented by the secular West. Thus, contrary to appearances, those societies are no longer Muslim. Islam has, in a sense, withdrawn from them; or, rather, they have rejected Islam. So, to the question "What has become of those societies?" the answer is simple: they have regressed to the period of barbarism and ignorance of divine law, that is, to a pre-Islamic period.[31] In short, they have evolved backward and crossed the wall of time to a period before their beginning. The required action is derived from these premises: it is necessary to "re-Islamicize" Muslims who are, in a sense, only pseudo-Muslims. As a result, Islamist movements assume the responsibility of isolating a preoriginary period and having Muslims "pass through" to their origins again. This is what many emirs are doing now, going so far as to have Muslim men and women sign statements like the following: "Today [date] I have entered the Islamic religion with the help of emir [name]."[32] This theory, which for many Muslims means that they are suddenly cast outside an origin and which literally reflects Shakespeare's words in *Hamlet* "Time is out of joint," sanctions violent extremist groups to kill and massacre without scruple, as in Algeria, by repeating the argument of regression: these people are apostates, or, worse still, they are simulacra of Muslims, whose deaths will be a service to Islam. Furthermore, their murders will absolve them of the sin of having regressed to a preorigin and having become Muslims in appearance only. Therefore, the murderers, as they lean over their victims to kill them, pass on the good news of their victims' salvation and ask their pardon for the act they, the murderers, are about to commit.

Those emirs who are "re-Islamicizing" Muslims assume the position of being wrapped in a collective primal scene and clinging to the gateway of beginnings, where they can control death by taking the tithe of life and flesh. This could even be a radical definition of fanaticism, the very source of its terror and the mass delusion it engenders. In one sense, it brings about a form of incest that could be called "political incest": the belief in the integral and compact presence of origin bound to the satisfied community. That is why, in the case of Islamist ideology, there is not simply a *return to* something — an expression in which the notion of separation from a source indicates the presence of metaphor and interpretation — but a *delusional appeal to origin,* an appeal that is possible only to the extent that interpretation is destroyed.

If the uprooting of metaphor and the destruction of interpretation are constantly at work in civilization, how is it that they assume the form of group psychopathology, organized by means of a delusion constructed as a theory? Obviously, the answer to this question is not straightforward, for the underlying act, namely, the abrogation of origin, has not been conceptualized in the social and political-science discourse on Islamist ideology. The same is true of the fundamental mechanism associated with the notion of return, which lends itself well both to the process of theoretical development and to delusion. Of course, we can say that "return" in interpretation entails the invention of a relationship to the old, a relationship that does not claim to have access to origin other than through the metaphor of a metaphor; whereas delusional "return" presents itself as a going back in time, to the point of invagination, when metaphor withdraws to a point within the form of origin. Here, return is no longer traction but retraction toward the shapeless, where the imaginary function breaks down, revealing origin as a kind of fleshy substance, a collective organ, a mouth that opens onto some bottomless political anxiety. In this way a disoriented group or community can regress while losing the spiritual capacity of a shared commonality. Collective delusion gives it a kind of primitive body that escapes symbolic interpretation, as if there were an imperious need for the physical sensations of the originary thing to be felt directly on the body, through bodies entwined with one another. That is why Islamists are constantly using their own bodies to publicly display the multiple manifestations of this phenomenon, and to exhibit the organic resurgence of shared origin as stigma. Now, we need to examine the historical and structural conditions that lead to such states.

We might begin by comparing the abrogation of origin with the events that took place on August 8, 1164, in Alamut, when the grand master of the Ismali Shiites proclaimed the abolition of the Law. Is this event, which is brilliantly described in Christian Jambet's *La grande résurrection d'Alamût*,[33] comparable to what we find in contemporary Islamist theory? Can the actions of a sect that lived in an enclave in the Iranian mountains, where a master put an end to the positive law of Islam and announced to his followers the beginning of an interior, spiritual religion, be compared to the widespread activities associated with Islamist ideology?

The two decrees, which appear to be equally revocatory, are based on opposite premises. In the case of the Shiite sect, there is a messianic promise that opens a window of expectation on a future when the Law will no longer exist — because man, now fulfilled from within, will no longer be in conflict with the external world. In the Islamist movement, however, with its belief in the perfection of origin, there is no utopian future, there is no prospect of some new occurrence happening, because the best has already occurred, the apotheosis has already taken place. All that is possible was given in a distinguished past that the future can only break down. The sun of the Law has been at its zenith ever since the revelation, dissipating all shadows on Earth. Melancholy, then, becomes the only stance, aside from terror, to assume while waiting for the last judgment. The Islamist movement should be considered a reversal of messianism: antimessianism as despair over time.

Here, another question presents itself: Are there, in the Islamic system, in its originary formation, fundamental antimessianic elements that might explain, at least partially, the emergence from within of an ideology that views the origin of Islam as a golden age and a time of salvation? We might provisionally answer yes. On the one hand, recall that, from the beginning, the teachings of the founder of Islam claimed to be a return to the first religion of Abraham, which Judaism and Christianity are said to have transformed by betraying its literal meaning. There is also a shared reference to the universal monotheistic reconciliation around the father's act of renunciation in the sacrifice of the son. To this should be added the fact that Muhammad claimed to be the seal of the prophets, the final term in a chain that began with Adam. The return to origin is accompanied, therefore, with the closure of monotheistic history. Islam presents itself as the end that returns to the beginning, a new beginning that makes origin infinite. This closed circuit makes messianism impossible.

On the other hand, by affirming that Christ was not crucified, that he is not dead, that he is alive at god's side, waiting to return to Earth to establish the final reign of justice and peace, Islam makes messianism possible, to the point that it gives the end of the world a Christly meaning — Christly and not Christian, of course.

Messianism, then, is both possible and impossible in Islam. From this point of view, we could interpret the history of crises within this civilization as an oscillation, or an antagonistic struggle between messianism and antimessianism. It is even possible that this opposition determines a great number of the patterns of Islamic thought. My hypothesis, for which I cannot provide proof at this time, is that Sufism presents itself as a hyperbolic solution that joins these opposites in individual private experience, where melancholy and hope, the finite and the infinite, expose the possibility of contemplating the human subject as mortal-immortal, complete-incomplete. It culminates in a monument of mental and spiritual exposition in Ibn Arabi's theory of the "imaginal,"[34] of which I will later give several examples. However, the divisions that crisscross Islamic tradition, although they indicate faults, and sometimes syntactic expressions of catastrophe, are not enough to explain or account for the scope of the present upheaval.

## Bodily Decay

How can we evaluate the exposure of the subject to the excess of the real and of *jouissance,* which is, according to my hypothesis, the result of the modern loosening of solidarity between truth and the Law in tradition, other than by listening to those who voice their distress and their rage, those who bear on their bodies the stigmata of the breakdown of religion, primarily through the defeat of the forbidden? I want to make use of the example of a recent book by a woman author, several hundred thousand copies of which have been distributed in the Arab world. The text is part of a body of literature whose negligible cost and easy availability have done much to spread Islamist ideology among the people. That the author is a woman is not without significance, for the female body in this tradition is associated, almost in its entirety, with the power that terrifies truth and the Law (a topic I will address in the next section). That is why the veil is seen as the essence of the forbidden. What interests me most in this testament is that it exposes the cultural crisis as a question not of ideas or representations but, as one would say in the language of psychoanalysis, of "representance" — that is, the extent of its touching upon an element of psychic work that is imposed upon it by its connection to the physical. From this point of view, there is no civilizational challenge that can be separated from libidinal economy.

## *The Veil of Pain*

In Ni'mat Sidqī's book *al-Tabarruj,* which could be translated as "Display," the author makes use of a Koranic concept that goes straight to the heart of the matter.[35] The title is a pejorative term that designates a woman's attitude whenever she presents herself publicly with ostentation. It especially connotes the action of showing, and showing oneself to excess, of defying the view of the other by presenting oneself in a way that draws attention and that calls to mind the register of phallic obscenity. (*Burj,* the noun derived from the verb *baraja,* designates a tower.) We could combine all these meanings in the term *monstration,* which reflects the excess of showing and its abnormal, even terrifying, nature.

The following excerpts are taken from the book's introduction, and sufficiently reveal the most important issues. The book begins on a note of indignation and warning:

> I have been afflicted by the greatest suffering in seeing the degree of abasement and humiliation to which the Egyptian woman has fallen in shamelessly exposing her body and her femininity in the streets, in public places, and on beaches. I have seen our society, men and women included, close their eyes to this breakdown, even accept it, rejoice over it, and enjoy it, without realizing that it is leading them toward the abyss of error and infidelity to God and his book. Behind this lies a forthcoming calamity that will sweep away this society. Only those will be saved who prohibit evil and warn those who are unconscious of their fall.

The author goes on to justify the legitimacy of her argument by basing it on the theological encouragement to denounce evil and by acknowledging her personal discomfort in the face of the generalized collapse of the prohibition. It is at the intersection of these two arguments that the dread of a violated common body takes shape. Sidqī then presents the essential thrust of her argument: "No, gentlemen, we must lance this abscess with enough force to cleanse it of this pus and burn the wound to purify it if necessary. . . . The epidemic of cholera has spread among you, how is it that you remain silent? Its victims have multiplied, the contamination has spread, the living cadavers are among you, and you fear nothing?"

The common body is infected, sick, cadaverous; it has lost its immunity and, simultaneously, its dignity. However, the specific thrust of this text relies not solely on the presentation of a devastated political body but on the fact that it will reveal the devastation on the subject's own body. It is the voice of the martyr that makes itself heard, to bear witness before all of the manifestation of god in a decaying body:

> Allah has healed me of this epidemic, which has spread around me; he has healed me of a painful sickness in my body; he has restored my health and healed my soul. . . .
>
> After having a tooth pulled, I suffered uninterrupted pain, which deprived me of the enjoyment of sleep and food for an entire month, for the attacks of pain continued day and night.
>
> The tumor grew to the point that my cheek nearly burst; it extended from my neck to my head; my eye was closed. The doctors and surgeons were perplexed, medicine was powerless, and the treatment difficult to come by; there was no further hope to be found in a cure.

> But the hand of Allah the generous wiped away disease and
> pain, easily healed the wound, and chased away the tumor. The
> doctors were overcome with shock in the face of this incredible
> surprise. They said, with humility: truly, God is powerful and mer-
> ciful, he causes dusty bones to come to life.

The religious power of the political body of the forbidden, its ability to
bear evidence, resides in the body of the subject that offers itself, producing within it the living proof of divine torment and pardon. What does it
say? I swear by my body that god is there, that my body is not in my
body as flesh is in the flesh, welded to itself and compact. It is wounded,
open, separated by the evil that has infected it. It is because the body's
immunity has been affected that it can be saved subsequently, by accepting healing and salvation, health and holiness.

But the author does not content herself with bearing witness to this
quintessence of religious experience, which is the experience of the collapse of immunity and the return of the "unharmed," as Jacques Derrida
has pointed out.[36] Her goal is to bring forth, for others, another, more
radical and more decisive meaning:

> During my illness, a woman came to see me. She said to me, indul-
> gently: you do not deserve this suffering, you are a believer and
> you pray, you make the pilgrimage to the house of God. What sins
> did you commit that God should punish you with this suffering?
> I yelled at her in response: Do not say that. God does not oppress
> people, it is people who are unjust. . . . I am guilty, I deserve this
> punishment. This mouth that God has punished with disease and
> pain, once adorned itself with lipstick, it did not prevent evil, it
> did not recommend good. The face that is now so swollen, once
> adorned itself with powder; this body nailed to the bed once deco-
> rated itself with elegant clothing. And this throbbing head, burned
> by the fever's fire, did not hide behind the veil as God ordained,
> and now is completely covered with the medical bandage that sur-
> rounds it like a veil. I did not cover myself with the veil of mod-
> esty, so God has covered me with the veil of pain. I covered my
> mouth and my face with tinctures and creams; God has struck them
> with suffering and infamy.

Here the final meaning of the defeat of the forbidden and the decomposition of its political body is made clear: an increase of guilt and, therefore,
of sacrificial debt, and the rise of a vengeful god who manifests his desire
through suffering. The purpose of this text, as with Islamist preaching, is
to proclaim the reign of the anguished face of the "obscure god."[37] It is

both a consequence of the breakdown of religion and an attempt to re-store it by means of an action articulated in the final words of this text: "on those criminals we shall take our revenge."

Nonetheless, this proclamation of the reign of the obscure god is accompanied – and this is the very reason for its existence – by the desire to reestablish the religious economy between representation and drive, an economy disrupted by the contemporary transformation of society. The expression "veil of pain" clearly indicates this: whatever moral imperative was swept away returns through physical suffering. The body always pays the debts of the soul.

## Debt

It is important to note that the sacred and the forbidden are designated by the same term in Islam, the Arabic word *haram,* based on the root "hrm," which gives us *harim* (modesty, home, wife), from which the European word *harem* is derived. Other words based on the same root include *hurma* (dignity), *hiram* (veil), *mahrim* (taboo), and *mahrum* (frustrated, venerable, respectable). Ibn Manzūr, in his *Lisān,* provides the following definition, which combines most of these meanings: "that which it is forbidden to touch."[38]

The religious notion of the "untouchable" has at least three meanings. First, it is a reference to the physical dimension of a body one must not enter into contact with. This is the concept of taboo. Something is also untouchable to the extent that it is unharmed (or untouched), which corresponds to one of the meanings of the word *Islam.* The word is, in fact, derived from the root "slm," which means "to escape from danger," "to be safe and sound." Therefore, the word *Islam* designates being safe after exposure to danger. In this sense, the untouchable is someone who benefits from immunity. The concept of the untouchable relates to what Freud identified in *Totem and Taboo* (1912–1913; *SE,* 13:1–161) and *The Future of an Illusion* (1927; *SE,* 21:1–56) concerning the mental sources of religious representation. Confronted by the subject's vital distress and the threat he feels from the world's hostility, whether projected onto the world or coming from it, religion provides a shield of protective illusion, but not without a counterpart that indicates the third major dimension of the untouchable: that which is rendered abstract by substituting a metaphorical body for the physical body – in other words, the substitution of the intelligible for the sensible. These aspects are combined in the general requirements

of cleanliness, physical purification, and the withdrawal of the flesh —
which is what Ni'mat Sidqī describes, although in exaggerated fashion.

Whether it takes place simply through distancing or veiling, or more
radically by removal (circumcision, scarification, sacrifice), the withdrawal
of the flesh is what gives the shield of religion its credibility. Illusion becomes credible through the real of the body that has been marked, bored
out,[39] or opened; in short, by flesh that has been distanced and paralyzed
by redemptive destruction. This is the price the body pays to legitimate
its existence and to access a legality of pleasure, which, because of the
withdrawal, cannot be total. But although the mechanism to establish the
protective illusion is based on an association with real, physical loss, it
turns out that there is no loss that settles everything at once and balances
every account, for that loss, that onetime loss, is death. Thus, it becomes a
question of prolonging what is lost, as if it could be lost again. To pro-
long the loss is what creates faith in the subject's future reward, or the
illusion of his immunity. The longer the conviction that he still has something to lose remains, the longer he can maintain the impression that he
is saved. Immunity is the capacity for liability.

Such is the general organization of the debt that structures one of the
world's key religious concepts. What the tradition of Latin Christianity
has called *religio* is known as debt *(din)* in Islam, following the example
of the religions of India.[40] Debt establishes the obligation of withdrawal,
and, conversely, without withdrawal there is no debt. We could say: in
the beginning, was withdrawal. The statement should be understood in
the sense that nothing takes place unless the All One is entered into. The
tradition of Judaism suggests this in its idea of a god who withdraws to
allow room for his creation. From this it follows that there is an inexhaustible debt to the creator, whose act assumes a degree of self-limitation,
of self-sacrifice, and the experience of loss. If we consider the episode of
the opening *(fath)* and the withdrawal of flesh from the child Muhammad's heart, it is clear that it foreshadows the fact that the Koranic text
will be based on withdrawal during the period of infantile narcissism.
Reading is, therefore, a recognition of debt. In general, Muslim mystics
have commented endlessly on the *hadith* (the word of the Prophet) where
god says, "I was a hidden treasure and I desired to be known. Thus, I
created the creatures so that I would be known by them." Every creature
is a mirror of god,[41] resulting from the loss he felt in wishing to know
himself. Every existent is a reflection that bears witness to the divine
withdrawal intended to establish the exteriority that supports his image.

It is this structure that relates god's passion to be known to the pathos of infinite sorrow, for he hopes to find in the other a sympathetic subject. In this sense, every subject both has and is a debt of awareness toward god, because knowing is equivalent to recognizing the being whose sad sigh we are. Here, we are closer to the sublime god of Ibn Arabi than the obscure god of Ni'mat Sidqī.[42] To fully account for this problematic, we must conceptualize some arrangement that would simultaneously incorporate being and having a debt, because, for the subject, no debt is merely a simple having or participates solely in the register of being. There is a constant transition, excess, and overflow of one into the other.

As for the debt of substance, as with the debt of understanding, although the withdrawal imposes a condition of omnipotence, it creates at the same time a separation within the self, between self and other, where *jouissance* is mediated by an empty transition to language, where it loses itself and becomes *rejouissance*. This model also affects capital. The tithe each subject must withdraw from his assets has the power to increase his capital in the very act of decreasing it! This is, in fact, the sense of the word *tithe* in Arabic *(zakat)*. But this gain through loss is nothing if not the extension of a part of oneself outside oneself. Even if the part is impure or cursed (à la Bataille), payment of the debt creates a communication of the subject with the exterior, an expansion of his being through withdrawal. Therefore, it would be preferable to speak of the interplay between debt and withdrawal, and debt and extension, within a continuous movement of conversion.

All of these operations assume a sense of abstraction, as the Latin root *abstrahere* (pull) clearly indicates. The dictionary definition of the word *abstraction* ("the act or process of leaving out of consideration one or more qualities of a complex object so as to attend to others")[43] clearly reflects that it was only recently that the idea of pulling away or drawing away changed to that of isolating or removing something from a whole in thought, as if the withdrawal were both a removal and a gift: the gift of withdrawal produces thought. I will use the term *abstract* to refer to the act of withdrawal or the withdrawing-giving on which all faith is based.

I would like now to examine the Islamic meaning of this "religion" of debt. The definition of *din* as it is treated in the *Lisān* covers all the registers of the word and reveals its scope.[44] First, there is the register of debt in the accounting sense, where the root "dyn" has given us the words meaning "claim," "stewardship," "recompense," "borrower," "debtor," "lender," and "seller," it being understood that the borrower-payer *(dayyan)* is god. With respect to debt as power, the same root has produced words meaning "to force," "to constrain," "to oblige," "to serve," "to obey," and "to submit to." In terms of debt as rectitude, the root "dyn" has generated words meaning "third party," "judge" (also known as "indebtor"), "judgment," "loyalty," "fidelity," and "issuance of a sentence." In terms of debt as evil and disease, we find words meaning the following: "to be damaged," "to be struck by evil," "to become sick," and "to die," because, as the *Lisān* specifies, "death is a debt for each of us." In terms of debt as a conduit for dogma, the root "dyn" has given us the words meaning "belief," "religion," and "preaching." Debt as policy covers the terms for "polity," "citizen," "civility," "civil," and "city" (*Medina* is derived from *madina* [city]). In each article, the *Lisān* provides, at one point or another, in an explosive sentence, the fundamental orientation of every inflection along a chain of signifiers. Concerning debt, we read: "Every thing *(chay')* not present is *din*." We can also say that, in the universe of the Arab language, what is called religion in the Christian world is clearly presented as a system of obligations, wherever the thing has been withdrawn. The withdrawal of the thing is the cause of religion.

Religion is within the limits of the thing: it orders, commands, and guards absence, the void or abstraction of the thing, with a halo of piety and prohibition. If, as Freud believed, religion is an imaginary that has an actuality *(Wirchlichkeit)*, we have to conceptualize the category of that imaginary (which is not fantasy) without hastily turning to the symbolic to conclude the matter.

It is quite clear that what we encounter here is the challenge underlying *das Ding*, as theorized by psychoanalysis, to the extent that it refers to the maternal thing that must remain the exclusive object of *jouissance* and from which arises the most fundamental of human laws as absolute distance from this thing.[45] Although the name of the community in Islam, *umma*, implies, through proximity to the word for "mother" *('um)*,[46] the kind of nostalgia that the common in community consists of, we nonetheless perceive a phonemic difference (the open mouth that terminates the word), which finds its full scope in these words' common root *(amm)*, "to strive for," "to approach without reaching the object or goal," or "to move forward" (which gave us *imam*). Debt is thus presented as the guardian of the asymptotic position of the members of the community with respect to the thing.

How can we maintain the asymptote? By hollowing out the prohibited *jouissance,* by cleaning it, by creating a desert around the thing. This hollowing out would target both an intimate region of the subject and his point of contact with the community. This would be the pivot point between narcissism and ideals, between the ideal ego and the ego ideal — except that this void is not a place but "no place"; it is atopic. In the traditional world, debt (religion) is the guardian of this circle of emptiness, whereas in so-called modern societies we can assume that this function is accomplished by politics.

Whenever the function of hollowing out can no longer be maintained, there appear in the body those points of rot and horror that are experienced as the points of *jouissance* of a cruel god. The abscess must be lanced, says the author of this *texte-cri,* who wishes to bear witness to the fact that the real of the putrid body has become amalgamated with the imaginary of the political body. From this point of view, we can consider Islamist ideology as the symptom of the collapse, in various parts of the Muslim world, of this function of removal that had, until then, been provided by debt, without its being replaced, or replaced only piecemeal, and that this ideology constitutes a desperate attempt to rediscover the lost indemnity through "autoimmunization." Ni'mat Sidqī's text falls within this logic of cleaning out the rot to recover the health and safety that the community supposedly lost during the epidemic of the flight of the forbidden.

As Jacques Derrida noted in the aforementioned conference on faith and knowledge, the process of autoimmunization "consists, in the case of a living organism, as we know, in protecting itself against its self-protective mechanism by destroying its own immune defenses."[47] I now want to examine how this process functions in Islamist ideology.

### Autoimmunization

Over the years, the Islamist movement has come to be seen as a form of fundamentalism. The terms *fundamentalist* and *Islamist* have been used interchangeably in speech, and to a large extent this is still true today. From the outset, political science has accredited this idea and analyzed it accordingly. A great deal of ink has been spilled about the "return to god." One gets the feeling that the Islamist movement is trying to reconnect with an older system in its totality and to apply its dogmas in their entirety, which is basically the definition of fundamentalism.

## Decomposition and Recomposition

Parallels between the Islamist movement and fundamentalism have been made by focusing on the way Islamists express themselves, especially the young, who account for a large percentage of the population in Islamic societies. Naturally, Islamists often refer to religion (debt) and emphasize a return to ritual practices. But this approach is not the only one; other registers are often present, including science.

Until the 1960s, the credo of a believer was based on the Koran and on tradition; it was very rare to see modern science invoked to support such claims. Of course, there has always been an appreciation for knowledge within the tradition, which goes back to the time of the Prophet, but the contemporary situation is quite different. Formerly, knowledge of science was congruent with the order of divine truth, and theology was its vigilant guardian. This was, in fact, the subject of Averroës' celebrated *Decisive Treatise*, written at a time (the thirteenth century) when the contradiction between religion and philosophy had begun to disturb the sleep of Islamic metaphysics,[48] before being dissolved by a theology that plunged the Islamic world into a state of lethargy that lasted several centuries. Yet if today I were to attempt to discuss with a young Islamist his religious beliefs and conception of the world, scientific or pseudoscientific arguments would soon fuse and blend with theological reasoning. If he doesn't eat pork, it's not only because his religion forbids it but also because medicine has proved that pigs develop a dangerous parasite (taenia) in their muscle tissue. Hygiene is used to justify the rites of ablution. Purity is related not only to cleanliness but especially to asepsis. The prohibition against incest is justified by the laws of genetics, to prevent the multiplication of recessive genes. The very truth of the Koran is said to be attested by the fact that recent discoveries in embryology correspond, point by point, to what the Koran describes concerning the development of the fetus. Such arguments cover a large number of religious requirements, which are frequently justified by quoting Koranic texts and scientific references together.

Generalized education has certainly given science its authority, to which popularization has managed to assign a value of transcendent truth. But, in fact, this mixture of discourses has been spread through the sermons and writings of Islamist leaders themselves. This discursive strategy has given rise to an explosion of books and audiovisual documents that are available at low cost. Their authors are scientists, sometimes famous ones, who are called upon, or feel called upon, to support not only the conformity of the truth of religion with that of science but also the way in which the Koran anticipated the discoveries and technical and scientific inventions characteristic of modernity. Examination of these documents leaves the impression of an immense interpretive delusion, which, like all delusions, arises from a destructive anxiety and attempts to shore up from the outside what has been weakened on the inside. In one audiovisual document, the presenter's gestures provide food for thought: carried away by his impassioned comparison between the Koran and a scientific work, he ends up by confusing the two books and holds up the latter in place of the former.[49]

The scientism that has infiltrated religious speech is extremely significant; it is as if religion had become incapable of ensuring believers of the order of truth that once existed. In short, we could apply to this generation Freud's remark in *The Future of an Illusion* according to which people no longer simply believe but "make it a duty to believe" (*SE*, 21:1–56), invoking arguments that are external to the register of faith. Isn't it the uncertainty of religious belief that should be discussed rather than one's fundamental attachment to it?

The same is true of the nationalist and populist dimension in this type of speech. Although the theological-political conception of Islam is universal, proscribing any distinction of ethnic identity, regional or racial, between one Muslim and another, Islamist movements are rarely separable from a powerful nationalist expression, and we might well wonder if the thrust of national fanaticism isn't drawing religious fanaticism along with it. In reality, Islamist ideology inherits this sacralization of the national that characterizes contemporary history nearly everywhere. For example, in Muslim countries the word used to designate nationalist combatants who have died during the struggle against colonialism is the religious term *chahid*, which is to say, a "martyr living with god," following the status assigned to him by the Koran. This has assumed considerable dimension in Algeria, where the unverifiable figure of a million and a half dead during the war of liberation has been advanced. The reference to this mass of martyrs constituted, in the discourse of the FLN (Front de libération nationale, or National Liberation Front) regime, one of the major elements for legitimizing its power, which helped accredit the idea that martyrology is the basis of politics. Thus, during the nationalization of the Algerian oil industry and the subsequent confrontation with the

French government, President Boumediene did not hesitate to proclaim that oil was the blood of the martyrs.[50] This nationalist and religious transubstantiation of the political body is not without consequences. The Islamists in Algeria will bear full responsibility for the nationalization of the sacred or the sacralization of the national, including the use of sacrifice that extremist movements have resorted to. No doubt there is more theology in politics than is generally realized. Nonetheless, the Islamist movements, far from being satisfied with using older theological-political conceptions of Islam, have also annexed modern political concepts of the nation-state without ever abandoning the spectral power of the religious martyr, for their leaders recognize the magnetic pull contained in the perspective of life after death.

It is in the platform of the Algerian FIS (Front islamique du salut, or Islamic Salvation Front) that we encounter the clearest and most direct formulation of what this is about. In its preamble, the group defines "the Front's methodological characteristics" as follows: "Collective effort based on the will of the Umma is one of the characteristics of the Front's scientific method." The platform then specifies, in its introduction, the three branches of its political activity, or the sources of its inspiration. The first is *sharia*, Islamic theological law. The second is science: "to use the resources of science methodically for a healthy approach to pending questions, so as to better identify problems." The third is "the aspiration of the Muslim people of Algeria." There is little doubt: the three principal ideological sources of the FIS are theology, science, and the people. Its entire platform is based on the intersection between these three concepts. And, in the event there was some misunderstanding, its own mission statement refers to these concepts and goes on to enumerate them individually. I quote its text here:

> Methodological elements:
>
> The methodological criteria for the development of a scientific political plan are:
>
> 1. Sharia
> 2. Science
> 3. The transitory state of mind of the Algerian people.[51]

Islamist ideology is not intelligible within the limits of what is customarily called religion; it is a blend of theology, scientism, and populism. Strictly speaking, only the reference to theological law *(sharia)* is Islamic. The two other components, science in the modern sense (its planning and methodology) and the people (a Greco-Latin concept), are foreign to its traditional corpus. In Islam, it's not the people but the community of the 'umma that constitutes the theological-political foundation of the collective being. Although it is mentioned in passing in this document, it is seen not as a means of transcending politics, as it should be in principle within traditional discourse, but as a part of the process of work, that is to say, part of the effort of negating and transforming nature. Would fundamentalist discourse have accepted associating the sovereignty of divine law with other sovereignties and placing its conception of community under the primacy of negativity and history? Aren't we faced, in this instance, with the illusion of the integral return of *the* religion, after having nourished the illusion of its end?

Theology, scientism, populism. Regardless of the proportion of these elements in the cauldron of Islamist ideology — and no doubt there are variations from one group to another — we are confronted not with a simple discourse for a return to the integrity of religion but with an invention, a new, modern myth unknown to the history of Islam. Blindness to this fact is one of the unexplained phenomena of contemporary political awareness.

How is it that in Islamist ideology Islamic religion *(din)* is no longer the only referent? We can make a first attempt at interpretation using the elements that have so far been identified. It seems that this ideology was possible, as a new, composite myth, only in societies where the breakdown of religion had been under way; to the extent that it was no longer possible to restore its former authority and thus became necessary to incorporate other elements and sources of authority. A comprehensive Islam, a cohesive world, belongs to the past. The expression of a Muslim scholar for whom Islamists are not "real Muslims" illustrates the concerns of a man of an older era — the early twentieth century — who is disturbed in his vision of an Islam equal to itself.[52] It is the avowal of a shocking truth: we have entered the age of the inevidence of the Islamic Self and the lack, not of homogeneity, which has never existed, but of its former coherence. The inevidence of self is always a mark of the confusion of modern identity. One Islam has ended.

It may come as a surprise to see science associated with theology. But we need to bear in mind that ever since the decline of Catholicism, scientistic belief has had, and still has, extensive support in Europe. Like anything else, science can be used for religious purposes. Indeed, many leaders and ideologues, active members of Islamist movements, belong to the world of science and technology. They have no hesitation in stating the need to appropriate "Western" technology, believing that it will have no effect on the essence of their identity. It is supposedly somehow neutral. Better yet, it will confer power upon them, pure force without word or meaning, or so they believe, and it will lead to the realization of a renewal of the Islamic beginning. With one hand, Islamic discourse denounces the expropriation it encourages, unawares, with the other. In this way, through the illusion of the neutrality of technology, it feeds the scandal of fanaticism and its fury.

Consequently, Islamist ideology is not simply a fundamentalist religious movement. Certainly, part of its platform belongs to religious tradition, whose importance varies from one movement to another, depending on the emphasis placed on the return to the literalness of the text and the rite; but the whole is the product of historic mutation, a new species of identity myth that I suggest calling national-theo-scientism. Without question, this myth, which seeks to bind and consolidate the three sovereignties of theology, science, and the people, is totalitarian. "The specifically national tradition or the particular spiritual source of its ideology matters little," wrote Hannah Arendt in her discussion of totalitarianism.[53] Like other historical examples in Europe and elsewhere, Islamist discourse is the Islamic version of the modern crisis that has engendered an ideology containing all the characteristics of totalitarianism.

That there are fundamentalist or dogmatic groups, sects, even movements, like the Taliban in Afghanistan, does not alter this situation, which affects the very basis of what we understand by tradition, experience, and religious institutions. Should the fact of having given the name Islamism to these movements be seen as one of the characteristic effects of this situation?

Until quite recently, "Islamism" referred to the Islamic religion as such, on the model of Judaism and Christianity. Given that the term expanded to cover activism and extremism, however, we no longer have a term to refer to the religion of Islam in the strict sense. There remains the word *Islam*, but this has the inconvenience of being a catchall, referring to the aggregate of peoples who profess the faith, Islamic civilization, and the religion itself. It's as if we could no longer distinguish, in language, between Judaism and Jewishness, Christianism and Christianity. Even if, by convention, we agree to refer to the civilization as "Islam," the result is that we are confronted with a perversion of language that deliberately restricts the scope of the term, just as we might refer, for example, to certain fascist movements that promoted the Christian religion as forms of "Christianism," or to a totalitarian ideology based on the idea of Europeanness as "Europeanism."

When Olivier Roy, one of the most highly regarded specialists in contemporary Islam, suggests, in a recent work, that "Islamism" be used to refer to both the Islamic religion and the political movements whose ideology claims to be derived from Islam, the ensuing confusion prevents us from distinguishing between the phenomenon of faith, along with its rites and dogmas, on the one hand, and the militant political movements that are inspired by that religion, on the other.[54] This kind of linguistic assimilation would be inappropriate if we were to use "Christianism" to refer both to Christian dogma and liturgy and to the Opus Dei movement, for example, or, in the best of cases, to Christian Democrats.

Islamism, therefore, is a damaged concept that has ceased to exist, having been dragged to its destruction by the desire to continue to treat Islam as a homogeneous whole, as a totality unified by religion, at the cost of great confusion. At the very moment when history is accelerating the process of internal differentiation, as well as the decomposition and recomposition of ideas and forces, resistance to the intelligibility of Islam in Europe has been strengthened by imposing the figure of a massive and compact alterity, leading ultimately to the murder of a concept. The great recent event in the order of discourse is, consequently, the death of ~~Islamism~~ — the strike-through is intentional. We can now begin to work with new words, such as *Islamicness* and *din,* and refer to Islams rather than Islam. We must think of Islam as both finite and infinite, in order to distinguish the Islam of theology, whose system is historically complete, from an extension that is stripped of religious manifestations but that incorporates certain fundamental characteristics — ethical and poetic — in its opening up to the world. We need to bear in mind that the signifier *opening (fth)* is the major signifier in Islam's initial infantile experience, being the hollowing out that disconnects the self from itself. In principle, it is juxtaposed to the healing that takes place through narcissism by adhesion to the ideal object of origin.

Following the illusion of the end of religion, we entered a period governed by a different illusion, that of the integral return of the religious. However, just as *din* did not disappear all at once, because of the simple desire of an elite to find itself in an afterlife, neither did it reappear or return in the form it had assumed for centuries, to govern according to its law and through its sovereign truth alone. Something else occurred, something unforeseeable that was inconsistent with the categories of political science, an unknown mixture, but one that wasn't the result of a deliberate volition knowing in advance what it wanted to do. This ideology results from a mutation in the symbolic and imaginary universe, comparable to what happens in living organisms whenever they are forced to transform themselves to keep up with changes in their environment, using both new information and the heritage of the past. What was it that forged this unexpected amalgam? How did the breakdown of religion arise?

## The Disruption of Meaning

Based on the preceding analysis of what I refer to as ~~Islamism~~, it appears that the breakdown is a form of unconscious demolition; for the substitution made by the speaker, who inadvertently displayed a scientific work in place of the Koran, is an emblematic gesture that condenses a self-destructive process. No doubt that process is more readily apparent among certain scientists, such as the speaker in the video, whose ideas support militants and in turn the people who listen to their speeches.

The following example describes a man who has acquired scientific skills and who holds a position of responsibility in the world of research. He is not one of the organic intellectuals known to Islamist movements, but he is one author among hundreds whose books — sold at very low prices — have proliferated during the last twenty years. In general, these books are intended to defend Islam and its accommodation to technological and scientific development. In the present case, the author also defends the other two monotheistic religions and goes so far as to recognize that "profane and absurd meaning does not prevent certain miscreants from respecting and protecting life," although, he goes on to specify, through a form of animal instinct rather than the moral convictions known to the faithful. His book *Les cinq valeurs universelles et les quatre superbombes* is intended as a plea for the protection of life and the environment, which are threatened by Western capitalism and industrialism, by associating science with the Koran.[55]

This association consists in identifying correspondences between scientific notions of the environment and ideas about nature found in the Koran. For example, at the beginning of his book, the author attempts to demonstrate that the idea of an ecosystem has an equivalent in the text of the Koran. The procedure is commonplace in this type of literature. In a section titled "Prevention Is Always Better than Healing," he begins by quoting a Koranic text on the prohibition against incest: "Unlawful are your mothers and daughters and your sisters to you, and the sisters of your fathers and your mothers, and the daughters of your brothers and sisters, and foster mothers, foster sisters,[56] and the mothers of your wives, and the daughters of the wives you have slept with who are under your charge" (4:23, "The Women"). He goes on to comment, "At present genetics has confirmed the reasonableness of these prohibitions, except with respect to marriage with foster mothers and sisters. Genetics has shown that every human being, like every living creature, has cells that contain chromosomes, containing genes. These genes, written biochemically on the DNA chain, encode all the characteristics of the living being." There follows a lengthy summary of genetic theory, along with diagrams, before he continues thus: "Fifteen centuries ago, this genetic knowledge did not exist, and it was because of the sexual prohibitions of religion that a large number of defects and diseases were avoided in Judeo-Christian and Islamic societies, as well as in societies in which those prohibitions were applied."

What's the point of this maneuver? It is intended to explain and justify the truth of the prohibition through biology. Having done so, the author, without realizing it, brings the prohibition found in Koranic discourse before the court of biological reason. This translation of the sacred utterance into scientific knowledge is "autoimmune" in two ways: it dismantles the linguistic logic of the prohibition to the benefit of the language of genetics, and it shifts the causal reference, because the biological becomes the rationale for the truth of the utterance. God supposedly promulgated the prohibition against incest to avoid the multiplication of genetic defects — this is the subtext of this maneuver. A true fundamentalist would have rebuffed such a translation, along with the interpretation that follows from it. In general, fundamentalists shun translations, for they know the price there is to pay. Their fundamentalism, as Émile Poulat noted, is not absurd from the point of view of the strict defense of a religious system.[57] Once a text has been translated, the specificity of the source language disappears and the meaning shifts according to the laws of the language of reception.

The generalization of this practice of translating religion into biology results not only in placing religious signifiers beneath the bar of scientific speech but also in repressing from the causal register the prohibition's status as interpositional statement. The language of prohibition (*inter-dit*, in the words of Pierre Legendre) is no longer the cause of the separation of subject and act, of the differentiation of the self with itself and the other, but a prescription that is secondary to the recognition of a biologically determined cause. It's plausible that eventually the religious signifiers will become a kind of dead language, dragging with them, in their wreckage, the interdictory or separative function of speech, that is, of language as fundamental mediation.

This may be one of the consequences of the historical process that governed the emergence of the modern subject, a process that went on to conceal the function of language as it had been transmitted for generations. Certainly, the condition of the modern subject in Europe cannot be reduced to this rupture, because the function was reinvented, primarily in politics. But this is a different context. The invention of the modern subject in Europe issues from a long period of historical gestation marked by numerous mutations and crises that took place over several centuries. Since the Renaissance, in every area of civilization, the work of transformation has required the repeated efforts of a large number of interpreters, until the Freudian disclosure of the unconscious mind. Nothing of the sort happened in Islam. Its entrance into the historical world has been sudden and stressful because of the anticolonial struggle, leaving little room for the work of interpretation. The acceptance of science and technology did not occur through a process of creative integration but took place passively and was accompanied by amazement, and discoveries were grasped as if they had fallen from the sky. In the absence of any critical function, without any accompanying ethics or aesthetics, we could say that this modernization took place without the necessary work of culture (*Kulturarbeit*, as Freud expressed it).

However, the European political invention was not free of accidents or destructive events with tragic consequences. A modern form of obscurantism born of biologism has infiltrated various areas of political and social life, with its most radical expression in Nazism. We could even consider the necessity of the emergence of psychoanalysis from this point of view, as it rediscovered the function of a devastated language through an archaeology of subjectivity caught up in the release of the maelstrom of biotechnological genius. Here, it was a question of inventing something to confront historical violence of enormous scope, which attacked the root of the psychic metaphor; for despair and barbarism are lodged in this expulsion of the function of language in the name of science. Freud did not view this problem as one of the sources of the discontent of modern civilization. Although he perceived it at a given point in *The Future of an*

*Illusion,* he quickly abandoned it. Nevertheless, the invention of psycho-analysis is, in its ethical modality, the response to this expropriation and the individual and collective madness it entails.

The preceding example reveals the collapse of the coherence of the prohibited as the kernel of religion *(din)* at work, operating through a subversion that saps its foundations and dissolves the logic of the symbol in the mechanism of life. The question we can now ask is the following: What is it that leads believers to dismantle a religion they venerate and honor? Rather, what is the force that causes the object of their passion to come apart in their hands, in the presence of the love they shower upon it? How can we conceptualize this extended and systematic contamination of religion by the discourse of science? An all-encompassing response referring to a lessening of intellectual qualities or the aptitude for rationality in men is inapposite, for, although these ideas have been popularized, there also exist circles of intellectuals within which such problems are discussed, and where we find the same practices but on a different level. Nor can we be satisfied with the peremptory explanation that where there is science, religion is forced to withdraw. First of all, according to our hypothesis, religion has not withdrawn, it is decomposing, and decomposition is a different phenomenon, more complex than withdrawal. Second, this does not explain how a man of faith comes to introduce, within his supposedly sufficient belief, another form of reasoning considered to contradict that belief. How are we to understand the unconscious motivations for this behavior, its desire and its risk?

If we return to the introduction of the book discussed earlier, we find elements we can use to orient our analysis toward the logic of autoimmunization, notably a montage of Koranic verses that the author makes use of in insets alongside the main text. The purpose of this arrangement (referred to as a schema) is to illustrate the author's introductory remarks: "By asking the question 'why life,' we seek to give meaning to life and grasp its principal goal. Generally, two opposite senses are given to it by men; a first, sacred sense, transcendent and eternal, and a profane sense, absurd and ephemeral. Both senses are mentioned in the sacred book of Islam, the Koran."[58]

The author's interpretation of this schema is simple: the ongoing destruction of the world, which he refers to as "global genocide" (quoting Costeau), is due to the invasion of the sense of the sacred by the sense of the absurd and profane, brought about by the development of technology from the capitalist West. The proposed solution is to stuff science with the sacred sense of the Koran, in order to strangle the absurd sense. In short, according to the author, the mix of science and religion we find in Islamist ideology would be the response to a disruption of the meaning of life. What is the nature of this disruption?

Let us assume that the claims of the author's text are capable of providing insight into the confusion that has given rise to Islamist ideology. Let's begin by examining what appears to be the least complicated sense based on the schema, the absurd sense. The expression "this world" clearly indicates that we are talking about this world. The "sense of the world" would then be absurd — not an absence of sense but one that is contrary to reason, inaudible to it *(ab-surdum)*.[59] The world would thus have nonsense for sense; or, rather, non-sense would be the sense of the world. According to one of the passages from the Koran quoted earlier (the third in the schema), atheism is the belief in the non-sense of the world. However, this claim is made from the point of view of the sacred sense, which gives the world meaning through religion or, if one prefers, based on an afterlife — in other words, metaphysics.

The source of meaning for religion is based on the purpose of mankind's creation, which is "to worship god." God created mankind to receive mankind's love in return. Mankind is thus a mirror of god, as the Muslim mystics said in interpreting the Koran. For religion, the subject is subjected to this primary orientation of meaning, this meaning of meaning, which is the capture of mankind in the specular *jouissance* of the Other. As for death, it constitutes a second orientation of meaning, namely, the challenge that defines an individual ethical course here below, at the end of which man, as a creature, returns to his creator ("to Us you will return"). The system functions according to the principle of a twofold return to god in love and in death. It is this that the two excerpts from the Koran in the schema attempt to demonstrate under the category of the "sacred sense."

So where is the problem? The author's confusion arises from the fact that, through technology and science, the world is no longer subject to the orientation of meaning on the basis of the twofold return but has transformed itself into a source of meaning, that is, "a world that becomes its own meaning" (Jean-Luc Nancy). This meaning is obtained at the cost of a work of terrifying negativity (production + consumption = destruction), which detaches mankind from the specular relationship to the Other. Thus, not only does god no longer constitute the unique source toward which meaning returns, and not only does the world produce its own meaning, but this meaning no longer has an identifiable destination; it overflows we don't know where, nowhere, never to return. Consequently, there is, at the same time, an excess of meaning and a terrifying loss of meaning in overwhelming infinity.

If we attempt to clarify the disruption of meaning from a metapsychological point of view, everything in this author's text tends to express — in its own way and in its own language — the idea of a historical modification, not only of the relationship to death but also of the actuality of the death drive.[60] If, given the way religion is organized, death is contained within the symbolic order by orienting meaning toward the Other, in a situation where the world is its own meaning, then death escapes the grasp of the symbolic, provides no orientation, and is at the service of no alterity.[61] Its destructiveness consists not only in taking life but also in a radical expropriation of the differential ethical qualities established by tradition, including mankind as the mirror of his creator. In short, in this world, death would no longer be death, just as man no longer reflects any other face but his own as it exists in the world. That is why the author, like other religious scientists, seeks to encase scientific and technical meanings within the sacred meaning, so as to contain an uncontrollable negativity and restore the theological structure of cross-referencing and circularity.

But this operation was destined to fail from the start, for it is based on a desperate attempt to control a trauma of faith in the religious subject. In the present text, as in all of this literature, and, in general, in the Islamist order of discourse that tries to capture science, we perceive something like a fatal encounter with the apparatus of scientific truth. As a result of this encounter, the mental coherence of religiosity can no longer be preserved. The following quotation is from a physicist in the Islamist movement: "From the start, I understood that the truth of science does not contradict the truth of religion, but clarifies it with a blinding light. For science shows in the real (waqi'), in detail and in the present, the truth that the Koran had already prepared and promised. It simply provides the proof of what was contained in the noble verses. We no longer have any excuse, as our forerunners, who had to put up with the hidden meaning until the last judgment. Now, the love of science must be equal to [fi mustawa, "at the level of"] the worship of God."[62] Based on this statement, the fatal encounter can be situated in the establishment of a hitherto unknown relation between truth and science, where a challenge (to live with the hidden meaning) is abolished in favor of a proof, and deferral relinquishes its position to the immediacy of revelation. It is this fascination with encountering truth in the real that subjugates the subject, causing him to experience love for science as equal to the worship of god. Something like an earth-shattering experience with the nakedness of truth has taken place.

This example clearly reveals the mechanism of autoimmunization. In the religious system, the subject must yield to the revealed signs behind which the truth remains hidden from all proof, whereas the scientific approach proceeds from an explanatory unveiling of reason; it introduces a truth of the real that shows itself directly every time it is convoked by calculation or through experiment. It is this truth of the real, whose manifestation is sufficient, that seduces believers, leading them to hand over the keys to the divine signs. For them, science has "realized" sacred writing, or stripped truth bare.

From this point on, a structural mutation in the foundations of faith has been at work. The procedures of legitimacy shudder beneath the prerogatives of science, which is invested with an authority that authenticates the truth of religion. Consequently, the incest prohibition receives its validity as a biological solution, and we have a literature in which the discourse of science continuously vouches for revelation. Science can do this because it presumably has the power to produce a pure truth, truth without an interpositional statement. Inherent in this is a belief that lies at the root of the mutation toward modern civilization, a belief in the abdication of language before a subjectless truth of the real.

### The Modern Caesura and the Despair of the Masses

In the preceding developments I do not claim to provide an exhaustive explanation of a phenomenon as considerable as the disruption of the Muslim world. My intent, rather, has been to identify certain areas of tension, rupture, or transformation whose center of gravity has been identified as the torment of origin. Behind the attempt at a forced restoration of the control of origin is concealed the dislocation of the relation to its sovereign myth. The *tourmentum* signifies the torment, suffering, and pain that resonate from a thousand cries heard across this world, like a collective attack of narcissism. Both the Rushdie affair and the abrogation of origin provide insight into the key challenges involved. These two events illustrate the historic and structural scope of this torment. On the one hand, we have a subversive use of metaphors of origin, implying a reworking of the textual body of the father, whose shards are projected across the world's stage in the name of a literary justice that would provide all with equal access to the text, and its truth, as fiction. This is literature as the subjective sharing of origin, as the diaspora of a story, any story. On the other hand, we have a dangerous maneuver that expels the community outside the metaphor of origin, forcing it to work its way backward through a time in which it is assumed to have strayed. We find in this a furious reprisal against modern history, accused of exposing the faithful, of locking them out within an unknown disbelief.

The return to origin should be understood not as a movement of the present toward the past nor as a past that must be made present, but as the return of a past from before the beginning, an anachronic and anarchic antecedence toward the matrical ark of the law. It is a question of being born again into origin from a preorigin. To paraphrase Hamlet, Islam is out of joint.

What does this unhinging mean for psychoanalysis, other than that the psychic metaphor has been attacked, that its mirror no longer pivots around the axis of eternal origin, and that a series of events has precipitated it into another temporality? Gilles Deleuze evokes Hamlet and the work of Kant in pointing out that time is no longer that of cosmic and celestial movement around an origin, or the meteorological time of the rural world, but that of the city, which is not subject to any condition but its own, thus introducing the order of pure time as an order of interminable change.[63]

It is a fact that the "vertical exile" resulting from Rushdie's pulverized origin coincides with the "horizontal exile" of the peasant masses to the outlying areas of urban agglomerations. But the Muslim world has known neither the figure of Hamlet nor the work of Kant, and hardly any of those markers of the passage of time. When time turns in the unnameable and unthinkable, becoming encounters fury, the delirium of theft, and the desire for vengeance. This is the reign of the martyr.

And it is precisely through the analysis of torment that we have been led toward the storm of turmoil. Our reading of the Islamist discourse that subjugates the masses reveals that, contrary to popular conceptions, what we are witnessing, far from being a simple return of the religious, is the confused manifestation of the decomposition of religion and its recomposition as a new, modern totalitarian ideology: national-theoscientism. Decomposition and recomposition are determined not by the interplay of contemporary ideas but by a system that regulates the life of bodies. In this case we are witnessing the undoing of the entire economy of *jouissance* that the theological order once so powerfully structured.

A civilization can become sick if the resistance to instinctual demands it has erected is no longer adequate. The failure to create new modes of subjectivization through which a more appropriate distribution of limits might take place has led to the appearance of morbid and cruel forces, along with a reactive appeal to radical forms of instinctual repression, such as the establishment of the reign of the obscure god, as we have seen in the example of the veil of sorrow. This is practically a textbook example of Freud's warning in *Civilization and Its Discontents* (1930), where he writes, "The sense of guilt [is] the most important problem in the development of civilization" (*SE*, 21:57–145).

The decomposition of religion and its ideological recomposition harbor another challenge alongside that of *jouissance:* behind the disruption of meaning we find a modification of the field of alterity, death, and truth. The result is the pathetic attempt to reestablish the protective orientation of the finality of meaning in a closed circuit that leads from god to god. When meaning is no longer oriented by the other world, when man is no longer the mirror of the One, when death no longer leads him to god, then the system begins to leak from all sides and "takes on nothingness" the way a sinking ship takes on water. In desperation, science is called upon to plug the holes, but the metal of its truth, which appears to lend itself to forming a new alloy with theological matter, merely corrodes it more intensely by attacking the nucleus of its truth: language. In the face of a truth of the real that can only result in authorized brutality, the illusion that science pursues the same goals as religion blithely signs the protocol of abdication of names.

## Mutation and Civilization

A new temporal order, modification of the economy of *jouissance,* transformation of the field of alterity and death, the emergence of a new regime of truth — by examining these elements as part of a larger context, we are in a better position to understand the nature of the mutation of civilization. Starting with Islam, we can give this notion a precise meaning. A civilizational mutation occurs whenever change affects the constituents of the pentahedron (time, *jouissance,* alterity, death, and truth) and brings about a new status quo in the connections among men and in their relation to the world. As a result, cultural work *(Kulturarbeit)* is necessary so that the new status quo can be assimilated by the psychic life of the individual and can ensure its unconscious anchorage in the human collectivity. Herein lies the capacity for subjectivization in the living being known as man, without which he is like any other animal, except perhaps in his power of destruction. We know, furthermore, that there is a point of desubjectivization beyond which man becomes the most fearful animal known.

Although Europe has undergone a similar mutation, leading to the emergence of the modern subject, not only did this occur over a long period of time but it was also guided, and sometimes anticipated, by works of art in all areas of culture, works that provided a way of conceptualizing change, or at least of making it available to individual and collective representation. For a long time large swaths of this mutation remained unimagined, especially when it involved the invisible architecture of culture and its instinctual foundations. The emergence of psychoanalysis finds its roots in the urgent need to clarify the radical transformation of subjectivity and its truths, which I have suggested referring to as the transition from the psyche of god to the psyche of the unconscious. This change is not only associated with representation, however, for that assumption neglects the physical upheaval, more specifically, the instinctual mechanisms whose moral and legal order was able, at one point, to govern the general economy of *jouissance.* For psychoanalysis, the work of culture, as a function of representativeness between the subject and the collectivity, cannot be separated from the question of the drives.[64]

The process of mutation in the Islamic world, although it reflects that of Europe in some respects, has taken place in historical, social, and political conditions of an entirely different nature. Succinctly, it is characterized by three traits: the element of colonial violence that marked its entrance into the modern world;[65] the electrifying speed of transformational processes and the way they have been obscured by the economic ideology of development; and the scarcity of works that illuminate the present and outline the future. As a result, we can consider the Islamists' cry of revolt as a mass protest brought about by the painful effects of the transformation of their world and the failure to implement *Kulturarbeit,* a transformation thus made unthinkable, absurd, and traumatic.

The following lines from the Seventh Elegy of Rainer Maria Rilke, one of the European poets most sharply attuned to the distress that accompanied the mutation of the modern world, reveal the tragedy of this condition:

> Each sluggish revolution of the world
> leaves its dispossessed — heirs neither
> of things past nor of those impending.
> The immediate future is distant for man.

The masses find themselves doubly dispossessed: by the poverty of the desolate urban landscapes into which they were thrust and in the indigence of representation of their newly imposed human situation. Powerful processes of subjective revocation appeared on a scale previously unknown. By this I am referring to the forms of massive destitution that are produced whenever the conditions of mankind's world can no longer be apprehended by the signposts of truth found in subjectivity. The masses then find that their self-interest, the perseverance of their being, and the consistency of what is common to their community are threatened.

Although men can endure extreme situations of material poverty, as a result of such destitution they begin to despair, become delusional, rebel, and sometimes end up in such a state of need that they will accept any transfusion of meaning. The shame of being subjectively revoked leads to the desire to bypass the present world to see whether, behind it, origin as inaugural paradise of truth is still accessible. Clearly, this presumes that the interruption provoked by mutation will be met by regression. Rilke's phrase "heirs neither / of things past nor of those impending" refers to a suspension and a divestment that evoke what Hölderlin called the "caesura," namely, the empty and untethered moment of tragic transport when every connection and every alternate fail.[66]

The elegy's following line, "The immediate future is distant for man," relates the caesura to the radical alienation of mankind from the essence of his being. However, this is hardly a consolation, for what is at play here are the fragility of the human form and our disorientation in recognizing it. And for Rilke, these are terrifyingly threatened in mass concentrations of men.

By claiming there has been a violent caesura in contemporary Islam that has disturbed traditional modes of subjectivization, we expose the crucial problem of identification and ideals: through this caesura, psychoanalysis views the nature of each man's adhesion to the human species as a process that makes use of the work of culture, a process that can, under certain circumstances, be arrested.

For a number of years, from the point of view of both clinical observation and events on the global scene, the contemporary development of civilization has gone hand in hand with the intensification of a generalized crisis of identity. The masses — and not only in the case of Islam — have been dragged in all directions toward unreasonable claims of identity, which can result in the cruelest acts of violence under the guise of appropriating the proper of who they are. By the same token, we willingly proclaim the destruction of the proper of the other, hoping to deprive him and his humanity of it, leaving him as exposed as a skinned animal. I have suggested using the term *expropriation* to refer to this sense of threat to the proper of what one is, as well as to the desire to dispossess the other because he might prevent the "Self" or the "Us" of the community from remaining the same. Expropriation appears to overflow the classic concept of the death drive, to the extent that it does not cease with the reduction to inanimacy but aims at the annihilation of qualities relative to identification, symbolic genealogy, and alterity. Thus, expropriation would be at the root of any transindividual processes that feed genocidal hatred.[67]

If we wish to avoid the frequent use of the word *fascism* to describe this phenomenon and want to go further in explaining what is happening, we must follow the trace of a historical truth that intersects this point of hatred and *jouissance* of identity. At this point we can formulate, with particular reference to the Muslim world, a three-part analysis:

First, the modern mutation necessarily brings about a caesura in the identificatory anchorages wherever it occurs. This caesura is not accidental; it characterizes modernity as such. It is systematic. It corresponds to a wide-ranging evolutionary process in the transformation of human subjectivity, which will continue throughout a lengthy historical period, from which the West itself has not yet broken out. We cannot comment about its ends, in the sense of both finality and limit. Nor do we know if humanity has undergone a mutation of this scope in the order of subjectivity, because the history and anthropology, the historicity of the modes of "being subject," have not yet been undertaken. But at least one thing is certain, namely, that this is a high-risk process for all of humanity, exacerbated by our misunderstanding and our emphasis on ecological risks, which leads us to ignore subjective devastation. The negation of the psychic is a dependent exponential variable of those devastations that are manifested in individual and collective psychoses, in massacre and genocide.

Second, when the modern caesura of identification occurs suddenly, without the corresponding cultural work, and when the deconstructions it engenders go largely unnoticed, it is transformed into a disastrous process of subjective revocation on a large scale, which triggers the despair of the masses. This despair is even more devastating when it is combined with poverty and the destruction of living spaces, but its causes lie in the loss of unconscious individual-collective anchorages and are expressed in the identificatory fear of losing face.

Third, this despair can manifest itself in the regression of human formations toward archaic configurations, individual and collective, in which identificatory hatred is openly expressed. In general, this leads to a collective restoration of face and incriminates the other — the minority or the neighboring community — felt to be responsible for the loss of face. The resulting aggressiveness then strives to eradicate the "face" of the other.

From the point of view of psychoanalysis, we cannot restrict our analysis to the views developed by Freud in *Civilization and Its Discontents* and other texts on culture to address such contemporary problems. To see things from the point of view of *Civilization and Its Discontents* and "Beyond Discontent" is a fundamental challenge for psychoanalysis,[68] if we intend to consider, as Jacques Derrida suggests, that mental cruelty is, "without excuses," the business of psychoanalysis.[69] Moreover, recognition of this need is becoming increasingly more evident in psychoanalytic work in France.[70]

## Despair, with Freud and Beyond

Let us consider the problem that most interests us here, the one treated in *The Future of an Illusion*, where Freud addresses religion's place in civilization and its future (*SE*, 21:1–56). It is interesting to note that the concept of despair is used by Freud specifically to characterize what occurs when religious illusion collapses. Let's return to the comment by his imaginary interlocutor (Pastor Pfister) in the book's final pages: "You have to defend the religious illusion with all your might. If it becomes discredited — and indeed the threat to it is great enough — then your world collapses. There is nothing left for you but to despair of everything, of civilization and the future of mankind."

Certainly, Freud's remarks on religion are prudent when discussing issues that directly affect the contemporary crisis of Islam. While treating religion as an illusion, he nevertheless considers it a participant in the defense of civilization, for it supports mankind's ego ideal. Remember that his central thesis is that culture exists only to the extent that men succeed in imposing draconian libidinal restrictions on themselves, through repression and prohibition. Prohibition frustrates men, so that each becomes a virtual enemy of culture, which is, even so, a benefit for all. Of course, men find compensations for their frustrations, but Freud's point of view here is that modern culture demands many more restrictions, especially when it comes to those who are most disadvantaged; even more so when it asks that they have a rational rather than a religious understanding of the prohibition.

According to Freud, modern culture seeks to establish the prohibition socially, by providing it with a human and rational origin. He argues for this rational foundation, but the fact is that the psychoanalytic inquiry shows that man, both on the general level of the species and on the individual level, has access to this prohibition only through his drives, the very access through which religion approaches the prohibition. In other words, the power of religious representations stems from the fact that the shield of their illusion against distress is so close to the emotional and physical character of the human condition. This is why they are so effective, and why it is so difficult to quickly free oneself of them. "It is certainly senseless to begin by trying to do away with religion by force and at a single blow," writes Freud. Likewise, it would be illusory to believe that religious illusion would retreat in the face of a greater engagement of rational actuality if physical human despair were not managed by constructions that accommodate imperious and libidinal demands, recognizing them, limiting them, and providing alternative solutions.

In spite of his caution, Freud gave free rein to his conviction that the ideal of science would be substituted for that of religion, a childhood disease of the human race. Yet we see in the case of Islam that the problem is far more complicated, for religion does not collapse but enters a cycle of decomposition and recomposition, using elements borrowed from scientific discourse and scientific ideals. In reality, there is a blend of illusions: religiosity and scientism are amalgamated and strengthen one another. This leads to the creation of derivative products such as culturalism and results in the ruin of subjectivity, where one comes to regret the subject of the religious institution of old, when god did not hide behind the folds of differentialism and cultural identity.

Contrary to what Freud leads us to believe, despair is not the culmination of the misfortune of religious subjectivity; it is the point of departure for a new state, which is a blend of illusions. At the same time, Freud provides the key to the structural explanation when he denounces the gluttony of the superego. Unlike nature, which merely abhors a vacuum, the superego, rather than remain silent in the face of caesura, chooses to take advantage of the situation. This remark is true for the situation of the subject in Islam, but it is equally true for the subject in the West, who experiences a different kind of mutation, which also leads, although differently, to the collapse of ideals, to despair, and to the intermingling of illusions — for example, between hypersubjectivity and the foreclosure of the subject in a calculating reason, between the managerial and humanitarian modes, and between hypertechnicity and magico-ethnic fragments.

## The Despair of the Masses in the Islamic World

Despair is not a category of political science; there is no trace of the term in its language. However, the Islamist movement and, a fortiori, its extremist wing can be viewed only as the most powerful indication in the contemporary world of the "despair of the masses."

In a text titled "Les islamistes sont-ils les ennemis de la modernisation ou ses victimes?" (Are Islamists the Enemies or the Victims of Modernization?), the Islamic scholar Abdelmajid Charfi, after attempting to analyze the conditions leading to the emergence of the Islamist movement, concludes, "Is it fair, after all, to treat the Islamist problem without also considering the causes that created it, to limit ourselves to defending them [Islamists] or putting them in prison or detention camps? Wouldn't it be preferable to increase our efforts to save them and to save society as a whole from their desperate solution, by reducing the causes of that despair (ya's)?"[71]

In his analysis, Charfi, who combines scholarship with observation of the reality of his environment, suggests that we distinguish between modernity and modernism. Modernity is the type of civilization invented two centuries ago in Europe, which has spread across the globe. Modernism is the imitation of modernity, its blind application — and therefore its failure — because it is considered, dogmatically, as the best of all possible civilizations. In this sense, modernism is the misleading ideology of modernity. Charfi's analysis rests on the belief that Islamists are the reactive product of modernism seen as the failure of modernity.

In certain ways, this idea is similar to Michel Foucault's reading of the Iranian insurgency against the shah. In 1978, two years before the fall of the monarchy, he wrote, in an Italian daily, "I then thought I understood that recent events did not signify the withdrawal of the most backward groups in the face of a too sudden modernization; but the rejection, by a culture and a people, of a modernization that is in itself archaic." He went on to write, "With the current Iranian regime in its death throes, we are witnessing the final moments of an episode that began nearly sixty years ago: an attempt to modernize Islamic countries on the European model. The Shah still clings to that idea as his only justification. I don't know if he's already looking forward to 2000. But I do know that his so-called vision dates from the nineteen twenties."[72]

Charfi's remarks are essentially devoted to describing the genealogy of Islamist despair resulting from modernism. He begins by recalling the deplorable situation of Islamic societies at the beginning of the twentieth century, before the appearance of anticolonial national liberation movements. This was a world marked by the scourge of poverty, epidemics, and illiteracy. Exhausted societies entered a state of lethargy interspersed with periodic uprisings that the colonial powers brutally repressed. Only tradition, architected by religion, helped those human communities survive; they turned in on themselves in a subsistence economy, without help and without alternatives.

Segments of the intellectual and political elite were aware of the lethargic state of their societies, of the economic exploitation and denial of rights that colonialism imposed. Some of them were the product of the colonial educational system that had introduced modern education to certain schools to supply administrators capable of applying its policies. It is this elite that rebelled against the colonial system and wanted to reform society.

Because the religious referent was the dominant referent in the culture of the time, reform elites, to ensure they would be understood by the people and to mobilize them against colonialism, used a language impregnated with religion. This was a new kind of language, which differed from that of the traditionalists and conservatives, as well as from popular speech.

At this point I would say that Charfi's description is beginning to reveal the elements of the modern caesura of identification, in which we see how, through a vast interplay of historic contradictions, Rilke's line — "heirs neither / of things past nor of those impending" — is realized. This is reflected in the way religion was used in the discourse of colonial emancipation: the religion used for political purposes was no longer the religion of the past, and the politics was no longer modern politics, which established its autonomy from religion.

Most importantly, from the moment these elites achieved a national state, becoming the direct heirs of the colonial government, the process acquired tremendous power in terms of actuality and rapidity. In every sector of social life — family, school, authority, health, demographics, and law — Charfi shows how these efforts never succeeded, or succeeded only by preventing the transmission of the past and destroying its meaning, without being able to establish anything other than a modernity incapable of taking on the task of humanizing society. We are then openly confronted with the fearful structure of the double negation — "neither of things past nor of those impending" — within which, if we are attentive, we can hear the "neither . . . nor" of nihilism. This is not Charfi's conclusion, but if there exists an Islamist despair whose major configurations he describes, it has been able to produce itself only from an unsustainable exposure to the void of the caesura, to the mass subjective revocation it has brought about, becoming, in response, a headlong quest for truths that restore subjectivity, including the return to the paradise of origin.

But to what extent is the distinction between modernity and modernism viable? Aren't we exculpating historical processes that can be brought about only by considerable violence? Can we avoid the emergence of the modern state and its direct intervention in the caesura of identification?

## State and Ego

We can use patriarchy as an example. The power and legitimacy of its system of subjugation reside in the postulate that the institution of filiation and the institution of power are one and the same — which effectively means that the logic of birth rules. The father provides a mediating function that perpetuates the union of the two principles, transmitted by god through one's ancestors. For god is the primal coalescence of the beginning and the commandment, of life and power, of nature and law. It is through this coalescence that the individual's most fundamental and direct identification with the father is established, according to a logic that one Muslim author has called "the natural politics of God."[73] Thus, in the traditional system, paternal transmission is not affected by the separation between the logic of birth (family) and the logic of politics (the tribe), because it serves to unite the two. It is the founding of the patriarchy that gives the paternal function such energy, by making the sire a father and a leader: a patriarch. We also see how patriarchy is strengthened by what Freud calls the "*direct* identification of individual prehistory with the father," although Freud does not assimilate it to the masculine sex of the biological father. But the modern state can establish itself only by separating the logic of birth, which is that of the family, and the political logic of the tribe, to create another, broader political space, notably that of civil society.

This separation, without which we cannot understand the transformation of "family complexes"[74] and the waning of the patriarchy (which also had an effect on the paternal function, although in theory we should distinguish between them), has immediate consequences on the formation of the subject; for the structure of the ego and its ideals differs depending on whether there is a separation between the birth community and the political community. If there is no separation, the patriarchal energy of the paternal imago provides the ego ideal with a capacity for aggregation and belonging, giving the ego considerable potential for resistance to disintegration. In this situation, the ego has no need to struggle against or resist the multiplicity of identifications one encounters in the modern subject, for whom the state has brought about the separation between the family and the political space. That is why, in the case of premodern subjectivity, the ego does not assume the heroic aspect it manifests in the modern subject, and always seems to be in the background, to the extent that we can speak of the "de-egoization" of the subject. This is even more pronounced when such a subject is continuously encouraged to manifest its love and submission to the patriarch, to inevitably elevate him to the position of his ego ideal, so that the temptation of narcissistic reflux, the cause of serious mental illness, is continuously frustrated, to the benefit of this powerful enticement.

The liberation of the modern subject from the figure of the patriarch as father/leader (the orthography is intentional) obviously introduces large swaths of freedom, incorporating a multiplicity of objects of identification where anything is possible, including for leaders who want to be fathers, which is not at all the same thing as fathers who are leaders from the start. It is because there are no longer any father/leaders that crowds in modern mass societies can erect a leader in place of their ego ideal. In this case we could speak of a separation of the powers of identification that the traditional world confused, those between the procreative father, the symbolic father, and the master. Recall Freud's remark that comes after the famous passage on direct identification with the father of individual prehistory, an identification that would, according to Freud, provide resistance against the threatening diversity of object identifications:

> If they [object identifications] obtain the upper hand and become too numerous, unduly powerful and incompatible with one another, a pathological outcome will not be far off. It may come to a disruption of the ego in consequence of the different identifications becoming cut off from one another by resistances; perhaps the secret of the cases of what is described as "multiple personality" is that the different identifications seize hold of consciousness in turn. Even when things do not go so far as this, there remains the question of conflicts between the various identifications into which the ego comes apart, conflicts which cannot after all be described as entirely pathological. (*The Ego and the Id, SE,* 19:1–66)

The logic of universalization of the modern state correlates closely with the emergence of a subject for the heroic ego that is adequate to the diversity of object identifications it undertakes and to the divergence that consequently haunts it. Modern literature, from James Joyce to Salman Rushdie, consistently bears witness to this multiple ego. What could be more logical than that, eventually, this ego would become a servant and allow itself to be served by a blend of illusions? The confusion of our contemporary culture would then reflect the threat of divergence of the subject's ego. Consumption encourages the multiplication of objects of identification, for example, through the system of trademarks, whose name so aptly reflects its function.

But didn't Hegel already warn of this evolution, given that his philosophy of the state was initially a philosophy of the ego? If we reexamine the *Realphilosophie,* we can see the extent to which the foundations of the state and the ego are the same, and how the unity of the modern ego is conceivable only to the extent that it is multitude and movement in the surrounding night.[75]

There is nothing surprising about the fact that the state is the principal exponent of the modern caesura of identification. This is, in fact, the argument of Étienne Balibar in *La crainte des masses,* where he theorizes a form of civility that incorporates the issue of collective identification, especially during periods of mutation. He writes, "Hegel's idea is that primary identities and affiliations [family, clan, religion, region, etc.] must be virtually destroyed if they are to be, not only purely and simply eliminated, but reconstructed as particular expressions and mediations of collective political identity or adhesion to the state." He goes on to write, "The deconstruction of primary identities, even, and especially, as the price of liberation, is in itself an extremely violent process, a 'disintegration' or dismemberment of the individual and the affiliation that served as membership for him."[76]

To identify the despair of the masses in the Islamic world is to claim that the modern state in the hands of a postcolonial elite (with the relative exception of someone like Bourguiba) has triggered an uncontrollable process of hidden destruction of the old order of primary identification, replacing it with constructed simulacra, without managing to realize anything other than a series of disconnections. The immediacy of tradition to itself is broken and uncoupled from its awareness. However, there is no new *Kulturarbeit* available to compensate for the destroyed modes of transmission, bringing about a destructive interference by repressive substitutes that are fiercer than those of the patriarchate. Islamist ideology is the response, in the form of a blend of illusions, to the subjective revocation that this caesura has brought about en masse.

What is the position of the psychoanalyst in the face of this condition? For him or her, the brutality of the mutations and the accompanying privation are not negligible. Freud never accepted them as a sign of progress but, rather, considered that they were a danger to civilization. He rejected any restoration of the old order in any form, but, while recognizing the necessity and aridity of the loss, neither did he accept the contemporary condition. Here it is appropriate to quote Nietzsche: "One forbids oneself every kind of clandestine access to afterworlds and false divinities — but cannot endure this world though one does not want to deny it."[77] There is no return to the past, no submission to the actual, and no negation of the real, to which we should add the three positive acts that sustain the psychoanalyst's analysis: to be receptive to anger, to identify despair, and to analyze its figures.

### Postscript: After September 11

The shock in the face of horror and the incessant repetition of the terrifying images of the attack of September 11, 2001, soon gave way to a global forum that tried to explain the causes of the act and evaluate its significance. The actual crime has become part of contemporary thought, part of the universe of discourse. The words read and heard cut through the torpor of the last few years, when history had supposedly ended. Everywhere we turned, something akin to a desire to reread the world in the dust-laden darkness of the towers appeared before our staring eyes. Our frankness increased with the presentiment that today's evil may be only a portent of a more terrifying tomorrow. However, there is a risk that hasty interpretations that appear to supply a reasonable response to our painful questions may leave out a great deal and, more seriously, may produce the illusions that nourish the hateful myths of identity politics in the future.

One explanation that appeared shortly after the attacks seems to contribute to this risk. It was soon repeated and spread across the world by a large number of media outlets. It is in the process of becoming the truth of the event and the focus of what is coming. This is the theme of humiliation and Islam, a humiliated Islam that is said to respond through sacrificial terror, taking revenge on the United States — or even the whole of what is known as the West — which is accused of being the author of this humiliation.

The concept is being dangerously misused, especially since it contains an element of truth concerning "political affects" that have been taken out of context. Behind the facade of recognition of a wrong, a kind of mea culpa — "We have humiliated the Muslims" — a series of infernal traps are created that authenticate the idea of the clash of civilizations and provide unlimited credit for future terror.

This idea infers that those who planned the attack are an expression of Islam and Muslims, and that they are engaged in a logic of recovering their honor and dignity. It is a perfect alibi for not modifying one's behavior and serves as a bond with the despair of the masses. We know that humiliation by the other is a powerful affect that can move the masses and that drives the most extreme logic of sacrifice in the hope of recovering offended dignity. When the example of the humiliation of the Treaty of Versailles as a cause of the Second World War is used to support such an interpretation,[78] the legitimation of resentment and revenge is molded into the rock of historical truth.

This image also assumes that Islam or Muslims can be assimilated to a unified entity capable of the same feelings, desires, and experiences; capable of bowing the same collective head (the ecclesiastical sense of the Latin *humiliare*). Yet nothing could be further from the truth. Although Islam is the name of a single religion, its human, cultural, and political reality is manifold and diffracted. Current events proved this a few days after the attack, in the welcome that Muslims in Kazakhstan gave to the pope during his visit. They made up two-thirds of the crowd that attended Mass.[79]

Nor does the explanation take into account the theological-political void created in Islam at the beginning of the twentieth century, for, with the abolition of the caliphate (1924), no single entity had the sovereign power to declare war. Any appeal to *jihad* addressed to Muslims is a form of imposture. All wars now are national, or the business of ringleaders who dream of becoming the popes of a religion without popes. Islam has no unity, no center, no political sovereignty. Its only cohesion is based on a limited theological and ritual core that has become indistinguishable from the cultures it has penetrated. There is no single institution, like the Roman Catholic Church, that holds sway over the faithful.

Although it is true that the Arab populace has, for decades, endured degradation on every level, to reduce the causes to humiliation by the West or the United States would be a form of intellectual imposture insofar as the mechanisms that led to this condition are concerned. Victimization by outside forces alone can only deflect attention from internal causes and perpetuate the passivity that characterizes the posture of humility, to the extent that it remains fully wedded to its own desperate collapse.

For more than twenty years, current events have supplied us with signs of the profound political breakdown of the Arab world, which has affected its fundamental anthropological structures. A funereal process associated with the structure of power has fed a pathology whose energy has continued to sow suffering and desolation. We will be unable to identify the causes of this breakdown if we fail to confront one of the primary elements in the existence of every human community, namely, that the cruelty associated with the destruction of politics shatters human dignity.

In that sense, the Arab world is subject to its own humiliation. The primary responsibility undoubtedly lies with its governments. A generation of courageous politicians who helped their people confront the colonial powers, win their emancipation, and earn universal respect has been followed by a clique of "undesirables" characterized, with some exceptions, by a combination of contemptible traits: they are often uneducated, corrupt, and tyrannical.

These leaders have caused considerable harm to their people and have sown confusion among them. The list of their wrongs would be a lengthy one and is equal to the resentment and fury that are spreading openly among their populations. Simply because their brutality has not assumed the visible forms of internment camps and genocide (at least, for some) does not mean it is not destructive. What is this devastation made of? Of the monstrous banality of a machine for the enjoyment of power that brings together the archaic family, the repressive state, and the appropriation of wealth in the hands of a few.

The wealth of the Arab world, including the pseudorepublics, is held by two hundred ruling families. The largest, and most paradigmatic, is the Saud family, which has assimilated an entire country to its encampments. Arabia is the only state in the world whose name bears that of its leading family. For thirty years, this machine has continued to eradicate argument, opposition, and creativity through the use of imprisonment, torture, murder, the corruption of elites, and the imposition of the most brutal norms on the planet. Its functionaries have maintained and aggravated archaic forms of male domination and sexual repression. The majority of them have excluded women from political life and tolerate their public presence only when they are wrapped in sacks and muzzled. If there is humiliation to be found, it is essentially the result of the actions of this contemptible elite.

For years, sensing that the patience of their people was running out, these rulers have found means, through the media under their control, to deflect attention onto their principal protector by implicating it as responsible for the despair they have sown. The theme of humiliation by the United States or the West allows them to escape their primary responsibility. It should be pointed out that those superpowers, without whose complicity these regimes would not have survived, have not lost any opportunity to display their lack of interest in the people their protégés are supposed to represent. The malfeasance, inconsistency, and submission of the latter have allowed the sources of injustice and the failures of international law to perpetuate themselves.

The increasing vulgarity of these men, the offensiveness of their extensive wealth, and the repulsiveness of their manners, which they try to pass off as forms of cultural heritage, have given the world a highly negative view of Arabs. Although the United States is hated for the arrogance of its power, the representation of Arabs these rulers have propagated arouses contempt for its disgraceful mixture of inane impotence and shadowy farce. Of course, anti-Arab racism has found reasons to feed on this and has delayed global awareness of the injustice done to these people.

It cannot be emphasized enough the extent to which oil has supplied the means for perversion and manipulation that have led to unlikely historic configurations. The monopolization of wealth and the subjection of the state to the particular interests of families and rentier clans have propelled them, even with their archaism, into the avant-garde of free-market proponents in the globalized market. They were archaically in advance of the new global economic order. This is the reason for their powerful alliance with the American neoliberal camp.

But why has the modernity of the Arab world been so catastrophic? Unlike other regions of the globe, it shares such an important cultural background with Europe that a number of thinkers view the Arab-Islamic world as part of the West.

Although we know that civilizations are mortal, we need to remind ourselves that they are subject to torpors that can sometimes be fatal but that may also give rise to reawakenings that restore the desire to live. Europe underwent a period of darkness that lasted several centuries, during which the monotheistic ideal and the flame of Greek knowledge were maintained by Islamic civilization. Islam, in turn, fell into a state of lethargy between the fifteenth century and the first half of the nineteenth. From that point on, the Arab world experienced a period of awakening and a desire for modernity that became a kind of renaissance, where the forces of progress came to dominate society ideologically, leading to the emancipation from colonialism.

However, during the 1960s, the families that lived off oil wealth understood that the form this renaissance had taken was becoming dangerous to their existence, so they plotted to bring it to a halt. Taking advantage of the cold war, contradictions in the process of transformation, and strategic errors on the part of progressives, the ruling families financed the emergence of radical Islamist movements to destroy progressive forces, suspend the interpretation of ancient texts, and disseminate their own values. They succeeded beyond their wildest dreams. Once the Left had been destroyed, political demands had no way to express themselves other than to make use of the most emotionally charged conduit, a religious ideology crossed with nostalgia for a golden age. The exclusion of the masses was turned into a powerful feeling of resentment against modernity. The ideological acumen of the rentier families, once again led by the Saudi elites, was to fabricate a lie out of money and the sacred. The product of a faction that promotes a rigorous puritanism (Wahhabism) and repudiates the Islam of the enlightenment, it used Islamist movements to spread a literal conception of religion, haunted by a vengeful god who always requires greater self-denial. As we have known since Freud, such denial can lead only to an endless cycle of increased libidinal demands, greater repression, and a thirst for sacrificial satisfaction. This is another of the unlikely configurations that history has given rise to:

one of the ultraminority branches of Islam — practically a sect — succeeded, through its oil wealth and with the support of its American protector, in transforming an anomaly into a dominant ideology. The invention of the Taliban is part of the logic of this process that Saudi Arabia has orchestrated. To any attentive observer, it is obvious that there is no essential difference between the demiurge and his creature; it is only a matter of degree.

Any analysis that does not integrate the materiality of historic forces within the life space it studies is condemned to produce a dishonest analysis of the essence, the innocence, and the sentiments of the collective soul violated by the foreign. In short, it offers nothing but the eternal wheel of resentment.

# 2

# The Repudiation of Origin

## Appropriation and Translation of the Father

### Freud and Islam

In *Moses and Monotheism* (*SE*, 23:1–137), in the chapter titled "Difficulties," Freud confronts Islam. After excusing himself for his limited knowledge of the subject, he immediately eliminates it from his study. But in a short passage at the beginning of the chapter, he provides a quick interpretation of the founding of Islam and the reason for its expansion. It is important to note that his comments are based on accurate information, gathered from unquoted sources but no doubt drawn from the very rich field of German orientalism:

> I must regretfully admit that I am unable to give more than this one example [Judaism] and that my expert knowledge is insufficient to complete the enquiry. From my limited information I may perhaps add that the case of the founding of the Mohammedan religion seems to me like an abbreviated repetition of the Jewish one, of which it emerged as an imitation [*Nachtahmung*]. It appears, indeed, that the Prophet intended originally to accept Judaism completely for himself and his people. The recapture [*Wiedergewinnung*] of the single great primal father [*Urvater*] brought the Arabs an extraordinary exaltation of their self-confidence, which led to great worldly successes but exhausted itself in them. Allah showed himself far more grateful to his chosen people than Yahweh did to his. But the internal development of the new religion soon came to a stop, perhaps because it lacked the depth which had been caused in the Jewish case by the murder of the founder of their religion.

Although brief, Freud's comments considerably advance his ideas about Islam. Freud introduces it into the general framework of his theory of religion with reference to the central question of the father. This is done through the concept of repetition (*Wiederholung*), which is neither reproduction nor brooding *(Grübelzwang)*. Psychoanalysis approaches the phenomenon of repetition in two ways. The first is symbolic, where the principle of language assumes the use of the same signs: to the extent that the same sign serves to produce new meanings, we can say that repetition produces difference. The second way is through the encounter with a real that is impossible to symbolize. This is the case with trauma, where repetition seeks to control the trauma: repetition reflects the failure of the trauma's integration in mental life and the overflow of the unbearable event. The repetition is pointless and accommodates the return of the same. It was this return that led Freud to introduce the concept of the death drive. Consequently, repetition can be a sign of creative progress or its contrary, which impedes the vital flow of life.

Borrowing the concept of imitation, Freud makes use of one of the claims of European orientalism concerning the influence of Judaism on the founding of Islam, which contrasts with another current that associates its origin with the rise of Christianity. The history of European thought concerning Islam as imitation, that is, as having nothing intrinsic about it, nothing that is its own, goes back a long way. In its most radical expression, it connects this original impropriety to the propensity of its founder to appropriate what belonged to other religions. This gave rise to the themes of usurpation and the false prophet, which are found throughout this history. With its emergence, the last monotheistic religion entered into conflict with those that came before it. This focused the founder's preaching initially on the heritage of a first faith, that of Abraham, with Islam developing as a kind of reappropriation after it was deformed and forgotten by Judaism and Christianity. The return to Abraham was the key element in the Muhammedan refounding, a return that saw itself as the culmination of monotheism, binding its origin to its end. But as we have seen, originary appropriation is a very old story in monotheism. It is present in Genesis, within the patriarchal family, in the drama that occurs between Abraham, Sarah, and Hagar. In this chapter I want to discuss this question of the gift of origin, its apportionment, and its appropriation or reappropriation. The operations of writing and reading in monotheism, by all parties and at all times until the present day, have never stopped focusing on this point: the dread of the essence of origin, its propriety and purity, and its "originarity" and virginity. Isn't this one of the challenges of *Moses and Monotheism,* where Freud tries to show that the founder of Judaism is Egyptian, a stranger to the Hebrew people? Originally, nothing is "proper."

Also, although Freud associates the founding of Islam with the appropriation of Judaism, twice in *Moses and Monotheism* he returns to Meyer's thesis of the Jewish tribes' initial borrowing of their god from the Arabs: "There [in Arabia] they took over the worship of a god Yahweh, probably from the neighboring Arabian tribe of Midianites. It seems likely that other tribes in the vicinity were also followers of this god."

Primal appropriation, mimesis, and repetition — such is the complex problematic introduced by Freud's casual remarks about Islam, a sizable problem involving the formation of symbolic orders and the emergence of civilizations and their interrelationships, from one origin to another. From this point of view, *Moses and Monotheism* is an attempt to conceptualize the plurality of emergences and the resurgence of a single trace through space and time. The problem could, in fact, be formulated as the emergence and resurgence of origin. It is within this context that we must situate the final phase of Freud's affirmation of Islam: "The recapture *[Wiedergewinnung]* of the single great primal father brought the Arabs an extraordinary exaltation of their self-confidence, which led to great worldly successes but exhausted itself in them."

*Wiedergewinnung* can be broken down into *Gewinnung,* the act of obtaining, earning, or taking; and *wieder,* which means "again" or "once more." That is, *Wiedergewinnung* indicates, quite precisely, the fact of regaining or retaking, the idea of recurrent appropriation, which assumes an interruption and resumption of something that once belonged to oneself or to someone else. The adverb *again,* which marks the idea of a repetition or supplement, is found in the Freudian concept of repetition, *Wiederholung,* or *Wiederholungszwang,* translated as "repetition compulsion."

The idea of a reappropriation of the primal father in the founding of Islam is of great relevance to my investigation. I do not view it as the resolution of a problem but as an encouragement to consider the question of the father in Islam in relation to other monotheisms. Therefore, I want to conduct an experiment with Freud, by testing his claim about the Arabs' recapture of the primal father. In what sense was this *Wiedergewinnung* possible? How, in borrowing the facilitation of earlier monotheisms, did the founder of Islam reappropriate the primal father? How can we reconcile the reappropriation of the primal father, the mythic figure of unlimited *jouissance,* with the god of monotheistic law? Doesn't Freud contradict himself with his thesis concerning the origin of society and spirituality? If we turn to the primitive father of *Totem and Taboo* to explain the mechanism of Islam, we are faced with an alternative: One possibility is that Islam misunderstands the symbolic father, in which case the concepts of success, time, and monotheism have no meaning. (Here, it is useful to recall Hegel's thesis, which attributes the speed with which Islam became a "universal empire" to the high level of "abstraction of its principle" and to the "highest intuition of the One" in its awareness.[1] This abstraction necessarily assumes a withdrawal of the thing and a cleansing of the imaginary associated with the representation of god.) The other possibility is that the persistence of the primal father is omnipresent in spiritual systems through an ongoing antagonism with the figure of the symbolic father within them, a permanent struggle between the "obscure god" and the "sublime god." In this case Islam is no different than other monotheistic religions. We would then need to examine the historical phases during which the antagonism became virulent, when one of the two figures became prevalent. Between the sixth and fifteenth centuries, the reign of the universal Muslim empire gave rise to both the best and the worst along these lines. Christianity, which, according to Freud, came closest to acknowledging the murder of the father, experienced similar ups and downs. The god at work in the Spanish Inquisition, for example, was not characterized by his sublimity. The same is true of the god of the Algerian GIA (Armed Islamic Group) or the Taliban in contemporary Islam. For that matter, the Old Testament devotes considerable space to the presence of the two figures and their continual struggle in human desire. This may be the crux of the challenge of monotheistic repetitions, which collide with the impossibility of total symbolization in their originary relationship to the One.

There is another explanation for Freud's difficulty with Islam and his reliance on the solution of the primitive father: namely, contrary to Judaism and Christianity, Islam, from its origin, excluded god from the logic of paternity. The Koran is particularly careful to distance the representation of god from reference to the father, even symbolically. Proclamations of the uniqueness of god surely banish any notion of generation or divine procreation. In the sura of the "pure faith" (112), divine nature is described in these abrupt terms:

> Say: HE IS God
> the one, the most unique,
> God the immanently indispensable.
> He has begotten no one,
> and is begotten of none.
> There is no one comparable to Him.

The problem is, therefore, the following: How can we conceptualize the question of the father in a religion in which god is not the father? I will use the exploration of the position of the father in Islam to explicate a monotheistic repetition that, while borrowing the materials of those that preceded it, culminates in a difference at the center of what Freudian theory considers to be the genesis of symbolization and spirituality.

## Genesis of the Father, Gift of Place

If a reappropriation of the primal father is conceivable in Islam, it must certainly involve the figure of Abraham, the father that monotheism places at the beginning, or *entête,* of its archive,[2] whom I will refer to as the "Father-of-Genesis." It should be pointed out that the formation of Islam would have been inconceivable without this figure, without those aspects of the problematic of origins it was able to engage with. It is through the Father-of-Genesis that the Prophet of Islam provides access to the Unique and the Great. As the Koranic text illustrates on several occasions, Muhammad's preaching is connected to the Abrahamic Genesis through three fundamental symbolic functions.

The first is naming. The Prophet of Islam attributes to Abraham the gift of the name Muslim before Islam came to be: "He named you Muslim earlier, and in this [Koran]" (22:78). The term *Muslim (al-muslimin)* here signifies subjection to the unique god of Abraham, submission to his law, and abandonment to his intentions, as Abraham reveals.

The second function is paternal filiation. Muhammad defines Islam as the closure of monotheism, to the extent that he identifies "the faith of your forbear Abraham" (22:78). That is why we can say that Islam, from its inception, saw itself as the religion of the return to the Father-of-Genesis.

The third function is ritual inscription. Islam is the only one of the three monotheistic religions to make commemoration of Abraham's sacrifice a ritual annual obligation, during which every father must sacrifice a ram as a substitute for his son. This element is crucial for the formation of the paternal complex in Islam, because the renunciation of the murder of the son is continuously staged and reenacted. In this case we can speak of a reactualization, more than a remembering, of the renunciation of the murder of the son and of Abraham's pact. (I will return to this idea on several occasions, especially in the section of chapter 4 titled "Sacrifice and Interpretation.") But if this staging of the sacrifice — its *actus,* in the theatrical sense of the term — recalls the renunciation, at the same time it also calls to mind its origin, or the reason it has constituted itself as a renunciation.

If the Father-of-Genesis is not the "primal father," it is because the spiritual and symbolic order that the latter establishes is based on the acceptance of unlimited *jouissance* and recognition of the radical alterity of the Other. We know how the biblical story relates Abraham's moving effort to constitute the antinomic ideal of the primal father and his imaginary omnipotence, concluding in circumcision and the covenant. But isn't it in this very desire to tear himself away from the primal father that Abraham transmits the affects attached to his archaicness, such as the scene of the sacrificial substitution of the ram, which establishes the pact of renunciation? The Father-of-Genesis is haunted by the specter of the primal father he wants to see triumph. This specter serves as the foundation of Abraham's *archiécriture*.

In short, the Father-of-Genesis reveals the genesis of the father as detachment from the primal father. We can speculate that this figure of the father in Genesis is necessary for the intelligibility of the father, his writing, his transmission. The Abrahamic literature, which is present in this part of the Bible, serves to generate the father, which can be considered a critical element for any text claiming to affect thought or culture, especially during periods of civilizational mutation. It is this function and its transmission of the biblical text to the Koranic text that I want to discuss here.

For the Arabs, Ishmael could be designated as the Father in the sense that, with this name, something that is assumed to be essentially Arab begins. This beginning occurs in Genesis, during the dramatic episode when Abraham sends Hagar and her son, Ishmael, into the desert at Sarah's prompting because she wants the family heritage to go exclusively to her own son, Isaac. At the moment of extreme abandonment, when the child Ishmael is on the point of dying of thirst, god reveals to Hagar a spring that saves them both from death. It is at this point that the promise is made: "For I will make of you a great nation." Before the promise, Ishmael was a child who cried, a son abandoned in the desert by his father and nearly dying of thirst; but, at the moment the promise is made, he becomes the Father of a nation to come. The act of promising doesn't go into effect only in the future toward which it tends; at the very instant it is made, it produces a rupture through which the son is separated from the father who abandoned him. He is lifted up and saved, propelled toward a destiny of his own. Ishmael becomes the national son-father, drawing upon the promise that serves as the gift of the institution of origin. But this gift is offered only when being is abandoned to death or the unknown. More specifically, the gift of being assumes a being abandoned.

Gift and abandonment — these terms are the basis of the monotheistic ontology of father and son, the emotional mechanism of their dialectic. It is in the conjunction of love and death that their mutual union is revealed, because there is no abandonment without love, and there is radical abandonment only with death.[3] Christ's cry "My God, my God, why have you abandoned me?" may be not so much an appeal to provide a reason, or a reproach addressed to the Father, as a terrible cry before the mystery of a form of abandonment, where grace is revealed through cruelty.[4] Whereas in Judaism the son is brought to the brink of sacrifice by the father, and in Islam relief occurs in the cessation of wandering in the company of the mother, with the dying and resurrected Christ there appears the absolute dialecticalization of abandonment and relief, based on the logic of *Aufhebung*,[5] for the barrier of death has been breached in order to complete the manifestation of the mutual affiliation of father and son.

"What aileth thee, Hagar? fear not; for God hath heard the voice of the lad where he *is*. Arise, lift up the lad, and hold him in thine hand; for I will make him a great nation" (Genesis 21:17–18). This passage from Genesis indicates a twofold gift of place. While divine hearing reveals a place in the desert where the child is saved from death, the promise projects, against the erasure of memory, a place in time; a place toward which the transmission of a son in the process of becoming the national Father is directed. Jewish, Christian, and subsequent Muslim traditions have preserved, starting with this promise, the memory of Ishmael as an ancestor of the Arabs — to such an extent that the name Ishmael has become synonymous with Arabs. The spot where the spring is presumed to have been found is identified in the narrative of Islam as the very site where Mecca was built.

The revelatory hearing *(entente ouvrante)* of the voice, therefore, existed at the origin of Islam, an origin emerging from the origin of the other or its writing. Believing himself to be the recipient of this transmission, Muhammad later established Islam as faith in a god who presented himself originally by embracing the childish voice expressed in the distress of abandonment. This is one of the sources of the religion. The status of alterity in Islam is marked by the voice, by a "letter-voice," the voice found in the composition of the name Ishmael: god hears and understands. The father bears the Name of the Other's hearing.

The association of the principle of the father with origin presupposes several figures of the father. Their relation to one another should not be considered linear or fixed but should, rather, be seen as an interplay of the transappropriation of the father. Abraham sits at the summit of the monotheistic genealogy, as the father who engenders himself through his ability to detach himself from the tyrannical and murderous figure of the primal father. It is the Father-of-Genesis who, through his renunciation, invokes the specter of the primal father upon the scene. But Abraham cannot be a father without the son who will make him a father. This is the point of the story of Genesis, which shows him waiting for a promised paternity that is slow in coming. The expectation of the son is part of the genesis of the Father, to the extent that it leads to crucial maneuvering and a vast dramaturgy, in order to illustrate the engendering of the son and, at the same time, the generation of the father through the arrival of the son. To the extent that the promise of the god of the Bible to Abraham is the promise of a posterity, the Father is determined by his goal, and it is clear that this goal is national, because the son (each of the sons, Ishmael and Isaac) becomes the Father of a nation.

## The Father as Translation

In monotheism the national and the filial are closely connected in establishing the genesis of the Father, yet the writing of this genesis through the son requires a third element and a different time. Jahiz, a ninth-century Arab rationalist author, indicates this with his usual acuity: "If the Prophet hadn't said: 'Ishmael was an Arab,' he could only be, to our eyes, non-Arab, because the non-Arab cannot become Arab and vice-versa; and we know that Ishmael became Arab after having been non-Arab solely because the Prophet said it."[6]

What Jahiz brings out is the nature of the operation of establishing the national-Father-son as an operation of displacement of the non-Arab toward the Arab — of the nonproper toward the proper — that relies only on the power of the word: "solely because the Prophet said it." There is no natural paternity at the origin, no manipulation of any substance; the original paternity is the result of a speech act by the founding Prophet;[7] it is displacement through speech. How can we qualify this displacement?

It would be tempting to speak of a metaphor of the founding Father. But, in fact, the operation is not simply metaphoric; it does not effect a transport within a given language. Rather, it enacts a border crossing to another people and another language. What is speech that displaces the foreign and appropriates it, other than translation? The founder intervenes as a third father, a father who translates the story of the genesis of father and son, of another people. He establishes through an appropriating translation.

It is hard not to imagine that Freud, in transferring the circumcision and covenant from Abraham to Moses, and in making Moses an Egyptian, produced the father at the origin by means of translation. Freud does not call foundation "translation." Yet he approaches this point, given that the first chapter of *Moses and Monotheism* is devoted to showing how the name Moses is a Hebraization of the Egyptian *mose,* which refers to a child.[8] He goes straight to the heart of the matter in trying to prove that the proper name of the founder is not proper to the Hebrews, and that it is the product of a translation. But this demonstration will serve as the basis for what will be, for Freud, his task of translation, namely, the transition from myth to metapsychology. He proceeds through a series of transpositions that leads from the child in Moses's name to the psychic figure of the infantile, and from the myth of the birth of the hero to the family romance, resulting in a historical configuration of origin that is approached through a form of writing qualified as novelistic. (The book's subtitle should be "A Historical Novel.") For Freud, "historical truth" would be, in some sense, the referent that circulates from one translation to the other through the vector of the foreign child or the child who becomes foreign to his family. Fiction appears to be the site of transposition: here, *Moses and Monotheism* has the status of a historical novel, but previously *Totem and Taboo* was considered by Freud as a scientific myth. This relationship between the infantile, the foreign, and the fictional relies on a critical articulation involving the psychic status of translation as an originary operation. It commits us to viewing the modern myth of the psychoanalytic psyche as being correlative to that of translation.

And yet, in spite of the boldness of his gesture, Freud does not feel the need to theorize about translation in the process of the formation of origin, in the genesis of institutions and their symbolic order. No doubt, this is the reason why he remains a prisoner of the ethnocentric view of orientalism, making Islam an *imitation* where he should have seen *translation.* The work of conceiving translation as foundation is one of the consequences we must draw from Freud's final operation, which consists in making the founder of Judaism a stranger to his people.[9]

For what Freud does with Moses turns out to involve a threefold translation. First, there is a translation of Moses into the other origin, the Egyptian origin; then, to the extent that Moses is foreign, the Mosaic founding of Judaism necessarily entails a translation from Egyptian to Hebrew. Why has this need for translation not occurred to psychoanalysis? It should be obvious, for as soon as the foreign is part of origin, the basis of its experience in language is inevitably translation, the translation that becomes the corollary of foundation.[10]

In fact, it's the third translation that obscures the first two: the specific translation of psychoanalysis, which consists in translating Moses into the metapsychological language of the murder of the father. The murder of the father in Freud serves as the universal operator of his translation of metaphysics into metapsychological language, because metaphysics in religion is supposed to deny and repress the murder of the father. But doesn't translation contain murder within itself, to the extent that it necessarily involves the destruction of the literary body of the language of origin and the reappearance of what is translated in the literary body of the receiving language? The translation of the father as process of appropriation signifies that the father dies at his origin in the transition from one language to the other.[11] Wouldn't this be one of the events characteristic of an origin: a translation that provides the dead father with a grave in a different literary body? Through the exogamy of language known as translation, origins are indefinitely produced from one another.

Jahiz, in affirming that Ishmael becomes Father by appropriating the non-Arab to the Arab, confronts the clergy who wish to keep the father as is, to hold him as holding himself *in himself* since the origin. Jahiz implicitly bases the Muhammedan operation of filiation and affiliation on an utterance that is an appropriating translation. In terms of the symbolic institution, the challenge of translation should be thought of as the process of transposing the father through a strategy of mourning necessary to foundation. And couldn't we view Saint Paul's Epistle to the Hebrews, by the very fact that it was given in Greek to its people of origin, as a founding translation of the Christian institution (Saul was Paul's Jewish name)? Antoine Berman has shown how Luther created a foundational work through his translation of the Bible into German.[12] What Berman refers to as the "historical power of translation" we also encounter in the emergence of Islam. Its founding Prophet had a heightened awareness of this, as the Koran illustrates: "If We had made it a discourse in an obscure tongue, they would have said: 'Why were its revelations not expounded distinctly? A foreign tongue and an Arab [audience]?'" (41:44).

But monotheism erases the originary translation of the father of its conception; it establishes paternity and origin on the basis of a virginal relation of identity and consubstantiality: the Father-of-Genesis (the basis of the *archiécriture* of the primal father), the national Father (the son), and the translator-father (the reader) develop out of one another and are reciprocally inclusive. The metaphysical construction of originary filiation claims to be proper in all its aspects: it is monolingual, exclusive, immaculate, and unisexual. Psychoanalysis, through the concept of the primal father, has only partly broken with this theological notion of origins. However, examination of the Islamic version of the father encounters, aside from the unavoidable question of translation, the subversion of monotheistic theology through the figure of Hagar, Hagar who rises up from between the lines, the disturber of originary paternity and its triumvirate conception.

Hagar appears with the beginning of monotheism (more specifically, with the writing of its beginning), within the heart of the patriarchal family, whose irreparable rupture she caused. The subversive impact of the figure of Hagar in the concept of origin has remained unnoticed throughout the lengthy tradition of monotheistic commentary and philosophical and psychoanalytic interpretations of the religion; for these have restricted themselves to the anecdotal aspects of female jealousy and Hagar's wandering in the desert with her son, and have perpetuated the need to sanitize the slave, in contrast to the spiritual purity of the masters. However, once we interrogate Genesis with respect to the possibility of being-Father, not as a given but as a genesis, Hagar's presence reveals the most crucial aspect of the event of the Father: origin as crisis of the gift, as blockage of *jouissance*. But to approach this, we must change our point of view and move from that of the masters, which has prevailed until now, to a reading of the Genesis of monotheism from Hagar's point of view.

### Genesis according to Hagar

It was Jacques Derrida who revealed the importance of the distinction between the biblical archive and memory.[13] This distinction must be maintained if we want to understand what Islam transmits in the story of Hagar.

Genesis tells the story of Hagar as two narratives. The first is the narrative of her flight and return to her mistress upon the angel's orders; the second is the staging of her expulsion into the desert by Abram in the company of her son.

## The Impasse of the Gift

Sarai, having reached advanced age, has not given a child to Abram, who, at eighty-six years of age, is still awaiting the fulfillment of the promise of numerous progeny that god made to him. Desperate to have a child, Sarai offers her servant Hagar to Abram so she might bear him a child. Hagar was an Egyptian slave, and the commentaries claim she once belonged to Pharaoh, who offered her to Sarai as a gift when he returned Sarai to Abram.[14] (During their stay in Egypt, fearing that he would be killed and Sarai taken from him because of her great beauty, Abram claimed she was his sister and gave her up to Pharaoh.[15] Once Pharaoh learned of their true relationship, he returned Sarai and her servant to Abram, and all three left for the land of Canaan.)

Let's recapitulate. Here we have a man who gives his wife to another man, who gives her back to him, further giving this wife a woman of her own. Unable to bear a child for her husband, the wife gives him the servant given to her by the other man so that this servant will give him what the Giver (Yahweh) has not yet given. It is striking that, from the beginning of this story, Hagar finds herself at the tail end of a succession of gifts, countergifts, and withholdings between masters and lords, a succession that results in the old couple's being deprived of posterity. And the slave is asked to provide the gift that will restore the patriarch, without which there would be no father, no origin, no memory. One has to ask, Why does the monotheist archive place this impasse of the gift, this inscription through which the future of origin could not be accomplished without the womb of the slave, in Genesis, its first written book?

Genesis puts the following words in the mouth of Sarai as she addresses Abram: "And Sarai said unto Abram, Behold now, the Lord hath restrained me from bearing; I pray thee, go in unto my maid; it may be that I may obtain children by her" (Genesis 16:2).[16] It is clear that, in giving Hagar to Abram, Sarai wishes to give herself a child, to have herself given a child by another woman. *Sarai wants Hagar to give her a child.* At this point, all the commentaries stick to a legal interpretation, according to which this practice corresponded to the legal customs of the time.[17]

But there may be another dimension to the phrase "it may be that I may obtain children by her," namely, that Sarai is saying, What god has not given me, the other woman will give me. This complementary meaning (in the sense of what Freud calls the complementary series, where there is no choosing between two factors) has not drawn the attention of those who have taken an interest in this episode of Genesis, including psychoanalysts. However, it exposes the crucial dimension of contempt in the request, where we see the mistress put the slave in the place of the Other, the Giver who withholds the gift. In short, Sarai lends Hagar the gift to overcome the lack of god in herself.[18]

The subsequent events flow from this contempt. The Bible indicates that, when Hagar finds herself pregnant, "her mistress was despised in her eyes," and points out Sarai's anger and spite in these words to Abram: "My wrong *be* upon thee." But the servant's insolence and Sarai's jealousy at seeing her made pregnant by the patriarch are made unbearable for Sarai only because of the situation she herself has placed Hagar in, elevating her servant to the omnipotence of *the* woman who gives the gift of origin to the father, while Yahweh continues to withhold it. If we fail to identify this dimension of the transfer of generative power from god to the "other woman," who thereby becomes the Other woman where she once was a *sugetum* (concubine), we miss the maneuver by which Genesis makes the transition from the initial lack of origin to the question of female *jouissance* in its relation to the establishment of the father. The collapse of her assurance of obtaining a child from god leads Sarai to put an other (woman) in the place of the Other, using Hagar as a surrogate womb and taking from her the son who will make Abram the father. Why does the scripture of origin present the mistress as asking for life from a slave? How should we view this initial withholding of origin, the open struggle between the two women, and the subsequent rupture, when it would have been possible for the absolute god of monotheism to offer the gift of a single origin, within a united family — in short, the perfect gift? What is the meaning of this originary economy?

## The Promise and the Name

When confronted by Sarai, Abram rejects Hagar the first time, but this initial rejection anticipates the second: "Behold the maid *is* in thy hand; do to her as it pleaseth thee." And, as if to demonstrate a relation of cause and effect, the biblical text continues: "And when Sarai dealt hardly

with her, she fled from her face." But Yahweh's angel finds her and orders, "Return to thy mistress, and submit thyself under her hands." The
requirement of submission comes from several sources; Hagar has no recourse, not even in heaven above, from where the angel descends to ad-
monish her: "Hagar, Sarai's maid, whence camest thou? and whither wilt
thou go?" That is to say, Hagar, outside of your servitude, you have
nowhere to go.

Yet once the angel enjoins her to return to her mistress, as if Hagar's
rebellion could now be stopped by simple decree, the scene of flight becomes one of promise, of annunciation, of gift and countergift, which
radically modifies Hagar's position. Speaking for Yahweh, the angel pre-
dicts, "I will multiply thy seed exceedingly, that it shall not be numbered
for multitude." This can be understood as saying that Hagar is no longer
simply a womb at the service of her master's posterity but that she herself will be the origin of descendants beyond number: "Behold, thou *art*
with child, and shalt bear a son, and shalt call his name Ishmael; because
the Lord hath heard thy affliction." Not only is Hagar recognized in her
suffering, but also the child will bear the proof of this recognition in his
name (Isma'El means "god hears/understands"). God has given, has
recognized, has signed. It is not insignificant that he wishes to leave a
trace of his recognition in the name, and that the name Ishmael is the
writing of the recognition of the "other woman" in the biblical archive.
This naming, which consists in inscribing the gift in the name, later
shows the gift to be a debt, proof of an unforgettable obligation. God
does not give without counting, without archiving. The name is the
archive of both the gift and the debt.

Before her return to servitude, Hagar performs an act that will distinguish her from all the other women in the Bible: she gives a name to
god — Lord (El).[19] This name, which signifies the "god of vision," appears to arrive as Hagar's countergift to the gift of the name of Ishmael:
you have heard me and I have seen you; or rather, you have given my
son the name of your comprehension, and I, Hagar, call you by the name
of my vision. For that matter, Hagar's eyes appear to have special power,
for they will see in the desert the fountain that will save her and her
child. Hagar will have seen the farthest reaches of heaven and the opening in the depths of the earth.

Perhaps Spinoza was thinking of this scene of the sight of god, when
in the *Theological-Political Treatise* he refers to Hagar as a prophet, with all
that prophecy assumes for Spinoza as a modality of thought dominated

by imagination.[20] To my knowledge, Spinoza is the only author to have attributed this dignity to Hagar, for the fate of this woman, as we shall see, was to be eradicated, scratched out, forgotten, as if her rejection continued to pursue her into the trap of monotheistic memory. However, her archive reveals a less categorical inscription, because the figure of Hagar is connected to a fundamental question that implies the possibility of origin and its writing from below.

The figure of Hagar will remain present in the exegetic and theological tradition of Judaism and Christianity, but often marked by disapproval and contempt. Hagar is condemned for her attitude toward her mistress, whereas Sarai is pitied for her suffering, and her ill treatment of her servant is made to seem justified. The commentaries have consistently attempted to actualize the reasons for rejecting this aspect of origin. Later, we shall see how this works its way into Saint Paul. Here are two more recent examples:

Louis Pirot and Albert Clamer, in their translation of and commentary on the Bible, write, with respect to Hagar's mistreatment and flight: "It is understandable that Sarah was no longer able to bear such an attitude on the part of her servant; she remained her mistress and, therefore, it was up to her to act and punish the insolence of her slave."[21] In *Les matriarches,* the philosopher Catherine Chaliez, after noting that Sarai's gesture is "not exactly charitable," adds a lengthy analysis, from which I quote the following:

> If suffering signifies neither expiation nor chastisement, why would Sarah submit, without comment, to someone who ridicules her sterility? Would she accept such cruel derision, such infamy, from a woman who was fortunate enough to conceive? Rather than keep silent, rather than feel contempt for such malice, or cower before Hagar's provocative triumph, Sarah chooses to send her away, thereby renouncing any hope for the infant about to be born. The text reveals her [Sarah's] solitude. She expects neither compassion nor sympathy, but cannot accept humiliation. The excessiveness of her suffering is equaled only by her abandonment. No doubt, her beauty, her wealth, and her virtuous reputation arouse more jealousy than friendship, and of that she had none at all, other than from Abraham, who obeys her and shares her sorrow. Rather, it appears that Hagar uses her not only to demonstrate her turpitude, but also to justify what she, Hagar, is.... As if there were people like Hagar who needed the other's suffering to provide a justification for their life.[22]

Chaliez's passage is inspired by a single sentence in the biblical text: "And when she saw that she had conceived, her mistress was despised in her eyes" (Genesis 16:4).[23] Therefore, the slave has caused her masters to suffer, so she has forced them to mistreat her, to send her away, exposing herself and her child to the elements. She bears not only responsibility for what they inflict upon her but also responsibility for having nearly compromised them morally.

Between the story of Hagar's first and second departures (the second being her wandering in the desert with Ishmael), there appears the caesura of the circumcision and the covenant, the announcement of Isaac and his birth; in other words, events that imbalance the Abrahamic family structure and set the stage, so to speak, for the rejection of Hagar. Once again, as with Ishmael, god will inscribe his acts — the promise and the gift — in their names. Abram will become Abraham, gaining the letter *h*, and Sarai will be known as Sarah. This change, which elides the *i* of the possessive (Hebrew *yod*) and substitutes the letter *h*, means that Abraham will no longer refer to her as "my Princess" (or "my Mistress"),[24] but "Princess." Since the declaration of this change occurs shortly before the announcement that Sarai will have a son, there is reason to believe that the Bible is trying to establish a connection between the gift of the child and the expropriation inherent in the name. Elimination of the possessive *my* has introduced indeterminacy to the name, returning it to the radical impropriety of its bearer, that is, to what is common in the proper noun. The called is freed from any hint of subjection before the caller, especially Sarah herself, for when called upon to name herself she will no longer say, "I am my Princess" or "my Mistress." We could refer to this event as Sarah's dispossession. The expropriation of the name assumes the significance of an opening to the Other who will announce to her the arrival of the child. Sarah is no longer her own mistress, is no longer in possession of herself. She has accepted the dispossession of self as a gift in the call of the name. If this is the case, the maneuver would assume that Sarai is more subservient than her servant and that the servitude inscribed in her name is a more radical form of slavery than Hagar's, for it is correlative in Sarah's case to her confinement within herself and resistance to the gift of the Other.

Marie Balmary interprets the loss of the possessive as a way for Sarah to free herself of possession by the father who named her, as well as her husband, who followed suit. The transition from "the possessive to the genitive" supposedly provided a way for her to appropriate herself.[25] In reality, the question is more complex. On the one hand, in spite of this mark of the possessive, Sarah behaves, from the beginning to the end of the story, as a possessive rather than a possessed mistress. This includes her actions in her relationship to Abraham, who obeys her, even when he disagrees with her about Hagar. On the other hand, the possessive in the name is far from being the index of a simple appropriation by someone, for "my Princess" conjoins enslavement and sovereignty in an oxymoron and refers to a self that appears to be its own master and slave. Rather, it seems that Genesis wants to suggest a process of transformation in Sarah, which consists in the literal loss of the asset, that is, the withdrawal of the mark of narcissistic and phallic omnipotence that resides in *yod*, the first letter of the name of god, YHWH, and the equal sharing of *hey*, the second and fourth letters of the tetragrammaton, with Abraham.

Isn't this unmarking-marking, this incision in the name, comparable to a circumcision? The circumcision of the name repeats, reinscribes, calls to mind that any name is an expropriation of the living being, its appropriation by language, its marking by the Other. This situation would then imply an operation of symbolic castration, through which is established the mark of commonality with Abraham as a condition of generation. At least this is what the Hebrew tradition encourages us to believe.[26] One of the commentaries in the *Midrach Rabba* indicates that the loss of the *yod* serves to universalize Sarah. It is a procreative universalization, for it provides her with the fertility that will engender kings: "From her will come the kings of peoples. From Sarah alone, Abraham deduced, and not from the other woman whose children will not be the kings of peoples."[27] Thus, the removal turns out to be a gift, and loss turns out to be fecundity, to neither of which Hagar is entitled. The servant does not have access to the symbolic castration and universalization, that is, the resulting *jouissance*, which can now be qualified as "phallic *jouissance*" to the extent that it involves a *jouissance* that relies on a linguistic and signifying operation to replace an absence,[28] or a conception resulting from a lack.[29] Hagar's name, moreover, was not cut by the Other, nor was her flesh for a covenant of some kind; rather, she undergoes the other's — her mistress's — mistreatment. This dimension of being cut by (and subservient to) the Other, and not the other, will later assume importance for Muslim commentators in their interpretation of circumcision.

But we are not there yet. Hagar and Sarah are two figures of the maternal within the biblical logic of the genealogical construction of the father. The problem presented is that of the relationship of master and slave to the symbolic order. The appearance of the father unfolds as the writing of a foundational process, where the master is the one who agrees to transform his lack into phallic *jouissance,* whereas the slave remains captive in the flesh.

The biblical text presents the suspension of the gift of origin – god's delay in providing a child – as correlative to Sarah's position of mastery. This is to say that the father's originary lack is written from a position of female *jouissance,* which would block the Other's gift. It is Sarah's eviction from this omnipotent position of taking possession of herself that allows this breach to occur. Isaac's name bears the event of Sarah's flowering, for it comprises an abbreviated form of *Yçhq El,* which in Hebrew means "god has smiled." Thus, the relation to the Other would have shifted from lack to breach, from retention to the outburst of generalized laughter, for the name also refers to the laugh of astonishment of Abraham and Sarah when Yahweh announces that they have conceived a son although they are at an age that would make this impossible.

## The Possibility of the Impossible

The promise is nearly fulfilled. But it took a very long time, so long that a miracle was necessary. A miracle means that god has made the impossible happen – Abraham and Sarah can have a child. This impossible is staged as such by the Bible. Let us return to the passage in Genesis (17: 17) where Abraham reacts to the announcement of Isaac's future birth: "Then Abraham fell upon his face, and laughed, and said in his heart, Shall *a child* be born unto him that is an hundred years old? and shall Sarah, that is ninety years old, bear?" Abraham is stunned, literally falls to the ground, but believes that god is referring to Ishmael. Yahweh resolves the ambiguity for him: "And God said, Sarah thy wife shall bear thee a son indeed; and thou shalt call his name Isaac." Through Abraham's stupor and astonishment, the Bible theatricalizes the dimension of the impossible associated with the announcement of Isaac's birth.

Faced with the possibility of the impossible, the couple undergoes another challenge involving the gift and countergift, when Abraham repeats the episode with Pharaoh and gives Sarah to a king who will return her as a result of Yahweh's threats. Is this a fiction that seeks to reestablish exogamous exchange, that is, the staging of Abraham's desire to accept his wife from another? The context would indicate, rather, that we continue to pursue the reading we have given to the text. In light of the fact that Isaac's conception and birth occur immediately after this episode, that they fall outside the laws of nature, and that the commentators emphasize that Isaac is not the child of King Abimelech,[30] the episode appears to be haunted by the question of having the *other's* child. It is as if, at this point in the text, we were witnessing a response to the beginning of the story, as if Abraham's relationship to Abimelech was comparable to that of Sarah's relationship to Hagar.

From an other to the Other — this seems to be the decisive leap through which the promise will be fulfilled, because the Bible, as well as the commentaries, implicate god himself in Isaac's conception: "And the Lord visited *(paqad)* Sarah as he had said, and the Lord did unto Sarah as he had spoken. For Sarah conceived, and bare Abraham a son in his old age, at the set time at which God had spoken to him" (Genesis 21:1–2). André Chouraqui notes that the Hebrew *paqad*, which means both "split" and "visit," marks Isaac's miraculous conception and reminds us that Christian exegesis saw him as "an archetype of Jesus."[31] The biblical text seems to associate procreation through Sarah with her division, with her transition from being mistress of herself to becoming an object of the *jouissance* of the Other in order to receive from Him a son.

I want to stop here for a moment. The biblical text offers the possibility of perceiving Sarah as receiving the child that establishes the father, not from Abraham but from god, to the extent that here god is the Father. The son would not belong to the Father-of-Genesis but would directly implicate the primal, or originary, Father. Through his involvement in the conception, the god of Genesis puts Abraham in the position of being a father merely through adoption, accepting Yahweh as the real father. God's impossible gift dispossesses this father of what is proper to paternity, making him a father by proxy. Abraham *serves* as Isaac's father, as Joseph did for Jesus. The possibility of the impossible makes the father a representation of the real father.

At this point a division appears between the genealogical possibility found in Judaism and Christianity, and that found in Islam. On the one hand, we have a formation in which the son's conception is divine, or at least mixed, involving god in the paternity, which assumes for Sarah, as much as it does for Mary, a *jouissance* of the son that restricts them to the phallic absolute. In effect, the figure of the father harbors the ideal nature of the primal Father, a creative omnipotence outside the natural laws of the body.

On the other hand, in terms of filiation through Hagar, we have the prosaic dimension of sexual insemination through Abraham as the real father. If we stick to the biblical text, the symbolic father for Judaism and Christianity is the real father for Islam. Curiously, this aspect was not revealed by traditional exegesis or orientalism, not even by comparative studies of monotheism. Yet it has significant consequences. For example, it clarifies why in Islam one never speaks of "god-the-father," and any comparison of the divine with the paternal is proscribed. Allah is, in principle, neither the Father nor the god of the fathers, and this includes the Prophet, who is irrevocably an orphan, whom the Koran forbids in turn from being the Father of the members of his community.[32] The reason for this discontinuity between god and the father in Islam has not been considered. Yet we are beginning to understand that the god who hears Ishmael has nothing to do with the human sexuality of his parents, does not intervene in the signifying mechanism of phallic *jouissance*. The god of Islam is not an originary father, he is the impossible: transpaternal *(hors-père)*. In the beginning, there was the being-there, thrust into the womb of Hagar, then heard in the afterwardness of his emission. The verb is originally delayed with respect to the body. There is a discrepancy between Islam and the originary phallicism of the Judeo-Christian conception of the father, which leads Islam to position itself as "really" Abrahamic. This in no way means that it is devoid of all phallocentrism. Although the Ishmaelite genealogy in Islam precedes the emergence of the phallic mastery of life and being, the religious institution of Islam does not escape phallocentrism, as we'll see. The fact remains that the god of Islam is connected neither with a sexual relation nor with its absence or spiritualization through symbolic filiation. Rather, this god should be seen as being *in the background* of relation and nonrelation; he is the incommensurable withdrawal of the no-place, through which the place of the father finds its opening.[33] In other words, god is the originary withdrawal of the father. Although this idea may not be immediately easy to grasp and may lead to some misunderstanding, it should become clearer shortly.

To the impossibility of the gift between Abraham and Sarah, the originary god of monotheism responds with an impossible gift. Without being conclusive, this formulation helps us understand the extreme bib-lical solution employed for writing the origin of the father. This ex-treme – a book that is devoted to the question of the gift but that does not deal with the originary situation of monotheism – has at times come close to appearing written in the direction of its fundamental utterance. The following appears on the first pages of Jacques Derrida's *Given Time:*

> ... The gift is the impossible.
> Not impossible, but the impossible. The very figure of the impossible. It announces itself, gives itself to be thought as the impossible. It is proposed that we begin by this.[34]

These few lines concisely summarize the intense difficulties we have en-countered in adopting a different point of view – Hagar's – when ap-proaching a text that has been discussed for millennia. This approach exposes the originary challenge of the father not as a tale of sterility and jealous competition between two women but as the writing of the possi-bility of the impossible.

In fact, Genesis offers a history of originary paternity where not only is the father not given, holding himself in abeyance; where not only does his arrival seem impossible, given the age of the parents; but, addition-ally, where it is just when he is possible that it is necessary that he arrive by way of the impossible. Paternity began with Ishmael, who is Abra-ham's firstborn son; however, everything in this story tends to say, The possible has taken place, but it doesn't begin here; this is not the promised beginning. The origin that arrives through Ishmael is, certainly, a begin-ning, but it is a bastard beginning, dictated by trivial circumstances. We have at hand a servant who has complicated the script of the surrogate womb and rebelled against her mistress after having been made preg-nant by the master. Hagar's conception does not contradict any natural law of the living body, and the announced child is described in the bibli-cal text as "an onager of a man," that is, according to the commentaries, someone who lives like a wild ass, a nomad in the desert. This is all quite banal, reasonably human ... too human. Therefore, it isn't until the last moment that a purer, nobler, more spiritual beginning is produced, one satisfied with being not merely the gift of a child but the gift as the im-possible. Sarah's conception is that of the miracle of the dead body that suddenly comes to life, contradicting the laws of human procreation. Isaac first makes his appearance as the child of the community of laugh-ter between god and men – in other words, the child of spirit.

## *The Split between the Two Principles*

This gives us some idea of where the split in the family of Abraham occurs. It breaks apart not only over a jealous quarrel between two women but also over the split between two principles of origin. One, originating in Hagar, is the principle of the flesh, or the gift of the possible; the other, coming through Sarah, is that of the spirit, or the gift of the impossible. It is the radical difference between these two principles that Saint Paul, in his Epistle to the Galatians, recalls. I quote the passage concerning Hagar and Sarah in full:

> Tell me, ye that desire to be under the law, do ye not hear the law? For it is written, that Abraham had two sons, the one by a bond-maid, the other by a freewoman. But he *who was* of the bondwoman was born after the flesh; but he of the freewoman *was* by promise. Which things are an allegory: for these are the two covenants; the one from the mount Sinai, which gendereth to bondage, which is Agar. For this Agar is mount Sinai in Arabia, and answereth to Jerusalem which now is, and is in bondage with her children. But Jerusalem which is above is free, which is the mother of us all. For it is written, Rejoice, *thou* barren that bearest not; break forth and cry, thou that travailest not: for the desolate hath many more children than she which hath an husband. Now we, brethren, as Isaac was, are the children of promise. But as then he *that was born after* the flesh persecuted him that was born after the Spirit, even so *it is* now. Nevertheless what saith the scripture? Cast out the bondwoman and her son; for the son of the bondwoman shall not be heir with the son of the freewoman. So then, brethren, we are not children of the bondwoman, but of the free. (Gal. 4:21)

Saint Paul suggests repeating Abraham's gesture in Genesis. This should be understood as unfolding within the relationship between Judaism and a nascent Christianity. Here, we begin to see how the gesture confirms the incompatibility between two modalities of origin, one of which, namely, that of Hagar, must be repudiated. Repudiated. Not eliminated or repressed, but rejected. To the extent that the scission and the repudiation are correlative to the premises of the archive, we could consider that monotheism has been built on the writing of the originary rent between two principles embodied by two maternal figures. However, this approach is not unique to Christianity, which simply radicalized it, for the difference between Hagar-Ishmael and Sarah-Isaac is understood, by some commentators of Judaism, as a conceptual difference between two substances. To explain the speed with which Hagar "became pregnant," the metaphor of the weed and the grass, of the thorn and the wheat, is used. For example, the commentary of the *Midrach Rabba* on the passage in Genesis 16:4 ("And he went in unto Hagar, and she conceived") is as follows: "She became pregnant during their first encounter. Rabbi Elezar relates: a woman never becomes pregnant during her first encounter.... Rabbi Hanina ben Pazi relates: Concerning thorns, there is no need to hoe or even to sow, they rise up, they grow and increase by themselves; for wheat, however, much difficulty and effort is required before it will grow."[35]

The circumstances of the expulsion of Hagar and her son, as given in Genesis, provide other elements for this reading. The event takes place the day Isaac is weaned, when Abraham serves a great feast. It is not without relevance that what follows takes place during the first separation between mother and child, between Sarah and her son: "And Sarah saw the son of Hagar the Egyptian, which she had born unto Abraham, mocking [variant translations give "laughing" or "playing"]. Wherefore she said unto Abraham, Cast out this bondwoman and her son; for the son of this bondwoman shall not be heir with my son, *even* with Isaac" (Genesis 21:9). As the commentators note, it is significant that the term *mocking* is a translation of Hebrew *shhaq,* meaning "to laugh," which alludes to Isaac's name, because it stems from the same verb.[36] It seems that this mention of Ishmael "playing" *(mshaheq)* with Isaac generated considerable commentary in the rabbinic tradition and among Jews of the Late Period, for it has been interpreted as meaning "to mock and ridicule," and even as referring to Ishmael's physical abuse of his brother and his perverse acts, which we find in Rashi, for example.[37] As we have seen, Saint Paul continues this tradition when he writes, "He *that was born after* the flesh persecuted him that was born after the Spirit." Modern exegetes have restored the meaning of the Hebrew text, which simply says that Hagar's son "played — laughed" with Sarah's son.[38] However, it is important to understand that, aside from the question of heritage, what Sarah could not bear was that, the first day her son was separated from her, he found himself with his brother in the community of laughter, or spirit. Hagar's repudiation has become inevitable with the first signs of the possible entanglement of the child of the promise and the child of the flesh. Therefore, it is the being together of these two brothers, these two modalities of origin, that is untenable, as if their union threatened the fundamental concepts of monotheistic logic — the father and origin.

According to Genesis, Abraham is displeased with Sarah's comments. But god takes her side and agrees to her request to expel Hagar, saying to Abraham, "Let it not be grievous in thy sight because of the lad, and because of thy bondwoman; in all that Sarah hath said unto thee, hearken unto her voice; for in Isaac shall thy seed be called" (Genesis 21:12). On one side we have the perpetuation of the name of Abraham through Isaac, or filiation through the Name of the Father; on the other side we have Ishmael, who represents filiation through race. In this we find the two covenants mentioned by Paul, which take on an additional determinant: origin through the name and the spirit; and origin through the substantial transmission of life.

There follows the episode of Hagar's expulsion, as she leaves with her son on her shoulder and a handful of provisions. A series of events ensues: the wandering in the desert, exhaustion, thirst; the child being placed beneath a bush, tears, the refusal to see the child die; the moment of revelatory hearing and promise; Hagar's eyes, which have seen the well; the child now safe. This is followed by mention of the son's later marriage to an Egyptian woman similar to his mother. The final biblical episode of this story is the presence of the two children at their father's burial. The Jewish tradition has left us several fine commentaries on this episode, on Hagar's tears and prayers, on the wandering of the foreign woman and her disarray. Some commentators have tried to see in Keturah (the perfumed woman), whom Abraham married after Sarah's death, a repetition of Hagar. This *Wiedergewinnung* of the other woman assumes the form of a *toilette,* the showering of praise on Hagar, whereby the servant's scent lingered, as we shall see, for centuries.

## There Is, There Is Not

What is it that determines the overall movement of these different moments of the problematic of the father in the archive of monotheism? What is their final destination?

Genesis opens on the impasse of the gift of life in the Abrahamic family, that is, the impasse of origin itself, because it occurred at the beginning. In the beginning, therefore, was the impasse of beginning. In the beginning, the archive preserves the lack of the father as beginning. Man is faithful, has been waiting for a very long time, but without the son who will make him father. The Donor had promised to give but holds on to his gift, as if he were expecting someone to make a move, a

condition to be fulfilled, before sending the anticipated gift. The asser-
tion is clear: at the origin, the father in the world is not given, there is not
yet a father; it is the holding back of the gift that constitutes his lack, or
that presents him as lacking and therefore as forthcoming. We are
gripped by the lack of the father to the extent that this lack is the son.
There is a need for the son to keep the father in suspense. For the archive,
there is only one way the father's lack and his arrival can be written,
and that is to withhold the son. Within this mechanism there is neither
father, nor son, nor origin without the suspense that constitutes the manifestation of "being father." In the beginning is "that which withholds." In
other words, there is that there-is-not. We cannot push origin further
back than this. "There is a there-is-not" is the abutment of the originary
impossible, the real of origin. Every paternity is preceded by an absolute
presupposition. Monotheism is initially presented as faith in this impossible that is the lack of the father in the world, or the originary lack of
origin. Naturally, it binds this lack to god's mercy, but god is then originally the god of what is lacking, which is the same as saying, "There is a
there-is-not." The Father of heaven, the Father of the lack, supplies the
father's lack, or the gift's lack. The statements "There is that there-is-
not," "There is a there-is-not," and "There is there-is-not"are only different variants of the same expression — namely, the limit of the writing of
origin. This limit constitutes the radical alterity of every origin. The
"Other" — what is written and conceptualized with this word — necessarily entails the idea this simple sentence harbors: There is a there-is-
not. It seems that originary formations, whether individual or collective,
must present, confront, unfold their existences based on this limit, and
continue, based on the impossible of this pose. We could call this sequence
"the deal of origin," in the distributive sense of a game (a card game being an illustrative example). The deal arranges the set of elements of the
originary game around the impossible. It is the place where the writing
of "being father," his *Arche*, is articulated.

In writing "father" and "being father," I am trying to clearly distinguish something that, in psychoanalytic thought, is often subsumed by
the notions of the manifest father and the manifestation of the father.
The manifest father is Abraham, the father of Ishmael and Isaac. The manifestation of the father is what proceeds from the impossible, starting with
Abram, the appearance of his proceeding, beginning with "There is a
there-is-not." "Being father" is missing since the origin, and its manifestation is forever forthcoming.

The Bible writes these premises of the impossible through a highly developed narrative and attempts to continue them through a resolvent construction of the deal of the impossible. Everything that is at stake in the story of Abraham is condensed in this notion. What originary monotheism enacts is a detour (no doubt its founding tour), which consists in appropriating the impossible through an impossible solution, that of Isaac's conception, which is nothing other than the phallic solution. The invention of biblical monotheism is the resolution of the impossible as real, in an impossible that reappears in the imaginary. It attempts to erect a phallic imaginary of the gift of the son in place of the originary impossible and to maintain the dissimulation of the latter in the former. Isaac fills the lack as the child of the promise that is realized. With him, the impossible is embodied and the father becomes definitively manifest; after him, retention ceases and origin closes over. We can now understand why Islam proposed the other solution, and sought to return to Abraham as father in reality and keep god on the side of the impossible.

Genesis indeed presents us with the originary cut (*entame*), but reduces it with a supplementary gift; it makes retention the possibility of the proper of the gift, even though it is a question not of proper or improper but of the originary withdrawal that exposes the possibility of saying and writing origin. "There is there-is-not" is this breach in the limit, the opening limit that does not belong to any order of signification or meaning; its withdrawal remains inalienable through everything that is and is to come. Through the logic of retention, religion seeks to accredit the permanent presence of the gift in its very absence, whereas withdrawal is neither presence nor absence but the impossible that no origin can enclose, retain, or possess. The impossible cannot be held back, because it prevents every origin from being given to itself and fulfilling the circle of the gift from self to self. Genesis turns the father into an operation of control of originary withdrawal through the phallus: the gift of the divine child.

And yet this appropriation of withdrawal, this dissimulation of the impossible, is not total, because we can read it in the very text of Genesis. The writing reveals the phallic turn that withdraws the withdrawal. It does not conceal the appropriation but reveals its mechanism, transmits its originary closure. This calls to mind an apparently enigmatic comment by Derrida in *Archive Fever:* "A priori, the archive always works against itself."[39] We could say that with the Bible monotheism made spiritual progress, an ethical advance. If such were the case, it would be not because monotheism had discovered the uniqueness, the transcendence, of "being father"; or because it preserved the memory of being father more carefully; but because it went on to write it, archived its manifestation, which writing illustrates the dissimulation of the impossible and reveals the phallic appropriation of originary withdrawal. Writing turns out to be complicit with the withdrawal rather than faithful to the phallic hypostasis of the impossible whose blind guardian we would like it to be. Writing wears the phallic veil of the primal Father only to reveal him. To entrust writing with the guardianship of origin is to entrust it to a veil that is an eye, an eye-veil. This is how monotheism begins to work against itself, by using the duplicity of writing to enter the play of history. We can read the repercussions of the originary deal of the father in Genesis in light of this hypothesis. We can start from the turning point of this reversal of writing, that is, the moment of the agrarian refusal.

## Originary Withdrawal

Faced with the originary withdrawal of the gift, the mistress, the princess, the woman above (in the sense of her self-appropriated sovereignty), attempts to get beyond the withdrawal by asking another woman, a slave, the woman below (and therefore dispossessed of herself), to offer the gift to the masters in abeyance and compensate for the withdrawal. A conflict then arises around the question of "originary withdrawal" — a concept that I want to propose in place of "originary castration" — its misunderstanding, its evasion, the forcing of its withdrawal using the slave as an instrument. The use of Hagar as a body, as a surrogate womb, is based on an instrumentalization of the other living being, of the use of the living being in its nudity, without recognizing its genealogical right. "For," writes Aristotle, "the body is the soul's tool born with it, a slave is as it were a member or tool of his master, a tool is a sort of inanimate slave."[40] Genesis in fact brings a case against itself, against those whose memory and genealogy it wishes to preserve. In my eyes this is an important ethical process, but one that has not yet been appreciated in its entirety, once again, because this story has been considered only from the point of view of the masters and the spiritual gift that overwhelms them. It entails what we can refer to as the instrumental *jouissance* of the other being as a naked body. Who could fail to see the relevance of this process, given the extent of the manipulation taking place, at an accelerated pace, before our astonished eyes? The instrumental *jouissance* of the other being does not seek only to use the physical strength of the other or its biological potential; nor does it seek solely to extract an economic or material surplus value, which may also be the case; but it also is supported by the powerful metaphysical desire to appropriate the impossible and overwhelm the originary withdrawal.

Yet the Bible, through the figure of Hagar, reveals that she says no to this desire for forcing the withdrawal through Sarah. The slave's gift to the master cannot go without compensation, cannot be a present without a return, a pure sacrifice, that is, an absolute gift, after which Hagar would have to remove herself from the situation and make sure she was forgotten. The scribes of monotheism could have written a story in which Hagar, reduced to a womb at the service of her masters, withdraws without leaving a trace of her own posterity, after having given the son to the master, the son who would not have been called Ishmael, and so on. But Genesis denies the masters the mastery of origin, through the rebellion of the other woman and the recognition of her genealogical right; it divides the gift of the father between two women. Moreover, through this division of the *Arche* of the father, not only are the beginning and the commandment not combined in the same hands but, additionally, the woman who commands does not begin, leaving the primacy of the gift of the father to the woman who engenders through the flesh. Life is the primary deal in the face of power. In spite of the promise, no one commands the beginning; the beginning withdraws from the commandment.

Naturally, by denying the masters the ability to force the withdrawal, by preventing Hagar's disappearance, and by giving a head start to the slave-life, the Bible keeps god's hand on origin. The absolute gift could not have been produced in the beginning, for if the Donor had given such a gift from the beginning, we would not know that the giving had taken place, nor the beginning. Nor could the perfect gift have been allowed to be produced among men, who would then have done without god's gift. In every case, the disappearance of the donor implies the perpetual obliteration of the debt, the immediate fulfillment of origin. If the archive did not want to bequeath us a perfect gift, it is because it was unable to do so; otherwise there would have been neither place nor archive material. The imperfect gift comes by way of Hagar, the gift that does not close off the beginning before it begins. Hagar, then, is the distancing of origin from itself, the possibility of an archive of the father, the point from which the writing of his manifestation as originary sharing occurs. God needed the figure of Hagar to bring paternity into the world. Hagar is the internal stranger who "distends" origin in its intimacy, so that the expected father can arrive. She is the gift from below *(aban-don)*, without which there is no gift from above.

But once the impasse of origin is overcome, the foreigner becomes a burden and threatens the prerogatives of the Master's gift to the masters. Therefore, mastery of origin necessitates that the foreigner be chastised and expelled. The father, in the monotheistic archive, cannot retain both principles of his paternity; he chooses one and leaves the other. Hagar is the origin that has been repudiated in order to preserve filiation in accordance with the imaginarized impossible. The imaginarized impossible is the foundation of origin in metaphysics. The concept of the father in originary monotheism entails the repudiation of the foreigner and phallic choice of the proper.

Here, we arrive at the point at which Freud left us in *Moses and Monotheism*, except that the foreign originally turns out to be a foreign woman and the Egyptian an Egyptian woman. This difference has come to light based on an analysis that reveals that the father can appear only if there is a distancing of origin. Once we understand how Freud's suggestion concerning the foreign origin of Moses is a radical deconstruction of the originary mytheme (because it renders the separation of any origin from itself more originary than that origin), we cannot help but note that Freud chose to condense father, founder, and foreigner in a single figure. To make the father the foreigner through whom the originary differentiation prior to any foundation is effected is to confer upon the father the absolute omnipotence that produces the foundational act as institution and the breach in the preexisting originary space that harbors that foundation. Such a father, who, in thought, would enjoy every power, would be either a god or a figure of the archaic Father, before his murder, whose decisive overshadowing *Totem and Taboo* attempted to delineate. In short, the founding of the institution should not be confused with originary difference and should not be in its grip, at the risk of damaging the space of psychoanalytic thought and reverting to the theological as phallic appropriation of the impossible.

Ever since Freud, psychoanalysis has often been reproached for excluding women in its theorizing of the origins of the Law and society, or, worse yet, of assigning them the status of "booty" that men fight for

among themselves, as in *Totem and Taboo*. However, analysis of the monotheistic fiction enables us to formulate a structural function of the feminine
at the moment of origin, which conditions the genealogical establishment
of the father.

## Between-Two-Women

There isn't only contingency in this story of the originary duality of the
feminine. For the man to become father, a feminine pole other than that
of the phallic female (the omnipotent mistress wanting to command the
beginning) was needed. In this sense, Hagar is the name of the "other
woman" through whom the originary divergence between the beginning
and the commandment was established. As long as these two principles
remained in the hands of a single woman, the father remained submissive. Origin had to deploy itself within the divergence because of the
fold *(pli)* in which the impossible kept the father submissive. The "originary fold of the father" is the impossible as fusion of the beginning and
the commandment, the submission of life to control, the cause of the absence of the gift. The father unfolds through the defeat of this confusion,
in the difference of the "between-two-women."

In fact, we have followed and identified, in the agrarian gesture, the
deracination of monotheistic paternity from its domestic history, as it
transforms itself, through the disruption of the family of the patriarch
and the multiplication of his sons, into a universal structure of the father.
This is the appearance in scripture of the One, the architructural difference irreducible to any origin.

This structural difference can be read directly in the myth of Moses.
After being abandoned by his mother to drift along the Nile, it is another woman, an Egyptian (wife or sister of Pharaoh, depending on the
Judeo-Christian or Islamic version), who takes him and returns him to
his mother, posing as his nurse. But the son who will become father and
savior of his people does not owe his survival to this distance alone, to
this estrangement from his mother and adoption by the "other woman."
It is through the other woman that the mother can escape the omnipotence of the maternal (or the phallic) to become the nursing or adoptive
mother, to whom the infant is merely loaned. She is a surrogate mother,
metaphorized ("the metaphor is a surrogate residence," according to the
grammarian Du Marsais), thereby becoming a fictional mother and not

only the mother whose parturition can be witnessed by the senses. For the fiction of the mother to exist, the other woman — the foreigner — must exist. In this sense, Hagar enabled Sarah to become a mother in fiction rather than by trying to take another woman's child. These elements indicate the need for a reevaluation of the problematic of the mother in psychoanalysis, who is often reduced to the function of physical procreation, whereas the father is viewed as a metaphor. We can hypothesize that the mother does not fulfill her function unless she effects this transition, the fictive creation of a separation that allows her to make the leap from the procreative to the adoptive. Yet this separation is possible only if the structural role of the other woman is established.

The "between-two-women" cannot be reduced only to competition, reprisal, and revenge centered on phallic *jouissance*, as an entire body of psychoanalytic literature for the last twenty years has claimed. Consequently, we need to move from the anecdotal distinction between two conflicting figures of the feminine to what exists at their origin: the inappropriable impossible that is confirmed through radical difference, that of originary withdrawal; that is, the impossible that is in itself this difference, which I have indicated by the expression "There is there-is-not." Here, I want to emphasize that this expression attempts to describe the differential movement of an oscillation in which the bond between affirmation and negation is maintained, in order to indicate the unity of the impossible. Of course, it is through the impossible that the father is dealt, but for the deal to occur the *Arche* must be split in two. Consequently, there are two phases of the impossible: a phase in which it is the unity of opposites (There is there-is-not, the withdrawn inhuman unity), and a phase in which it comes into being humanly as father, in the structural separation of the "between-two."

### The Perpetuation of Repudiation

What was the relationship between the pre-Islamic Arabs and the memory that Jews and Christians had preserved of their agrarian or Ishmaelic origin? What did they think of this history, and how did they relate to it? Until the publication of René Dagorn's *La geste d'Ismaël*, some twenty-five years ago,[41] it was believed that the Arabs had always been familiar with this history, had referred to it and claimed it as their own, as shown by the Koran, Islamic tradition, and the Arab literature of the Middle Ages. However, the results of Dagorn's research have demonstrated that this evidence is misleading. In his research, Dagorn used Arab texts and onomastic techniques to determine whether references to Ishmael and Abraham existed before Islam, and whether pre-Islamic Arabs considered themselves descendants of Ishmael and Abraham, as has been mentioned in Jewish tradition at least since the second millennium BCE, and subsequently by many Christian authors.

## Transmission through Ishmael

Dagorn's book is impressive for the amount of documentation he supplies, his methodology, and his rigorous analysis. He studies the most important Arab genealogies, catalogs and counts proper names, and prepares tables of filiation and frequencies, which he compares with other sources. He concludes, "This examination, nearly exclusively based on the analysis of Arabic genealogies and the oldest Muslim tradition, leads me to formally conclude in the absolute and radical non-existence, within the pre-Islamic tradition, of Ishmael, Hagar, her mother, and even Abraham." And he goes on to write, "There is no record of the biblical patriarch and his exiled son that could serve as the basis for a theory claiming that the Arabs preserved the historical memory of a physical, or even spiritual, attachment to Abraham through Ishmael."[42]

At what point do the references to Ishmael and Abraham first appear? Dagorn writes, "The frequency of the use of these names increases the further one gets from the beginnings of Islam. As a result, there is reason to believe that, under the influence of the Koran and Islamic preaching, use of these names increased or simply began."[43] Therefore, it is with Muhammad that the Arabs' memory of their origin as it appears in Genesis begins. Jahiz, therefore, was quite literally correct: "Ishmael became Arab after having been non-Arab simply because the Prophet said so."

On the one hand, the contrast before and after the beginnings of Islam is striking: "Prior to Islam," Dagorn writes, "there is absolutely no one among the Qureshis [the Prophet's tribe] who are named who had been given the name 'Ibrahim, Isma'il, or Ishaq.'"[44] On the other hand, we have the Koran, where those names not only appear but are often claimed as being part of the unforgettable memory that joins the Arabs to the father of monotheism. Even the Prophet chose to give to the only son (the dead son) he had with Marie, the Copt, the name Ibrahim, which did not exist at the time, according to Arab tradition. Dagorn concludes with these remarks: "It is unquestionably the Prophet who has the honor of having perceived the link between his own monotheistic ideas and the religious ideal he intended to substitute for the ancestral paganism of his fellow Mekkites and the faith of the great biblical patriarch."[45]

How can we explain that, for centuries, nearby tribes retained knowledge about the origin and lineage of the Arabs, a knowledge that related them to the common ancestor of monotheism, without this knowledge leaving any imprint upon them? Here, we reach the limits of Dagorn's research — Freud might have said that it concerns the material truth rather than the historical truth — which maintains that there is "no trace of..." but does not delve further into the reasons for that absence. Is it a deliberate refusal to make use of this knowledge? Or is it an oversight?

In the preface to the book, one of the conclusions drawn from Dagorn's work by Maxime Rodinson is disturbing and raises many questions. Rodinson writes:

> Everything we know — and the mass of documentation so laboriously assembled and organized by René Dagorn should demonstrate this even to those most unwilling to see — indicates that there was a separation of more than a thousand years between theories that may have been developed in a handful of pre-Arab or proto-Arab tribes in the peri-Palestinian region, and in any case among the historians of Beni Yisrael, and the return of those theories, their incorporation in what were to become sacred texts, developed with the authority acquired by what had become global religions, Judaism and Christianity, and their adoption by Muhammad, who imposed them, not without considerable hesitation... upon the vast community of Muslims.[46]

If the Arabs had not begun to exist as such, in what sense would there have been a separation and return? What does a thousand years of interruption imply? Why, suddenly, did a man arrive on the scene who managed to transmit what had not been transmitted for so long? It will take more than listing proper nouns to understand the appropriation of something that was not proper. And, although we can say that there was a *Wiedergewinnung* of the Father, albeit in a different sense than the one contemplated by Freud, and that a single man attempted this, we still have to examine the operation of appropriation and the gift to his people.

It is not possible here to examine the Muhammadan operation in its full scope, for that would mean studying the foundation of Islam. I want to limit myself to the agrarian core of this operation, the "knot" as used in the language of tapestry, which will serve as the point of departure for establishing how the originary Islamic text was woven. However, I would like to briefly outline the hypothesis I presented in an earlier work, namely, that the intelligibility of the Muhammadan operation depended on an analysis of the injunction to read, which is the root of Muhammad's preaching. "Read," as the reader may recall, is the command of the angel who terrorized Muhammad into accepting the revelation. It is important to note, when it concerns the archive and memory, that the text began this way, that is to say, it did not begin, because it was assumed that the text existed; something had already been written and had to be read. Yet, given a situation that I compared to that of the Virgin Mary receiving the word (see the section in chapter 3 titled "The Veil"), it is interesting to give the injunction to read (qara'a) in the angel's command its meaning in ancient Arabic: the woman's retention of the man, forming the fetus, and casting him out when the act is completed.[47] To read is to conceive, to let oneself be penetrated by the trace or the writing of the Other. To conceive "the mother of the book" (the guarded tablet, of which the Koran is one of the revealed versions) is to receive the origin, the Arche, or archive, as gift of the Other and to give it life, a new life through language. Is this the modality of the translating Father, through which he appropriates the writing of the Father-of-Genesis and gives it back? It is not part of the register of citation or reproduction but, rather, part of the maternal reception of the word, which calls to mind the name of god in Islam, the name with which all the suras in the Koran begin and through which everything is undertaken: "In the Name of God the genatrix, the generative [arrahman arrahim] . . ."[48] The principle of insemination through the writing of the Father contains the message of life and the word, which appears in the very first lines of the Koran.[49]

## Transmissible and Intransmissible

To read the Muhammadan reading of the Wiedergewinnung of the Father entails an examination of the way Muhammad confronted certain crucial problems inherited from the biblical archive and its memory. The first and most important of these problems is, What do we do with the abandonment of the father when the father must be reclaimed? How can the man whose final act was to abandon mother and son be reclaimed? What do we do with the woman Saint Paul called the "abandoned": Hagar, the servant and rebel, slave and mother? How do we derive a monotheistic spirituality of the family, after what happened within the Abrahamic family and its final split? Didn't Hagar's expulsion lead Abraham to produce the spiritual antinomy of the family? Repudiation replaced the union provided by the family, expropriation replaced sharing and transmission, and abandonment of the child replaced caring and education. What kind of ethics can be derived from this antinomy? How can we assume there is love between father, mother, and son at the origin when hatred of the other woman and rejection of the other gift of origin exist?

The Koran is the first document in the Arab tradition to speak explicitly of Abraham, Ishmael, and his brother Isaac. Examination of the text shows that, until the Hegira, or exile at Medina, in 615 (five years after the beginning of revelation), the importance of descent through Ishmael is unclear. It is only after the Hegira (year 1 of the Muslim calendar) that such descent is confirmed, no doubt through the dialogue and confrontation between the Prophet and the Jews and Christians of Medina.

Although Ishmael is cited a dozen times in the Koran, and Abraham seventy-eight, Hagar is nowhere to be found. There is no mention of Hagar (*hajer* in Arabic, "the exiled one"), her flight, her expulsion, or the abandonment of the child. No element of the biblical story concerning this critical episode appears, except for the reference to an all-hearing god (*sami*) when Isma'il (Ishmael's Arabic name) is mentioned. We can explain this absence in terms of the situation at the time. To rally the Arab aristocracy, or even simply the proud people of the desert, by giving them for an ancestor a female slave expelled by the man one wishes to make the father of the new religion, was no doubt a difficult maneuver to enact — even more so given that the Jews and Christians of the region apparently did not fail to remind the Arabs of Ishmael's "impure" heritage. Is this the real reason? Whatever the case, the Muhammadan reclamation of the father maintains Hagar's repudiation in the form of her removal from the founding text. However, we encounter, in the Koran, several episodes where Isaac's birth is mentioned and, among them, at least twice, explicit reference to Sarah as "the wife of Abraham." It is worth quoting, as an example, sura 11, which refers to the announcement by the angels: "His wife who stood near, laughed as We gave her the good news of Isaac, and after Isaac of Jacob. She said: 'Woe betide me! Will I give birth when I am old and this my husband be aged? This is indeed surprising?' 'Why are you surprised at the command of God? God's mercy and blessings be upon you, O members of this household,' they said. 'Verily He is worthy of praise and glory'" (11:71–73). In this way the Koranic text also takes the side of Sarah, by making her present and by bearing witness to her emotion, while Hagar is kept out of the text, unreferenced. Hagar was intransmissible through the Koran.

Yet — and this is one of the fundamental acts of reclamation — the Koran adds a new sequence not found in the Bible. This entails the reconciliation of Abraham with Ishmael during the construction of the temple in Mecca: "And when Abraham was raising the plinth of the House with Ishmael, [he prayed]: 'Accept this from us, O Lord, for you hear and know every thing'" (2:127). Thus, the reclamation consisted in organizing the reconciliation of father and son in the place where the child was heard and saved, through their communion in the act of building the temple. Their love is manifested through a construction. To construct, stone by stone, what would come to be known in Islam as the "House of Abraham" (Mecca) is the response to the broken bond and the broken family found in the Bible. The basis of the communion of father and son, of their reconciliation and conciliation, Muhammad's *Wiedergewinnung*, is a foundation in stone. Thus, the father has not completely abandoned his son; he finds him in the hardness of the rock.

In an earlier verse, god reminds us that he has literally written the presence of the father in the stone: "Remember, We made the House [the temple of the Ka'bah] a place of congregation and safe retreat, and said: 'Make the spot where Abraham stood the place of worship'" (2:125). Régis Blachère, in a note to his translation of the Koran, writes, concerning this "site where Abraham stood" *(maqam Ibrahim)*, where something like an impression of the father in Islam occurs: "This refers to a sacred stone wider at the top and bottom and thinner in the center, of approximately 60 by 90 centimeters, on which can be distinguished, in relief, an imprint that is said to be the foot of Abraham. This stone, whose hollows may be receptacles intended to receive the blood of victims, is said to have served Abraham to raise himself up to the level of the terrace of the Kaaba when he began to build it."[50] Thus, the father returned, stepped onto his pedestal, built with the son, engraved his footprint, and left the stone of his pedestal as archive of his return. The notion of the *maqam*, which I have translated as "site" is also of interest. It signifies the place where one stands upright, from the verb *qama*, "to get up," to rise up, to lift oneself up, to stand up. So the foundational encounter appears to be a monumental erection. But from this stone erection of father and son together, Hagar is, naturally, excluded. Such is Muhammad's ethical solution:

holiness lies not within the family — there is no Holy Family in Islam — but in the construction of the temple, the third term between father and son, in which is monumentalized their reconciliation, their communion, their renewed love.

The reclamation of the father in the same place would be inscribed not only in this originary formation and its impression but in ritual as well, namely, in the pilgrimage, during which Abraham's gesture of substituting the sacrificial lamb for his son is renewed. Before completing this sacrifice, the pilgrims must go forth and return seven times between the hills of Safa and Marwah. This sequence, which is certainly pre-Islamic, is supposed to imitate Hagar in her desperate search for water for her son. It is the only point in the corpus of Islamic dogma and ritual where Hagar's memory is invoked, not through words but through the silent physical staging of identification with her disarray, without specifically naming her. So, on the one hand, the rite recalls the moment of the mother and son's distress and serves as its physical staging; and, on the other hand, it commemorates the pacifying gesture of substitution in the relation between father and son. The mother's disarray and the imminent death of the son are worked in with the suspense of the slaughter of the lamb and the symbolic embodiment of sacrifice. In this mechanism, reminiscence is for Hagar, whereas Abraham and his son are remembered.

The completion of the father's reclamation finds its final expression in an originary escalation that occurred whenever Muhammad's relations with the Jews and Christians who refused to recognize him became strained. This escalation consisted in claiming that he had rediscovered the first religion of Abraham, known as the religion of the Hanifs. For Muhammad, there was no longer any old or new text, no fulfillment through scripture, no writing to come. The true religion had already taken place; it was the religion of Abraham, whose reign Islam wished to restore. It is here that nostalgia for the father becomes organized into a doctrine of return to the religious and paternal origin of Abraham.

## From the Abandoned (Woman) to Abandonment

Hagar was evicted from the Islamic foundation so the father could be found and reconciled with the son. This resulted in an act by the Prophet that was essential to Islam's becoming a religion. This was his recognition of the trauma of abandonment in the story of Hagar and Ishmael as a universal originary experience shared by all humanity. The word *islam* names this trauma and the spiritual possibility of its transcendence. Most often, the sense of "submission" in the word has been emphasized and other important meanings obscured, namely, those involving abandonment and escape from danger, being saved, and finding safety. No doubt, the arc of Muhammad's life, in its infantile segment, shows the extent to which it is littered with experiences of abandonment. Having addressed this question at the beginning of this chapter, and more exhaustively elsewhere,[51] I will limit myself here to two aspects of the phenomenon.

Abandonment is to be understood through the multiplicity of Muhammad's experiences: orphaned, wandering, exiled, homeless, faithless, companionless, without ideals, and without a project. But in a more radical sense it is the experience of every man abandoned in existence. Existence as gift assumes abandonment; it is literally "the gift from below" *(le don du bas)*, that is, a coming into the world. Obviously, the abandonment of the mother and her child — which Muhammad experienced when his mother died during a trip through the desert — and their rescue when god hears and understands, revealing the site of their salvation, sustains the entire movement of the recognition of abandonment as originary trauma of the existent.

Because this history is overdetermined, there is in Islam a likely radicalization of the problematic of abandonment, which, for that matter, is common to all religions. Whereas, elsewhere, salvation (rescue) emerges directly from abandonment, as in Christianity, which presents us with the Resurrection following the abandonment and death of Christ on the cross, we do not find in Islam this dialectical relief, this desire to overcome death in its opposite, which is found in all European speculative thought. In Islam death is not tragic abandonment, it is abandonment only for the purpose of moving toward a more infinite abandonment, which is god himself. This belief implies a conception of abandonment that embodies a sense of mourning for change. Hagar, the abandoned woman, and her son have certainly marked the spiritual experience of Islam, even beyond our awareness of it today.

## Controversies surrounding Hagar

The effects of Islam's appropriation of the father did, of course, continue after the death of the founder. Certain aspects are worth pointing out. With Muhammad's first successors, Muslims sought to better familiarize themselves with the history of Ishmael in the Bible as well as in the Talmudic and Midrashic traditions, and they continued to construct the legend of the reconciled father and son. Initially, Hagar continued to be ignored. So, for a very long period, she was known not by her proper name but as the "mother of Ishmael." Then, gradually, her name began to appear, although its frequency was never greater than that of Sarah. For example, in a study of famous women in Islam, René Dagorn counts eighteen occurrences of Sarah for three of Hagar. Moreover, Hagar's name would never become a desirable first name.

Hagar was erased, but her servitude nonetheless remains at the heart of Muslims' relations with others. The historiographer Masudi mentions that the Byzantine emperor Nicephorus I (802–811) had to issue a decree whereby "he prevented his subjects from calling the Arabs Saracens, a name that meant 'slave of Sarah,' which the Greeks gave to the Arabs as a pejorative allusion to Hagar, mother of Ishmael, who had been Sarah's servant."[52]

But Hagar's servitude is not a topic for discussion only between Muslims, Jews, and Christians. It is within Islam that the real dispute is to be found: between Arab and non-Arab Muslims, such as the Persians and Nabataeans, known as *shu'ubi* (populace). Unlike the Arabs, who incorporated Ishmael and Abraham and began to introduce recognition of Hagar, the Nabataeans believed in Abrahamic descent through Isaac and considered Arabs to be the sons of *lakhna*, literally the sons of the "foulsmelling female." Ibn Qutayba writes, "Is a heretic, much less a Muslim, allowed to claim that a woman such as Hagar stinks, a woman whom god purified of all stain and perfumed, removing all unpleasant odors from her, whom he accepted as a wife for his friend Abraham ["friend of god" is one of Abraham's surnames in Islam] and as mother of the two virtuous men known as Ishmael and Muhammad, through whom his progeny flow?"[53] The nonrecognition of Hagar within her own family continues. But her defense grows stronger through her recognition as the "ancestral mother," outside her position as servant. We find another example in Ibn Garsiya's response to Hagar's detractors: "[Abraham] chose Hagar in preference to your mother [Sarah] as the recipient of his message and took her for concubine when he was already an octogenarian; she was the first to give him a child, the woman who received (in trust) our father Ishmael, may God extend his blessing upon him."[54]

This passage reflects a new position. The repudiation of Hagar and abandonment of Ishmael could no longer be completely erased, for access to Jewish and Christian texts had become widespread. Therefore, an attempt was made to minimize the effects of the repudiation and abandonment, until they were turned into no more than a temporary separation, where the patriarch, giving in to Sarah and fearing some irreparable act might be committed, led Hagar out of harm's way. The counterpart to this is that Abraham's responsibility is diminished and Sarah's greatly increased. The hatred of the other woman erupts, but from the other side.

Hagar is mentioned by the historiographer Tabari (ninth century) in his *Chronicles*, and his comments are typical of this attitude. The author attributes circumcision to Sarah: the cruelty toward Hagar is then generalized on god's command as a form of justice. He writes,

> Sarah became angry and violently jealous [after the birth of Ishmael]. No longer being in control of herself, she quarreled and argued with Abraham, and insulted him. Then, she swore: I will cut some part of Hagar's body, a hand, or a foot, or an ear, or nose. But after reconsidering, she said: I am the one who committed the fault, for I gave Hagar to Abraham. It would be unfair to cut a part of this young woman's body or to kill her; but I have sworn and it is essential that I cut something. After having reflected, she said: I will circumcise her to prevent her from seeking men.[55]

Sarah's wrongs continue: she does not give a son to the father; and she provides him with a woman, persecutes her, mutilates her, and provokes him to send her away. This is a reversal of the roles enacted in the primal scene of female rivalry: the perverse woman who insinuates herself between father and son, who divides the monotheistic patriarchal family, is now Sarah. Dread of the "other woman" changes masks but continues to do its work.

The reconciliation between father and son, according to Tabari, results in an episode that is highly characteristic of these issues. Having succeeded in obtaining from Sarah the authorization to visit his son in Mecca for the first time, Abraham arrives while Ishmael is away and meets his wife. The following dialogue takes place:

> Where is Ishmael? She answers: he is out hunting. Abraham says to Ishmael's wife: I cannot unmount my horse, have you nothing to eat? [Sarah had made Abraham promise not to get off his horse, most likely so his foot would leave no imprint.] The woman answered him: I have nothing. This place is a desert. Then Abraham wanted to return because of the oath he had made to Sarah. For he had asked to eat only to test the wife of Ishmael; for he had no need of food. He said to the woman: I'm going. When your husband

returns, describe me to him, and tell him for me that he should change the sill of his door and put another in place of the one that is there now.[56]

Ishmael's wife, when she relates the conversation to her husband, simply transmits the paternal recommendation that she be repudiated. On the following occasion, Abraham finds a suitable woman as Ishmael's wife and sets foot on the ground. It was necessary for the son to renew his father's gesture of rejecting his wife to reconcile with his father. In this way the repudiation of the other woman is perpetuated within the very heart of the space that denounces her or would free itself of her debasement, but which merely reproduces it in turn — as if every time the pact between father and son is about to be made, there reappears the Hagarian figure likely to divide them and prevent origin from closing in on itself.

# 3

## Destinies of the Other Woman

### Theorizing Disavowal

Hagar's eradication from Islam's founding texts presents us with two inevitable questions: What effect does this have on the constitution of Islam's symbolic order, and to what extent is there a relationship between this and the condition of women in Islamic societies?

It is obvious that Islam is not the only religion of the ancient world to marginalize the position of women in its spiritual structure, to exclude them from legal institutions of power, or to deprecate the female body. From this point of view, Islam is not fundamentally different from other monotheisms, which recognize women's symbolic dignity only through the conception of the son; more specifically, woman is seen as an intermediary who serves as a physical conduit for routing the form of the father to that of the son. The obliteration of the ancestral mother, of her name, of her existence, from the founding text (the Koran), while all the other protagonists in the same story are welcomed, leads us to conclude that Islam's originary establishment entails the disavowal of Hagar — regardless of the constraints inherited from her biblical situation and the conflicting attempts, shot through with ambivalence, to overcome this rejection from within the tradition. But what was eliminated at the beginning cannot be so easily restored. On the contrary, this event will continue to obsess the institution and haunt it throughout its history as long as it remains ignored. Islam arose from the (female) foreigner when monotheism originated, and she has remained estranged in Islam.

The mechanism of disavowal does not affect the truth, as is the case with denial; it is not associated with the action of rejecting or refusing to recognize an obligation, which belongs to the register of abjuration; nor is it a repudiation, which consists in rejecting what has already been accepted. Rather, it gives rise to a claim that refuses to recognize belonging.[1] Hagar's story is one of repudiation at monotheism's origin, which became disavowal when Islam began.[2]

This finding introduces a perspective likely to help conceptualize a body of facts inscribed in the symbolic possibility of Islam, which have marked its culture until the present day. My argument is that the specter of the woman who was repudiated, then disavowed, from the place of *Référence* continues to haunt Islamic thinking.[3]

In this chapter I will examine the formations that carry the unconscious determinations of disavowal and the dread of the "other woman," and all they imply. Because I want to pursue the multiple apparitions of the other woman's specter, I will consolidate and summarize the traits that constitute her figure, as identified in chapter 2 in my analysis of the monotheistic literature of the genesis of the father.

The "other woman" cannot be understood alone, without her other, without the other term of the structure of originary difference, represented by Sarah. That is why the other woman is always the wife's double: she doubles the official wife, precedes her, supplants her from the outset in the play of maternity, and disturbs the process of difference and division in the family. Although preempted, the mistress-wife still retains her titles: she is "the wife of Abraham" according to the Koranic expression, "the promise" according to Saint Paul, and the "annunciation" from the point of view of the angels in the books of the three monotheistic religions. Moreover, at the pinnacle of dignity, she receives god's seed: she is the divine Mother, the wife who has been sacralized, sanctified. That is why it is appropriate for her to be referred to as "the woman of the Other."

The other woman is the feminine to the extent that it is differentiated and distinct from the woman of the Other, which, at the same time, leads to the creation of femininity as a value of *jouissance*. The other woman is, first and foremost, the foreigner, whereas the woman of the Other is part of the same family and the same tribe, and often of a higher rank, than the man chosen to be the father or founder of the symbolic institution. We need to bear in mind that Sarah is Abraham's half sister. Of lowly birth, the other woman does not have statutory maternity; she can give birth, but she does not acquire the position of "Her Highness the Mother" (which is why Hagar is absent from the Koranic text), for her uterus, or womb, is borrowed; that is, it can circulate among men, which is why she is, in some sense, a prostitute. Yet the other woman is not without power; quite the contrary. Her power is hidden, disturbing, even shocking. It is related to a type of *jouissance* that can be divided into two, not necessarily distinct, segments.

The first segment is the *jouissance* of the knowledge of alterity: The Hagar of the Bible sees god and does not die, names him, then sees the resuscitating source in the ground (the source is the eye in Arabic: *'ayn*). Remember that this power is unique; no other woman in the Bible has it. It is a visionary power, a clairvoyant, mystical power, through which she accesses that which is hidden in the blinding light of the sky or the obscure depths of the earth. What is this knowledge of alterity that ranges from the highest to the lowest, which conjoins penetration and nomination?

The second segment of the *jouissance* of the other woman concerns the body. It is the capture of the seed and the proliferation of progeny. Rereading Saint Paul's letters and biblical commentaries on Hagar, we can describe this *jouissance*. It is most certainly associated with a life that is rough ("the thorn"), teeming ("for many are the children of the abandoned woman"), wandering and painful (the woman of the Other does not experience suffering), seductive, and, therefore, perverse. It revolts against the official wife, pushes her aside, usurps her place without occupying it completely, and forces her to undergo symbolic castration. It inserts itself between the mistress and her access to phallic *jouissance*, complicating it through the game of desire.[4]

These two segments are connected, and it is their bond that makes the other woman a disturbing and feared figure, for the conjunction of the knowledge of alterity and the *jouissance* of the body, as a body of desire and vital force, directs suspicion and fear toward her. What, then, is this knowledge that is intermediary between the intelligible and the sensible?

The other woman assists in constructing the woman of the Other and threatens her at the same time. She is both a woman and a female threat for any woman, at least to the extent that the mechanism of phallic *jouissance* establishes her in its power.

### The Glow

In many traditions, stories about origin contain a sequence involving the founder's birth. It is a way of framing the question, Where does he come from, and how was he conceived? The answer often includes the representation of a moment of vacillation before destiny compels a refractory chance to do its bidding and completes its fulfillment. That the father is not present at the outset but must appear through the fiction of his gene-sis indicates the need to stage an unfolding through which the language of origin tames the possibility of the impossible.

In Islam, the staging of this question is positioned, through the bio-graphical narrative of the Prophet, on a path between two women.[5] This choice, the specific scenario that it unfolds, contains information about the mechanism of the Islamic representation of origin, haunted by the attempt to control the other woman.

## The Coming into Being of the Founder

The story of Muhammad's conception is told by several authors.[6] The context is that Abdullah, the Prophet's father, has just escaped destruc-tion through the help of his own father, who has exchanged his vow to sacrifice the child against a considerable fortune: the slaughter of a large number of camels offered up to the pre-Islamic divinities of Mecca. Con-sequently, it is a survivor who accompanies his father to the woman his father has chosen for him as his wife — Amina, who will become the mother of the Prophet. The genesis of the father takes as its point of de-parture the refusal to kill the son and the transcendence of the tyrannical and cruel figure of the primal Father.

In a chapter titled "Mention of the Woman Who Proposed Inter-course to Abdullah," the biographer Ibn Hicham writes,

> [Abdullah] walked past a woman known as Ruqayya, the sister of Waraqa, who happened to be in the sanctuary. When she saw his face, she asked him, "Where are you going, Abdullah?" He replied, "With my father." She said "If you lie with me now, I will give you as many camels as served to redeem you." He said, "I am with my father and cannot go against my father or separate from him." He then went to the home of Amina, whose rank and lineage were among the highest in Quraysh, whom he married. It is said that he joined with her sexually and that she thus conceived the Prophet. He then left to see the woman who had offered herself to him: "Why do you not offer me today what you offered yesterday?" he asked her. She replied, "You no longer have the light you had yes-terday. I no longer have any desire for you today." Ruqayya knew from her brother Waraqa that there would be an Arab prophet.[7]

According to the same sources, there exists another, very similar, version:

> Abdullah entered the home of a woman whom he had in addition to Amina. He went to work at the Clay Works and bore the traces.

> He made advances to the woman but she did not immediately respond because of the traces of clay. He left, rose, and went to Amina. He returned to the woman, who called him to her, but he refused. He returned to Amina and took her. She then conceived Muhammad. He then returned to that woman and said to her, "Do you want to?" She replied "No. When you passed by me, there was a white glow between your eyes; I called you then and you refused; you entered the home of Amina, she has stolen you."

According to Tabari, Ruqayya, who was a seer and knew from scripture the coming birth of the Prophet, proposed intercourse to Abdullah. He agreed and said to her, "Stay here. I'm going home to speak to my father." When he entered his home, Amina threw herself upon his neck. Yielding to his passion, he coupled with her, and the Prophet was conceived within Amina. The light that had surrounded Abdullah's forehead had disappeared when he returned to Ruqayya. She, no longer seeing the glow on his face, realized that the treasure he had borne within him had departed his body. Having learned from him that he had a wife and had just coupled with her, she said to him, "Go. My desire is gone." Abdullah then left.[8]

Regardless of the variations among versions, what all the stories have in common is the space "between-two-women" as the site where the first acts of generation of the Prophet as a human being occur. It is in this space, through this back-and-forth from one woman to the other, that the Islamic narrative has chosen to set the stage for the most radical question of origin. Let's examine the elements of this mechanism.

The point of departure is the question of destination proposed by Ruqayya, "Where are you going?" Isn't this the enigma encountered on the road of existence for all of us, that of destination and knowledge? In a sense, the entire story is presented as a theatrical event — "Where are you going?" The protagonist is the son who becomes a father, and the "where" refers to the place of procreation of the child who establishes origin. The fiction that governs the organization of this narrative claims not only to answer this question but, especially, to answer for the truth and legality of the place.

## The Dimensions of the Mechanism

The first dimension of this mechanism is found in Abdullah's response to Ruqayya's question. His answer does not directly address her question, however, because it refers not to a destination but to a companion; he confirms at once that he will not leave his father. The reference to the father as the one who prevents him from satisfying the woman's request — and his own desire, if we are to judge by what follows — immediately establishes the question of the "between-two-women" as held in tension between the subject's desire and his father's choice. The narrative could have stopped there, ending with the man obeying his father's order. But if it goes on, it is because the paternal prescript does not stop the son. For as soon as he is subjected to his father's choice and deposits the "treasure" he carries with the approved woman, he turns around and returns to the first woman, to whom he is still attracted, the approved woman not having satisfied his desire. Nonetheless, there is no understanding possible between them: when she wants, he does not want, and when he wants, she does not want. Rather than an insurmountable obstacle, the father's prescript creates a discordance in the time of desire. Apparently, the between-two-women establishes the stage space for this discordance, through which is revealed the distinction between the procreation of the Prophet and his father's sexual desire, between this desire and the symbolic law represented by the father of this father.

The second dimension is related to the knowledge and desire of the woman with respect to the man. Ruqayya is referred to in several versions as the sister of Waraqa, a Christian monk who recognized the first prophetic signs of Muhammad's arrival. She is, therefore, both a foreigner and a seer, two Hagarian characteristics of the "other woman," to which is added the desire to "double" the legitimate woman and receive the father's child. In the background is the approved woman, the noble woman (from the same tribe as Abdullah but of the highest birth, according to the story), that is, the woman of the Other, recipient of the holy child. Yet, although the foreign woman is presented by the story as possessing the gift of prophecy — and what prophecy! that of phallic illumination — the father of the Prophet is characterized by ignorance and contempt. Contrary to what he believes, he is not the object of Ruqayya's desire, he is merely the *bearer* of the object of that desire. Abdullah does not know he carries the sign of fecundity that will produce the son, who will be the initiator of origin. There is a light or glow, which is perceived and deciphered by Ruqayya as "signifying" that the son is in the father. The other woman, because she is able to perceive "the son's glow," would like to take him into herself. But she is required to ask the father. She makes use of the fact that she knows what the other does not know, in order to capture his seed unawares. The other woman enjoys a knowledge about light and the body, about the body of light of infantile origin, that is invisible to the father who carries it. Abdullah, who does not know that he carries what Ruqayya wants, namely, the son, believes he is refusing something else. But, while he makes himself an object of desire only to reject the other, that other puts an Other in his place. Abdullah refuses something he is not asked for. The misunderstanding is complete. Through this misunderstanding, fiction stages the question of phallic appropriation. What does it say? That it is neither knowledge nor the possession of the phallus that determines destiny and destination, but the law of the father. No one is master of the light (semen) other than this law, which preexists the birth of the founder of the law.

The third dimension is related to the underlying rivalry between the two women. The narrative emphasizes that the glow Abdullah unknowingly carries refers to the "holy child," who will elevate its recipient to the rank of Mother of the Prophet, that is, woman of the Other. It tries to show that the rivalry between the two women revolves not so much around the man as sexual object as around access to the status of woman of the Other and to the phallic *jouissance* that access confers, that is, the supreme power of engendering the son who will become the founding father. Yet the scene seems to resolve the question: one woman has it and the other does not. One woman will become the Mother and the other will remain the foreigner — empty and "without desire," as she says in the story.

The interpretation of the episode is obvious: it is a fiction that reenacts the genesis of the father in Genesis, but with a "new deal," an originary deal that, while maintaining the separation between the two women, claims to better control the situation and succeeds in dismissing the other woman. The foreigner has not superseded the spouse, and the son has arrived at his legitimate destination; there is only one father and one son. The divine treasure is hidden in the body of the woman of the Other.

## A Comparison

Given these elements, the Islamic staging of the scene of the between-two-women differs from the Mosaic one. Here, it is important to note that what is most central is not saving the child. The Islamic fiction emphasizes the question of desire and the law rather than survival.

The element concerning the other woman's knowledge is not found in the Mosaic narrative, whereas it is central in the Muhammadan narrative. In the former, the foreign woman remains on the side of power in its most destructive form, because Pharaoh wants to exterminate the male children of Israel. But it is the return of this woman to the service of the Mother that allows Moses to escape death. The woman of the Other and the other woman are unknowing accomplices in saving the child, who is the savior of his people.

Comparing the two scenes, we find that each tradition is haunted by the risk of its origin, or its originary fault. Ever since the origin of Judaism, the god of the Bible has held out the threat of withdrawing the gift, a threat of the absence of filiation and the destruction of the son. Yet, for Moses, the space between-two-women, that is, the originary Mosaic structural difference, is presented as the site of the fiction of rescue, so that the source of destruction (Pharaoh) becomes the source of salvation.

Islam, ever since the originary repudiation, has been haunted by the other woman, who has threatened to capture the son, making him an illegitimate bastard. Here, the space between-two-women carries with it a fiction that establishes the nobility of the mother's birth, control of the other woman, and preservation of the son's seed through the father. The son's obedience to the father to avoid capture by the other woman goes so far as to risk breaking his ties to his desire, which persists all the same, yet not without a certain ingenuousness. The price of submission to the symbolic law of the father is misunderstanding of the other woman's real desire. That is why the Islamic scene emphasizes the rivalry between the two women — one has the man and the other does not — whereas, in the Mosaic scene, the woman who has him (the mother) allows him to drift toward the woman who does not (the wife of Pharaoh), who returns him to the woman who agreed to give him up, his mother as his nurse. We could say that in this case the child is originally in exile, allowed to wander or subjected to fate, and in that way origin is saved and kept alive, as if the holy child, by becoming a stranger to his mother, enabled origin to split, to separate from itself, escaping the fate of self-identification and mortal self-foundation. In a sense, Freud repeats this gesture by making Moses a stranger to his people. For Islam, born to a foreigner, the opposite is true: the holy child must go toward the destination identified by the father, allowing for the appropriation of origin. In every case, the originary fault watches over and threatens origin at the same time — watches over it through the threat that exposed it to its becoming.

## Between-Two-Women in Psychoanalysis

What does psychoanalysis have to say about this notion of "between-two-women"? You may recall that in the first part of his interpretation of the myth of Moses (*Moses and Monotheism, SE,* 23:1–137), Freud connects the two families — the family of high rank and the family of humble origins — to the family romance of the child who oscillates between overestimation and disappointment concerning his real family, especially his father. He then applies this interpretation to the myth of the hero who rebels against the father who exposed him, while a child, to the risk of death, from which the child escapes, later to return and kill the father.[9] How does the Oedipal reading relate to the present case? Abdullah is in a situation of transition or genealogical articulation between father and son, son and father. The sequence of exposing the child is, indeed, present in this version, because, according to the story, Abdullah's father wanted to implement his vow to sacrifice his son, but buys back his life. And the son, now indebted to his father for his life, obeys him, accompanies him, and submits to his law. Thus, we are faced with an Abrahamic counter-Oedipal situation, where the son is connected to his father through sacrificial debt. (See the section titled "Sacrifice and Interpretation" in chapter 4.) And it is this connection that enables him to avoid giving the holy child to the other woman, the foreign woman who sees and knows far too much. The law of the father is an economic law of reciprocity, wherein the son's sacrificial debt entails a phallic debt in favor of the woman of the Other.

Note that there exists, in Freud's self-analysis, an important episode in which he meets the figure of a woman who holds a particular kind of knowledge. She is mentioned in a letter to Wilhelm Fliess; this is the elderly woman who was his nursemaid. Freud situates her in relation to his mother, attributing to her the role of instructor. He describes her as a witch and calls her his "professor of sexuality" (*Extracts from the Fliess Papers, SE,* 1:173–280). Does this mean that Freud received from this woman positive encouragement in the knowledge of sexuality? To judge from the episode, the figure of the "knowing witch," the other woman, would, in some sense, be at the infantile psychic root of the invention of psychoanalysis.

In Jacques Lacan's "The Signification of the Phallus" (1958), there appears a reference that evokes the between-two-women: "If, indeed, man is able to satisfy his demand for love in his relationship with a woman, inasmuch as the phallic signifier clearly constitutes her as giving in love what she does not have, conversely, his own desire for the phallus will make its signifier emerge in its residual divergence toward 'another woman' who may signify this phallus in various ways, either as virgin or as a prostitute."[10] This statement could apply, in part, to the present case, for the narrative uses the "residual divergence toward 'another woman'" to illustrate that Abdullah bears on his face "the signifier" indicating that he possesses the holy child. The other woman reads "the signifier" and reveals it as such for Abdullah, who did not know what he had: "You no longer have the light you had yesterday," she says to him. In other words, it is only at the moment of loss that he knows what he had.

If the father, according to the story, is the one who gives what he did not realize he had, we can add some refinements to Lacan's statement: it is not only the gift of what one does not have that will define love, but the *unknown* gift.[11] On the one hand, to give what one does not have anchors the problem in the domain of ownership, whether the gift is treated as a debt or as the concealment of stolen goods. This leads us to the economical logic of credit. On the other hand, "not knowing" that one gives falls to one side or the other of the question of ownership of the gift and its economic justification; to give without knowing is an un-thinkable transappropriation in terms of credit, value, and consideration. This transappropriation is part of the logic of the noneconomizable, where the gift is inestimable because it is imperceptible as a gift — unless there is someone (such as Ruqayya) who is supposed to know there is a gift. But the noneconomizable, the inestimable, the imperceptible... is the impossible.

## The Father according to the Impossible

We have, therefore, two strata for the genesis of the father. The first is that of the economy of sacrifice, where the phallic gift is inscribed in the register of love as "giving what one doesn't have." This would refer to the life of the son who is the object of the concealment. We see it again in the gesture of Abdullah's father, who is ready to proffer death and divert it at the same time. The son, now indebted, releases his semen where his father tells him to. The second stratum reveals the son-father as being unaware of what he has or what he gives, but he does indeed give it to the appropriate recipient, in keeping with the father's preference. At this point, it is impossible to know that there was a gift before the gift took place, and before the other woman, supposed to know, tells him so. As long as there is no knowledge, the gift is confused with the impossible as elusive, inestimable, and noneconomizable. The formula I proposed in chapter 2 applies here as well: "There is there-is-not." We could also add a variant form of the expression: "There is he-does-not-know." But once Ruqayya knows of the gift, the law of the father goes into action. This law, as an economic law of debt, can legislate only ownership and destination, for the impossible escapes its jurisdiction — it predates the law of the *Pater economicus,* who needs to know that there is an *object* to manipulate somewhere.[12] In short, the impossible is not subject to patriarchal law.

It appears that the god of Islam, as the Prophet understands him at the very beginning, is located on the side of this impossible. Subsequently, the religious institution of which he is the founder will co-opt him, placing him at the service of domestic paternity and phallic *jouissance.* But, as noted previously, the Koranic text retains the trace of the affirmation of this god who is not father through a fulguration that Jacques Berque has compared to the Unique God in the poem of Parmenides: "unborn and indestructible... Whole, unique, and unmoving and complete."[13]

In the fiction of the founder's procreation, the inestimable impossible is manifested by "the glow." It is not the light itself but the consequences it brings about in manifesting itself that reveal the mark of the impossible. Note how this glow provokes a split among the protagonists, which results in the fact that what is represented as an object of their desire is negated or concealed: "He has it, but doesn't know it," "He knows he had it when it he no longer has it" (Abdullah); "She knows but doesn't have it" (Ruqayya); "She has what the other does not" (Amina). This last expression seems to indicate full possession; but this is only an illusion of belief in the phallic appropriation and interrogation of the impossible. In fact, even for Amina, there is a split: she has the son's seed but does not have the desire Abdullah feels for the other woman. The woman of the Other does not have what the other woman has, namely, this supplemental *jouissance* that the man demands of her, in being neither son nor father but someone who is reaching for a supplement that overflows phallic *jouissance.* The inestimable impossible is the result of the glow that produces a universal split and dispossesses everyone of some amount of *jouissance,* which is lost forever. If we follow Lacan's hypothesis, the glow would not be just any signifier but what he calls "the master signifier," to the extent that it exposes all of us to this crisis of lack.

## Between Emptiness and Fullness

Other psychoanalytic studies have examined the schema of the between-two-women from the point of view of the *jouissance* of the other woman, emphasizing the destructive hatred this figure may provoke whenever there is no working-off of the imaginary rivalry with this figure for a female subject. Michèle Montrelay's research has helped clarify this issue.[14] In an interview on female jealousy, she says,

> You lose all desire, you remain a body, a body that is only a body, and, at that moment, the body of the other woman — which is always seen as luminous, it is that body that bears the light of the other's desire, of the man's desire — that body attracts you and you want to dissolve into it. . . . At that moment, you try to reconstruct yourself, and this reconstruction involves the gaze, from the point of view of a woman's body. It is the body of a woman who is light — elsewhere, jealousy is said to be "blinding" — this brings us back to an altogether archaic period. What you need is the opportunity to give shape to this light, which is now on the other, to create the maternal body. You, you are nothing more than a body, you no longer have the words to express your jealousy, but there is the body of the other woman — it's highly enigmatic — which is like the first step you must take to reconstruct yourself. . . . This kind of blinding clarity that is nothing, which is the void of jealousy, you provide it with the contour of the body of that woman. But this implies that you have had constructive relations with your mother's body. That your experiences of jealousy with regard to your mother were fragmentary and not completely devastating.[15]

We should not be surprised that clinical research finds, through its own meanderings, the same issues expressed by the fiction of origin, sometimes even down to the details. I would like to focus for a moment on Montrelay's reference to light as a desire for the other, who is "void," "nothing," and at the same time something that needs to be given form by the body of the other woman. How does this light reveal voids and solids? By creating a feeling of destruction ("the void of jealousy") such that the only escape is through an appeal to the other woman, which establishes the structure of the between-two-women. The appearance of a binary modality — 0/1 or 1/0 — appeases the anxiety of destruction brought about by the light, providing the other woman is not destructive in turn.[16] Jealousy conceals both this anxiety of nothingness and the intent to free oneself by creating the pole of the other woman. This is the function of the glow in the narrative, because through it the two terms of the fundamental structure — "There is a woman who has it" and "The other woman does not have it" (there is there-is-not) — are manifested; as if the glow is an epiphany through which antagonistic forces are revealed, opposite and yet complementary places, so that the founder of the symbolic institution can come into being. However, although there is a place (a womb) that remains empty and another that is full, according to the 0/1 binary schema, it is from this empty place that the glow is visible. The empty place does not receive the glow but creates the gaze that reads it. If the other woman sees, it is because she is not phallically fulfilled, because the lack or persistence of the desire of the other makes her prophetic and knowing. However, we must be careful here when using the concept of emptiness. The emptiness of the other woman (Ruqayya's womb) is a void of privation and not the void of interval that falls between two, the void that indicates the glow, or the vertical bar between 0 and 1. The void of interval is not a place, it is the place beyond *(hors-lieu)* of the impossible. It is not metaphor but nothingness and epiphanic interval, the in-between through which the existence of the structure we are studying is set in motion and becomes possible. Naturally, this is made manifest through the privation of the other woman, who reveals it through the gaze, through desire, through a metapsychological knowledge within the negating struggle with the woman of the Other.[17] But the void of interval belongs to a different order of negativity, one beyond membership, identities, or essences; it is "neither one nor the other": neutral, therefore.

It should be clear that the Islamic fiction of the origin of the father differs from that in the Bible. By stressing the opposition between the two women, it allows the impossible, the void of interval, this withdrawal from which arises the very possibility of "fictionalizing" the father, to appear. This recalls what we found to occur at the beginning of Islam concerning a nonpaternal god: the original One is, in some sense, an infinite genealogical desert, out of which all origins and their imagination continually arrive. It is here that the ocean of illuminative philosophy and Muslim mysticism touch a (bottomless) bottom. But we also see how this idea is masked by the defensive stance against the other woman that arises from the originary disavowal and the phallocentric patriarchal co-optation of her gaze. By presenting the man as the bearer of the "glow," the father becomes "pregnant," phallically certain, whereas the mother, to the extent she may have been displaced by the other woman, appears uncertain: if the father of the father (the patriarch) had not been there to direct the son's seed toward her... Consequently, there is an inversion of the judgment of certainty that is customarily attributed to the mother. Here, paternity is attested by the evidence of the senses (sight) of the other woman.

## The Mother as Fiction

In spite of this reversal, or possibly because of it, the narrative contains a problem of interest to the female subject. By making the man uncertain, even for a moment, about his desire for the mother, the narrative introduces a separation into the affirmation of generative certainty, and it is through this separation that the mother as fiction is produced. For such an operation to be possible, a sequence was needed in which the originary "deal" revealed that another distribution was possible, and how the law of the father abolished the accident of the ignorant desire of fate. Conception according to fiction rends the unambiguous space of maternal certainty.

For a period of time, the mother was almost not the mother; another woman could have taken her place. In this "almost" of eventuality, this "caesura of pure jealousy," a story is produced, a narrative, a signifying construction. Because of the other woman, origin is not only a jet of sperm in the womb of the woman of the Other but also the emission of a fiction between two, that is, the story itself, or even the procreation of the fiction of the procreation of origin. Ruqayya had to delay Abdullah for a short while so there would be time for a story. This gift, through the attraction of the other woman, is necessary for instituting the origin of the founder. A kind of mediation takes place between Ruqayya and Amina, a *différance* (in Derrida's orthography), that is, the gift of temporality as fiction, in which the procreation of the body of the founder takes place, which is merely the imaginary of the symbolic. For the subject, it is belief in this fiction that *makes* the founder, as body of sanctity or truth. This sanctity resides not in the flesh of the child but in the fiction that confers it upon him. In this sense, fiction is the mother of the sanctity of the holy child, which is what all fiction tries to achieve and re-create, including in the form we now call literature.

But when we speak of "the possibility that a woman can take the place of an other," what is the status of this necessary eventuality that fiction is capable of introducing? As shown earlier, this necessary eventuality refers to a preexisting separation in which this permutation can occur, this alternative, a separation in which the possibility of the impossible arises. The "between-two" is a space that emerges not because there is one woman + one woman, an interval, a split created between them or by them; it is they who enter the separation that precedes all polarity, all alternatives, all paternal and maternal certainty. There is a separation that lies at the origin of all origin, an archistructural division around which originary meaning is constituted as jealousy of being. I have referred to this as the void of interval, and fiction is a garment for this void, from which arises the gift of time.[18] The fiction of jealousy is jealousy of the void (in the initial sense of the Italian *gelosia,* a trellis that protects the woman from the gaze of others); it conceals real sovereignty. Fictions are presented as the mothers of an origin of which they are the daughters. Like the crocus in the poem by Apollinaire, they would be "mothers daughters of their daughters."[19] Would the imaginary be the mother of a real of which it is the child? But the real of origin withdraws from all paternity and maternity; it holds itself back from everything that might be said or imagined about it that is only jealousy.

**The Veil**

The foreign woman sees the glow of sanctity and tries to appropriate it. The originary scene of the procreation of the founder may have shown that patriarchal law holds her in check; nevertheless, she will continue to disturb Islamic order, as if the eye (of Hagar), which since the origin has seen sovereignty without dying, continued to torment it.

That this eye is found in a body known as desire only adds to the power of vision, the enticement of the gaze, and turns the other woman into a clairvoyant power. It is clairvoyance in two senses: in the sense that she sees beyond the possible, and in the sense that she allows herself to be seen and reveals too much of herself. She thus conjugates the penetration of knowledge with the attraction of seduction.

When encountered, this clairvoyant power, by being embodied in the beginnings of Islamic history, crystallized a negating action that used the law to cast women into the night of the city. The threat had to have been significant for the response to be so intense. So what happened?

In concrete existence the "other woman" is not necessarily another woman; she may be the same woman split between two poles of the feminine, as the fiction of origins or unconscious fantasies present them. As long as the split exists, female *jouissance* retains its differential value on the scale of the law of desire. Some splitting may remain, and libidinal peace is preserved. But if the distance is closed, the two positions converge, confusion occurs, and anxiety or even delusion can take over the subject or group. This scheme, which I will describe further, is at the heart of the problem that Freud addressed in one of his most important texts: the relationship between sexuality and civilization.

Sometimes, at the base of the structure of a civilization, unreasonable demands are found to exist, which serve, beneath the mask of love of the law or our neighbor, as a continuous source of what Freud called the "psychological poverty of the masses." The veiling of women in Islam, through its unconscious mechanisms, and in light of the network of repression and social debasement with which it is associated, is most certainly one of those demands. The following quote from Freud is revelatory here: "The curb put upon love by civilization involves a universal tendency to debase sexual objects" ("On the Universal Tendency to Debasement in the Sphere of Love" [1912], *SE*, 11:177–90).

What I want to focus on is the mechanism for blinding the female body and its internal seclusion, which the Islamic institution of origins has imposed. I want to keep in perspective the disavowal of the other woman as a center around which a series of repressions at the base of the system revolves.

## The Actuality of the Veil

One of the dimensions of the modern crisis of Islam is precisely that which involves the place of woman in society. We are witnessing a virulent actualization of the question of the veil and its originary modalities at the very heart of the modern spaces that have broken away from her subjection. What this actualization shows most clearly is that the repression within a culture cannot be easily undone, and that resistance is organized by a variety of means: avoidance, displacement, eradication of the initial reason for the repression, and repressive activities. The coexistence, in one place, of representations of woman associated with her traditional status and her ultramodern condition introduces an additional complication that radicalizes the issue, for it exposes unknown conflicts that affect the foundations of political and linguistic systems.

The veil and the sign — in France, for the past ten years or so, a debate of unusual proportions has centered on the violent association of these words. I should, first of all, point out the scope of the discussions that have mobilized a number of participants for many years, giving rise to a profusion of written and audiovisual products that have implicated the institutions of government and resulted in both lawsuits and new laws. In examining the archive of those events, we cannot help being struck by the multiple fields of discourse that have been called upon: law, politics, ethics, religion, and language. With some hindsight, the disproportion suddenly appears obvious between the facts themselves — a handful of young women in specific schools in certain regions, and maybe a few hundred, at most, throughout the country — and the explanatory, theoretical, and polemical reaction they triggered. Between the veil and the sign, something akin to a semiological work site of foundations has suddenly been exposed.

Naturally, such a site cannot be opened at just any time or for just any reason. If so many forces have been put into play, it's because of the importance of what is at stake. But if we look for a formulation of the issues in this debate, we find it impossible to identify one in particular. A tangle of reasons and themes, all equally important and intercommunicating, is advanced, which effectively convokes the principles, values, even the identity of the entire political and cultural system. An expression by the French minister of education summarizes the issues nicely: "the face of France." And to signal that this is not just some expression thrown out randomly, he specifies: "I'm a believer, and naturally I respect believers. But we need to show that we are also believers in human rights, in France and the Republic. It's too bad if that seems a bit solemn and unfashionable."[20] The veil and the face of France: it looks like it's all up for grabs.

Beyond the position of the politician anxious to justify the ban he has just issued by referring to his "belief,"[21] it is possible to recognize the scope of the menacing shadow of the veil throughout the debate that has taken place. In it two key concepts have been continuously referred to: fundamentalism and integration. The first designates the evil that operates through the veil; the second, the good it implies, the political fiction of entering the shared body of the nation. Literally, these words reflect the integrity of a system that is apparently challenged by the integrality of another. Why is the veil presented as a question of the *whole,* that is, as a "panic question," as Maurice Blanchot put it?

It is significant that the debate crystallized around the sign and its ostentatious nature. Ostentation reflects a "pretentious display" (according to Webster's) that creates a disturbance that French law wants to protect its citizens from. But, as we know, the Conseil d'État (France's highest administrative court) has never considered a sign to be ostentatious in it-self; it is the essence of a sign to display, and the excess is determined not by the sign itself but by the subject who displays it. This calls to mind the West's problematic of the sign and "monstration," of the hand in the sense that it is intrinsic to man, who is capable of both greeting and mon-strosity. The *monstrare* of the sign inevitably culminates in the problem of meaning.[22]

In the Islamic tradition, it is not accidental that the hand (of Fatima) is contrasted with the eye, because excess is considered essential for the latter, whereas the hand symbolizes the ethical organ par excellence, ca-pable of compensating for the eye's overindulgence. The excess of the hand exists as well, but what is characteristic of man is the ability to limit such excess; however, no ethics is possible for the eye, other than to pit it against the real screen that blinds it. Yet the debate always returns to the following question: At what point does a sign begin to reveal too much? Is this the case for the cross, the Star of David, the *kippah* ? Is the veil an excessively demonstrative sign? The way in which the minister's order settled the matter — without appearing to explicitly address the veil, while nevertheless designating it — was to consider it an ostentatious religious sign in itself.

## The Theological Veil

From the point of view of Islamic theology, which prescribes its use, the veil is not a sign. It is a thing through which the female body is partially or wholly obscured because that body has the power to charm and fasci-nate. In other words, for religion it is the woman's *body* that is ostenta-tious, whereas the veil would serve as a *filter* that does away with and protects against the body's disturbing effects. From the beginning, the debate got off to a wrong start by treating the veil as a religious sign similar to the crucifix, whose Muslim equivalent is the calligraphy of the name of god and, more specifically, the Koran. For a believer, the Koran alone is the "treasury of signs" *('ayat)*, because that is the name of the fundamental constituents of the text, with which everyone is invited to identify: "Be Koran," in the words of the Prophet. The outward signs of identity for Muslims reside in the aestheticization of the divine letter. A minimum of investigation would have shown that the veil plays no part in this form of interpretation but is governed by a theological logic of real *control* over a woman's body for the purpose of subjugation. What was the purpose, then, of getting involved in a lengthy argument about signs, which culminated with the minister of education adopting the position of a "semiological censor"?[23]

Naturally, the veil can be viewed as a symbol — as it is among the mystics, for example — or as a simulacrum in Arabic aesthetics and erotics. Note that some Islamist movements do not impose the wearing of the veil, based on the strict requirements of Islamic law they claim to follow. They modify the law, limiting it to the wearing of a head scarf or the concealment of all of a woman's body except for her face and then only her face, for her hair and neck are completely covered, which gives the strange impression of looking at a mask or a model of flesh, behind which the real face is located. In this form, the veil has become one of the emblems of the conquest of public space by Islamism. It becomes semiologically overdetermined in terms of current political struggles. The real register of the veil remains preponderant, however, in historical references to the Islamic corpus of the law *(sharia)*.[24] At this level there is an obligation to conceal a woman's body by various means, which makes the veil the central element of a sophisticated system of concealment, which includes muffling the sound of the voice and the tinkling of jewelry. That is why all the Arabic lexicons, when discussing the word *hijab*, the canonical term referring to the veil, begin with this simple definition: "the forbidden," or "anything that forbids something."[25] Veiling is, therefore, an operation through which the woman's body, as a whole, is transformed into a thing we are forbidden from seeing, except for those familiars who are part of the domestic space.

At the beginning of his study *La sexualité en Islam*, Abdelwahab Bouhdiba makes this distressing remark: "The veil thrusts the Muslim woman into a state of total anonymity: to be a Muslim woman is to live incognito. And to make sure, Arab society has only to sequester the female sex. The Arab home will become nothing more than a veil of stone enclosing the veil of cotton or wool."[26] As we saw in chapter 1 with the example of Ni'mat Sidqī, what is at play in the veiling of the female body is the political body of the forbidden, for which the concept of *tabarruj* clearly illustrates the threat: woman, to the extent that she makes use of any public display that "seduces" and provokes "sedition" in the community. The concept of *fitna*, which controls the fields of individual and collective, moral and political experience, combines both these aspects. This seduction-sedition consists essentially in turning men away from their god by disturbing their faith in its signs *('ayat)*. It breaks the relation between man and the Koranic text. Woman embodies the perversion of the community and its laws. That is why Imam Ali, son-in-law and successor of the Prophet, considers woman to be a "necessary evil," an evil whose power operates primarily in the visual field. He is reported to have said, "The glances cast at women's charms are the arrows of Satan."[27] Along with signs there is "belief," as the minister of education so well understood for his own purposes. It is this belief, but from another point of view, that Islam would like to protect from female monstration through the imposition of the veil.

One of the key concepts in this system is 'awra, which is etymologically related to the act of putting out an eye. The term ended up generally referring to what is obscene and should therefore be hidden from sight. Because woman's body was declared to be taboo in its entirety, it is woman who became, essentially, an eye, an irradiating sexual eye that had to be shut. However, these arguments show that blinding this eye does not eliminate the dangerous charm; it merely shifts the eye's spectrum into obscurity. Its dark rays only become more threatening to the light of divine signs.

In this context the veil is not a sign but the thing that blinds the woman's body, that interferes with the signs of faith and the law in the visual field. Veiling is, therefore, a theological operation of concealing the woman in order to neutralize her. It entails a logic of interposition designed to prevent woman's monstration and to obliterate her as a monster of indecent and dangerous charms. In this sense, we could say that it derives from a "de-monstration" of woman, assuming we use the prefix de- as a privative rather than an intensifier. But as we shall see, privation and intensity come together whenever there is a question of truth, for there is no belief, no law, and, a fortiori, no unveiling without the intervention of truth.

If we now consider the current definition of the sign as a unit combining signifier and signified that serves for the thing itself, the veil is then the bar beneath which woman becomes an invisible and inaudible signified. In its canonical form, which does not allow any patch of skin to appear, it reduces every woman to an anonymous and undifferentiated entity insofar as she is a person. It totalizes women, abstracts them, ties them to a unique signifier: beneath the veil is *woman*. It is a ghostly apparition on a shapeless body making its way down the street, bearing, through the eradication of its face, either beauty or ugliness, youth or age, foreignness or familiarity. An undecidable, indeterminate, virtual woman who combines infinite attraction and repulsion, she becomes the subject of doubt, error, and speculation, a fiction for which opposites struggle.

But, through this ghostly presence, through a gaze one can only imagine, doesn't the act of theological concealment turn against its own control? For what is an invisible or imagined gaze if not the one we assume to be that of the visionary omnipotence of god?[28] The seclusion of the female subject beneath the veil establishes her as a being gifted with occult powers, because this signified is not only a mental image but also a living and mysterious presence, which acts within the straitjacket of its imprisonment.

## Woman as Clairvoyant Power

In clinical practice, women subjects, when they have been forced to occasionally wear the veil, often refer to the fantasy of being possessed by a powerful eye that adheres to their skin or intersects it, at the same time becoming entirely this eye that sees without being seen. In a way the veil creates a visual partner similar to the "cutaneous partner" Gaétan Clérambault (1872–1934) introduced on the basis of his observations of women's erotic attachment to fabric. What is striking, in examining the hundreds of photographs of traditional garments he brought back from a trip to Morocco, is the transformation of the veiled woman into a shapeless and swollen entity that repels and fascinates at the same time.[29] The visual partner would be that which, through the veil, envelops female clairvoyance, subjugating it from within and turning it into an anamorphic ghost on the outside. The veil, more than just a simple screen, creates a visual barrier, homologous in the visual field to the prohibition in the field of language. The veil *visually bars* the woman. Something like a mediated view takes hold of her body, establishing a separatory power between seeing and being seen, between the desire to see and what can be seen. The repression is twofold: for the woman, she tries to break the circularity of clairvoyance, the power that sees and allows one to see; while for the man, it is a question not only of concealing the woman as real object of desire but of transforming her through her concealment into an obviated fantasy, an ideational body with the promise of infinite unveiling, like a houri in paradise, whose hymen is continuously reconstituted. In short, through the veil the woman becomes a fable, an obscure mirage. In this way men's sight is protected.

In this narrative, man appears as an eye that desires its own blindness through the woman. In the Arab world, the theme of passion between the eye and the night is an old one. A legend summarizes it well. It is based on a phrase heard often in love songs, one that is repeated by listeners: *ya ein, ya leil,* "oh eye, oh night." Eye *(ein)* is the name of a man, Night *(leil)* is the name of a woman. Eye is hopelessly in love with Night; which is to say that he loses her as soon as he meets her, and looks for her in desperation. But when he finds her, he only loses her again, for the eye cannot see its night at night.[30] The passion of man's eye can be realized only through its own blindness. The woman, presented as a visual power that must be darkened, also appears as the obscure object of desire. The woman is, therefore, both the eye and the night of the eye.

It is in the sense of limiting woman's clairvoyant power that the legal requirements for the veil have been interpreted, even among the most indulgent authors, such as Ibn Hazm, in his famous treaty on love, *The Ring of the Dove* (eleventh century). There, after recalling the Koranic passage that recommends "lowering one's gaze and preserving one's sex," he writes, "Were it not that Allah is aware of the delicate way in which women lower their eyelids when striving to win the affection of men's hearts, and the subtle ruses they employ in contriving to attract men's desires, never would He have revealed *(kachf)* a notion so infinitely remote and abstruse. This is the limit beyond which one may not prudently expose oneself to danger: how then shall it be with a man if he adventure further?"[31] In this passage, there is an allusion to a kind of "virility of the eye" in the woman, which enables her to penetrate the man and subjugate him. The woman could be said to "play the pupil" like an instrument of erotic infraction.[32]

When a female college student who wore a veil wrote to a French newspaper to say that "being a believer is simply a question of modesty before God, which is important in my religion,"[33] it is impossible to ignore this "question of modesty before God." It forces us to ask with her, What is this feeling of shame that women feel before god? Why should they be more directly confronted by transcendence than men? Why would a veil suffice to ward off the gaze of god, when his eye is assumed to be all-seeing? What is so insolent and obscene about the female body to the deity?

Certain aspects of this idea are found in Jewish and Christian theology. For example, according to Saint Paul, "woman ought to have power *[exousia]* on her head because of the angels." Saint Paul interprets this "because of the angels," through which woman is uplifted, as a sign of power and freedom.[34] But why should an uncovered head undermine the cause of the angels? Why would covering her head elevate a woman? What does a woman have on her head? Is it that monotheism attributes to woman an imaginary eye at the top of her head that would constantly offend transcendence?

Within the Islamic context, both Hagar and Ruqayya possess an arrogant power of clairvoyance that enables one of them to see god without dying and name him with the name of that vision, and the other to perceive the glow of sanctity and want to capture it. The veil is the response in the real to this cranial eye that imaginarily defies divine alterity.

## Some Remarks about the Pineal Eye

The elements I have just laid out — the clairvoyance and obscenity of the woman's body, the virility of her eye, her threat to the divine signs, her modesty before god, and the veiling of her head — all suggest a detour through what Georges Bataille has called the "pineal eye."[35] There is not enough space here to fully examine Bataille's "pineal eye," which would lead me too far from the current investigation. Instead, I will limit myself to a few remarks.

"The Pineal Eye," published after Bataille's death, provides an entrance point for an examination of this enigmatic conjecture. Naturally, this eye is not specific to women; it affects the human species as a whole. Nonetheless, in Bataille's work it is almost always the attribute of a femininity eroticized through horror. In Bataille, the idea first emerges convulsively, almost delusionally, and subsequently follows the pathways of rationality, intersecting the analysis of fantasy, the study of myth, and anthropological, anatomical, and physiological data. I want to begin with this last dimension, from which we get the name "pineal eye." It refers to a gland that presents the characteristics of an embryonic eye located at the tip of the spinal column, at the top of the skull. Scientists assigned it a sexual function, which has been confirmed recently (Descartes said it was the seat of the soul); but this aspect is not the most important for my analysis. Bataille stressed the imaginary dimension and expressly considered the pineal eye to be a "purely psychological concept."[36]

I don't want to discuss the images of this eye rising from the cranium. It is sufficient to note that it combines, in a visceral impulse, obscenity with a feeling of repugnant modesty, blindness as well as incandescence, the virile protuberance and simultaneously the orificial breach, to crystallize in the vision of a hideous and terrifying black anti-sun. Bataille placed the first appearance of this hyperbolic eye, which remained in a sense incomplete but still fearfully efficient, at the moment when the human animal finally stood upright. To the extent that the eye came into existence just as mankind rose up like a tree, it is fundamentally erectile, therefore virile (the "ocular tree," Bataille sometimes called it). The object of its desire is the sun, for, unlike the eye of horizontal vision, it does not fear the fire of the sky, given that it is already blind. More exactly, its blindness is the basis for its power of imaginal vision.

This explains the element of defiance in this insolent visual erection of the skull. Verticalization created the drive for a range of mental activity toward regions opposite the ground, that is, toward the top of the head, which led this eye to challenge the sun of plenary light with the arrogance of a negative and spectral sun. Moreover, humanity's myths have always expressed the fulfillment of the function with which this eye is associated — the flight skyward and the flight of celestial fire (Icarus, Prometheus, who is himself an eagle), where "the erection of human flesh *sees* its completion."

Several themes involving the pineal eye coincide with woman's visionary power in the Islamic corpus, but one element decisively corroborates their inclusion in the same logical category. We find it in the concept of *tabarruj*, which designates the monstrations of the woman "whenever she exhibits herself to arouse man's desire." The term is derived from *baraja*, "to build a tower," "to make conspicuous and tall." From this root are derived words referring to the "split in the eye," the "distance that separates the eyebrows," the "size of the eye," the "alert gaze," "tower," "verve," "force," and "angle."[37] Could there be a better way of combining and expressing the erectile character of such monstrations, the clairvoyant erection that woman is assumed to possess? Similarly, *baraja* has also given us words meaning the "signs of the zodiac," the "planets," the "starry sky," and the "crest of plants," which confirms the polarization toward the sky Bataille speaks of. Thus, the veil is thrown over what is considered to be woman's visual evil or disease, erected between god, whom she defies, and man, whose desire she arouses and whose power she terrorizes through his obsession with the erect eye.

In the Islamic corpus we can also find examples of the mythic freedom found in the figure of Prometheus or that of the legendary eagle that can look the sun in the face, figures in which man projects the overarching function of a virtual eye. Mention is made by Ibn Arabi in the following terms: "Man is to God what the pupil is to the eye."[38] Relying on the fact that, in Arabic, the pupil is literally "the man in the eye" *(insān al-'ayn)*, Ibn Arabi makes man god's visual organ, his visionary quintessence. Not only does man see god, he is god's view of the world. Consequently, man's desire, his obsession with the virtual eye, leads him to make himself the orifice of the all-seeing absolute. But Ibn Arabi isn't the only mystic to have erected the human eye to such heights; there are other examples. Hallaj, for example, in addressing god, says, "The eye through which you see me is the eye through which I see you." Similarly, we can see why, according to the terms of this system, woman is a threat to this grandeur. If she turns man away from his god, she deflects the pupil of his eye. She brings about absolute blindness.

The provenance of the archaic belief in woman's possession of an eye on her head could arise from the infantile memory marked by the close involvement with the mother and the incorporation of her fascinating and all-seeing eye. Woman preserves the primitive character of an eye imprinted by the source (the womb or female sex), which threatens, through its omnipotence, the grandeur of transcendent origin as godlike point of view. It is this unconscious assumption of defiance and arrogance before the divine eye of truth that causes the student quoted earlier to state that she wears the Islamic veil out of "modesty before god." That is also the reason Saint Paul states that woman must cover her head "because of the angels" and that this act raises her up, as if, uncovered, she were low or constituted a point of attraction downward.

## The Demonstration of Woman

There is a scene in Islamic tradition that provides us with a front-row seat to the angel's cause, a scene in which the veil appears for the first time in Islam's founding narrative.[39] The episode, reported by all of Muhammad's biographers, occurs before the beginning of the revelation, during the difficult early period, when the future Prophet had doubts about his mental state and discussed this with his wife:

> That year, Muhammad, upon leaving the mountain, came to Khadija and said to her: "Oh, Khadija, I'm afraid I'm going mad." "Why?" she asked him. "Because," he said, "I see in myself the signs of the possessed. When I walk on the road, I hear voices coming from each stone and from each hill; and at night I see in

dreams an enormous being who comes to me, a being whose head touches the sky and whose feet touch the ground; I do not know him and he comes forward to grab me. . . ." Khadija said to him: "Tell me when you see something like that. . . ." So one day, finding himself in the house with Khadija, Muhammad said: "Oh Khadija, the being appears before me, I see it." Khadija approached Muhammad, sat down, held him to her breast and said to him: "Do you still see it?" "Yes," he said. Then Khadija exposed her head and her hair and said: "Do you see it now?" "No," said Muhammad. Khadija said: "Rejoice, it is not a demon but an angel."[40]

It goes without saying that the historical reality of this scene is of little importance. What is important is that it is presented as part of the larger narrative and borrows the language of scenes of origin to illustrate, reveal, and convince us of the demonstration of woman. What does it show? First, that the history of truth in Islam begins with the unveiling of a woman and, second, that it also begins with an attempt upon the modesty of an angel. These two claims are two sides of the same coin, namely, the theological fabric hiding the body of the woman who would threaten the view from above. Everything in this story rests on the final act and affirmation that, when the woman uncovers herself, the angel hides. The angel, who no longer appears in the Prophet's visual field at the moment of unveiling, disappears only because it is assumed that, as an angel, it cannot support the sight of Khadija's uncovered head. Had it been a demon, it would not have turned away from her, because what she reveals and the demonic are assumed to be the same. Because it is an angel who transmits the veridical word of the Koran (the archangel Gabriel), the demonstration of the woman turns out to be a demonstration of truth and, simultaneously, an attempt against that truth in the very act of demonstrating it. The angel who flees is the truth that conceals itself through the unveiling of the woman, but the concealment of truth is the verification of truth.

Second, the woman's situation originally appears tied to a prohibition "against looking," upon which belief is established. The woman believes what she does not see, whereas the man does not believe what he sees. Therefore, his ability to believe must rely on her. What I will refer to as the "scene of demonstration" (which has no name in Islamic tradition) inevitably leads toward the conclusion that man, if he is to believe in god, must rely upon belief in a woman, one who has access to a knowledge of truth that precedes and exceeds the knowledge of the founder himself. She verifies the founder's truth. She verifies it through an offense against that truth and through the defective insight of the man-Prophet's visionary excess. The woman seems possessed of a "negativity" that can be used to prove the truth of the Other. The veil separates truth from its negation.

To the man terrorized by his vision, incapable of judging the nature of what is haunting him, Khadija offers an active interpretation that brings the unknown to light. Her unveiling gives rise to a decision in the man's indecisive subjectivity. She provides him with the certainty of the Other that he is unable to recognize by himself. Man is inhabited by the Other but does not recognize it. Without the woman's unveiling, and therefore without the veil, he would have remained indecisive, living but doubting god. The woman makes him a gift of decisive judgment. Man misunderstands the truth (of the castration) he bears. These are the extreme consequences of the assumptions harbored by this scene. Theology confers upon the woman's veiling-unveiling the status of a rescue, of giving man access to an identification of the divine, as if the difference of the woman's body enables him to grasp the difference that haunts him.

But if man can access the certainty of the Other only through woman, doesn't such a theological construction amount to the same thing as saying that man's narcissism is more problematic than woman's? If woman is presented as already knowing the truth of the Other, or already blindly opened to it, man must first work through the female operation in order to recognize the sign in himself and thereby acquire the certainty of that Other. The veiling of the woman would be a bulwark against man's narcissistic stupidity.

According to Islamic historiography, Khadija was the first person to believe in the Prophet. The first Muslim, therefore, was a woman. The woman who causes the angel of truth to flee is the first to believe. Through her, man is able to affirm his god. That is why tradition relates that after this episode, Muhammad said to Khadija, "The angel sends you his greeting." But how can we fail to see the change of position here: the woman through whom he believes becomes the woman who believes in him? The woman would then be the antiorigin upon which the initial faith in origin resided.

Veiled, unveiled, reveiled — these are the three stages in the female operation of theology: initially veiled, unveiled to demonstrate originary truth, then reveiled by order of the belief in that truth of origin. For, once established, truth aspires to conceal the nothingness through which it has passed.

## The Reversal

This is the path that gradually led to the massive imposition of the Islamic prohibition concerning the veil. Just as the man who doubts his sanity has been transformed into the man who institutes theological principles, the angel's greeting has been transformed into an incredibly suspicious form of mistrust. Belief in woman, in the foundation of the demonstration of truth, has been reversed, turned into a dangerous mechanism through which she appears as a being who "lacks reason and religion" *(hadith)*, as a sex whose "wiles . . . are great" (Koran 12:28). The scene harbored the possibility of such a reversal because the demonstration was obtained through monstration (unveiling), and the identity of the angel was confirmed by its flight. But we also see why, in this system, there is no need to burn the witch — burning at the stake is unknown in the history of Islam — the lie and the capacity for reversal that theology attributes to woman will remain firmly associated with the truth of the Other and will cling to her through the veil that holds them in suspension in mystery. Would the veil prevent woman from being burned? Isn't one of the slogans in the current campaign by Islamists to promote the wearing of the veil "the veil or hell"?

I cannot provide a detailed examination here of the profound reasons for Muhammad's change. Certainly, after Khadija's death he became, when he was nearly fifty, polygamous, loving "women, perfume, and prayer" *(hadith)*. To believe in the woman (who believes him) and to love women — the entire breadth of the transformation is inscribed between those two statements. We can state succinctly that they correspond to a modification of the libidinal and political economy of the Prophet — a subject to which I will return later in this chapter.

The theater of the theological forbidden begins when the veil descends. The complex machinery, some of whose workings we've just explored, often supports powerful interpenetrations, drawn from the obscure dramas of the body, its life and death. In the case of Islam, the script is known and the episodes concerning woman's concealment or elimination are too visible for us not to see that their divinity is their humanity, that their strength is found in their rootedness in human (all too human) dramas.

These dramas correspond, point by point, to the problems of Muhammad's desire as a man during the last fifteen years of his life, a period that completely overlaps the building of Islamic society. This may seem simplistic, but it's verifiable in every case. Whenever the man-Prophet encountered a conflict of desire or found himself at an impasse of *jouissance*, god supplied a Koranic solution that had the value of law. The first act unfolds with the story of Aisha, his favorite wife, who, during a trip, separates from the caravan, followed by a man named Safwan, to search throughout the night for a pearl necklace lost in the desert. She is accused of adultery, for Safwan is a handsome man and witnesses are said to have mentioned the existence of a relationship between them in the past.[41] For several months the Prophet experiences terrible doubt, but he loves Aisha. When the verses that exculpate her and release her from suspicion appear (in the sura called "Light"), the theological curtain inexorably begins its descent. It is obvious that the veil is not only the piece of fabric thrown over the woman's body but the organizing hand of an order that is rigorously maintained between the subject of desire as visionary substance and the political institution of society. Veiling turns out to be a powerful system for structuring the body of *jouissance* in space, in time, and in interpersonal relations. At the time of Aisha's accusation (in the same sura, "Light"), private and public are delimited. Entry into the home is subject to authorization during the three prayers (dawn, noon, evening) that necessitate disrobing for the ablutions. The persons to whom women may reveal "their charms" are strictly limited, based on their blood relationship. The principle of major prohibition makes its appearance: the veil as prohibition coincides with the ban against incest.

This becomes clear with the second scandal that occurred in the early Muslim community.[42] One day, the Prophet, entering without permission and unannounced into the home of his adopted son Zaid, surprised Zaid's wife, who was only partly clothed. He was disturbed and captivated by the sight of this woman, who was said to be very beautiful. Anticipating the Prophet's desire and god's intent, Zaid divorced his wife, whom the Prophet immediately questioned, for he lived with the fear and torment of his desire. What was to be done? Not only did god authorize their marriage, it was celebrated by the angels. Nothing less would suffice to address the Prophet's confusion and legitimize their union. This unique case of celestial celebration in Islam was the Prophet's final marriage. Just as the Koran (30:3, "The Romans") makes him a gift of the other's wife, it forbids him to take any other wives: "No other women are lawful for you after this . . . even though their beauty should appeal to you" (33:52). At the same time, adoption is banned as being anti-Islamic, and Zaid was no longer the son of Muhammad: "Muhammad is not the father of any man among you" (33:40). Having brushed aside any complaint of incest against the Prophet through this genealogical maneuver, the law attacked the root of the risk and generalized the restriction of the veil: "Oh, Prophet, tell your wives and daughters and the women of the faithful to draw their wraps a little over them. They will thus be recognized and no harm will come to them" (33:59).

We could summarize the question of the veil as structure by referring to the following two Koranic fragments: "though their beauty should appeal to you" and "draw their wraps a little over them." To the extent that women delight men to the point of leading them to risk incest, the wearing of the veil finds its rationale in the more serious threat to the social order brought about by the extremity of human desire. The statement assumes the incrimination of woman, of her beauty or her monstration, but it also harbors signs of a passive position of the man-pupil who is, in a way, incapable of controlling his focus. He examines women rather than examining himself. In this sense, man is unable to regulate his vision in the presence of women. Like an uncontrollable visual orifice, he can be penetrated by female monstrations, which possess and subjugate him to the extent that he forgets his law. Theological representation is tied to the necessity of overcoming an originary weakness in men, who allow themselves to be captivated by women's clairvoyant power.

Veiled, unveiled, reveiled — the three terms can be seen as movements that establish theological principles whenever man's vision is excessively receptive. But aren't those same movements found in the night of the world into which mankind descended during the fall from paradise?

According to the Islamic version (sura 7), in the beginning a veil of light separated Adam and Eve from the sight of their sex. When they transgressed god's order and ate of the forbidden fruit, the veil of light disappeared and they discovered their nakedness. They had to wear clothing to hide it. The three movements — veiling, unveiling, reveiling — correspond to the three stages of theological representation: the blinding light, the darkness that allows one to see, and the screen that blinds the seen object.

If we follow the terms of the theological argument, men and women after the fall would have been equal during the night of the world. Their visual disturbances coincident with the fall were the same and exposed them both to the unbearable sight of their sexual organs. But something else occurred that managed to change that equality, eventually requiring that men impose the addition of the veil to free themselves of women's charms. So what happened?

To this question, the scene of the first dialogue between Eve and Adam, as reported in certain narratives, seems to suggest a response: "When Adam opened his eyes, he saw Eve on the bed he occupied; as is said in the Koran: 'We have said: Oh Adam, inhabit paradise, you and your wife.' When Adam looked at Eve, he was astonished and said to her: Who are you? She answered: I am your wife; God created me from you and for you, so that your heart should find rest. The angels said to Adam: what sort of thing is that, what name does she have and why did he create her? Adam answered: it is Eve."[43] What is striking in this story is that Adam does not recognize Eve when he opens his eyes, although he knows her name, for god had taught Adam every name. Adam's knowledge is, therefore, nominal and not associated with the female thing as alterity. Eve, however, who does not possess the knowledge of names, knows who the other is and answers his question in terms not of identity but of attachment and desire:[44] "I am your wife; God created me from you and for you, so that your heart should find rest." The story seems to say that man originally misunderstood the alterity of gender that derived from him as species (since Eve was created from Adam) and that his direct and violent question about the identity of the woman remains unanswered.

Theological discourse has continued to present us with man's confusion around woman, a disturbance that is related to woman's clairvoyant power, her knowledge of alterity, and the originary confusion in the face of the identity of her being.[45] These disturbances and the imbalances inherent in them crystallize around woman's relation to the truth; for woman, as a challenge to truth, is truth and the attack on truth, its confirmation and simultaneous flight. There is nothing proper (propre) about woman, for what characterizes her essential characteristic is the ability to discriminate between proper and nonproper. The essential characteristic of woman is to be withdrawn from the proper, to be undecidable. We might conclude that at this point the trap closes on the hand of theology, leading it to the desperate solution of the veil. But what if this were the cause of man's fascination, this withdrawal of the proper, in what appears to be properly undecidable about truth in woman? What if the extremity of men's desire were to seek enjoyment in the place where truth and untruth communicate with one another? To want *the* truth would turn out to be incestuous, because to want all of it necessarily includes the desire for untruth that truth, in its essence, contains.[46] Theological representation, therefore, proposes snatching men away from this fascination, interceding for them, with their dilated pupils, invaded in invisibility by god and subjugated in visibility by women. To men it assigns a salutary task: the task of truth or the veiling of woman.

## Return to the Actual

The incident of the veil now appears in a new light. The problem must be posed in terms not of signs but of the forbidden to which those signs refer. This forbidden cannot be reduced to a prohibition; it is, rather, a truth mechanism, which digs its roots into the lower depths of the drives to establish, on the surface, a legality of *jouissance* whose imperative is a *jouissance* in legality. As long as young women are found in the space conquered by god's political idleness and they reactivate theological imperatives, we find ourselves in the presence of a conflict between two prohibitions and two beliefs that sustain them, which are necessarily beliefs in a certain position of woman and truth. Those beliefs are represented here by the young woman who defends her "modesty before god" and by the minister who responds with "the face of France," at least a face of France associated with his belief in human rights. The young woman believes in the de-monstration of woman, which indicates that in her system's unconscious she is represented by the monster of erectile visual power and enigmatic knowledge. This is what we encounter in the imaginary of ancient civilizations in the figure of the sphinx, as found in the myth of Oedipus, for example. Arab-Islamic culture abounds in enigmatic and dangerous sphinxes, always found along the initiatory path of the male hero. The theological solution, as we have seen, consists in imposing on woman the prohibition of the veil as a ban on the monstration of her head (the hair, according to tradition), which challenges the originary view of truth. The minister believed that de-monstration was monstration (the veil as ostentatious sign) and banned it. *In doing so, he banned* this act. By making it one sign among many, the veil was hidden behind a curtain of religious semiology to avoid confronting the fearful question of the prohibition of the prohibition of the other.

What exactly is the position of the woman in the minister's belief when he bans the prohibition of the other woman: a monster who has the right to the monstration of its signs, or a being who will be definitively de-monstrated, no longer under the jurisdiction of any prohibition of the veil? And what is a woman, according to this belief? We need to examine the reference corpus, in this case the text defining human rights (*les droits de l'homme,* literally, "the rights of man"). We know that the textuality of those rights is more extensive than the declaration that goes by that name. But principles are laid out and, in this respect, it is clear that woman is a Man, Man as anthropos or characteristic singularity for the species. Not only is sexual difference not an essential characteristic of this textuality, but it is precisely one of the forms of discrimination the textuality wants to suppress. What is important here is humanity insofar as it is different from other species. The man of those rights does not, in principle, refer to a man or a woman but to the singular identity of their identity and their difference. Here, the originary division of sex is no longer current, which means that, essentially, the question of truth does not depend, in this reference universe, on the difference between the sexes. In principle, this system intends for the truth of sexual difference to become, like religious truth, a private and subjective matter.

It's easy to understand why the display of the veil is such a touchy question. Not only do veiled young women not harbor religious signs, they have placed the highest bet on a system at war with another: a mechanism for producing truth, even if it assumes the mode of untruth. The stakes have been raised in the competing myths of a modernist West and a traditionalist Islam that are everywhere at war. This war is not the old confrontation between two beliefs in one and the same truth, as the Crusades were and still are in our memories, but a war between two uncrossed truths. In the case of Rushdie, the war for truth took place through fiction and operated in the textual field of origin, whereas, in the case of the veil, it is the mechanism of the prohibition concerning woman that is shattered. It is no accident that fiction and woman are at stake in the most important conflict in the world today between belief and identity; for in one and the other conjointly, it is the *truth of the body and the body of truth* as determinants of the limits of what is essential to a system, a person, or a community that are at stake. This is, consequently, the most crucial element when considering relationships in the world and between worlds. Such is the question of the prohibition of the prohibition of the other.

It is an unanswerable question. There is no other without the prohibition that changes it as other for itself and for the other. The prohibition is the institution of the other. To prohibit its prohibition is to prohibit it as other. From this point of view, there is no doubt that de-institution is one of the forms of human destruction. At present there are many signs throughout the world of the increase in this mode of destruction. The growth of identity politics is the most obvious symptom, the sign of widespread global anxiety in the face of the question of the forbidden — providing we do not interpret this anxiety in the moralizing sense of a relaxation of mores, and so on.

This anxiety arises from the fact that we all appear to be facing something like an ineluctable deadline, namely, the imposition of a universal law for all humanity and the institution of a global legislator. This is not the place for a detailed discussion of the growth of this project in the West, or the many versions of such a law, which gravitate around the idea of a humanity centered on a community of universal prohibition and a universality of prohibitions. This project is currently present in military, economic, political, scientific, and humanitarian discourse and can be experienced on a daily basis.

What characterizes these discourses, along with the terror and hope they embody or arouse, is that the law is treated as technology and the prohibition as order. This notion avoids the essential question of the prohibition, namely, that it is based on an interpositional statement[47] supported (implied) by a truth mechanism. What would the universal statement be that could impose itself on all humanity? In what language would it be articulated? From what place could it be uttered? The universal prohibition would assume that there is an INTER position among all the "inter's" of human communities, embodied by an absolute femininity, a world-Woman without an identity who would undo all identities in order to dispense with the difference between truth and nontruth for all people; a deferred mother of humanity whose language would be maternal within every language.

Although there is material for combating the servitude or injustice produced by the prohibition of the other, there can be no place from which to announce the prohibition that would strike its prohibition. There is no universal interposer because there is no master of language. There are only statements of interposition. But the identity myth of the modern West is bound to the idea of producing the prohibition of prohibitions, of becoming the difference of differences, thereby connecting with an absolute femininity of the species. Given its radical perspective, the freedom this myth promotes is the advance toward a destiny where the truth that conforms to this freedom would reestablish the modern West's identity, which would be *woman*.

The final pages of Claude Lévi-Strauss's *Tristes tropiques* provide the most limpid formulation of the West's identity mythemes concerning this subject:

> Now I can see, beyond Islam, to India, but it is the India of Buddha, before Muhammad. For me as a European, and because I am a European, Muhammad intervenes with uncouth clumsiness, between our thought and Indian doctrines that are very close to it, in such a way as to prevent East and West joining hands, as they might well have done, in harmonious collaboration. . . .
>
> If the West traces its internal tensions back to their source, it will see that Islam, by coming between Buddhism and Christianity, Islamized us at the time when the West, by taking part in the crusades, was involved in opposing it and therefore came to resemble it, instead of undergoing — had Islam never come into being — a slow process of osmosis with Buddhism, which would have Christianized us still further, and would have made us all the more Christian in that we would have gone back beyond Christianity itself. It was then that the West lost the opportunity of remaining female.[48]

Through Islam, therefore, the West could be said to have encountered the interposer who prevents it from realizing its identifying destiny as woman. The cry of the mythifying mythologue is heartrending; he laments a West that is unable to connect with its Far East or to close the circle of the identity of identity and difference. The other as misfortune, as co-optation, as male cutting the woman from herself — this is how the anthropological myth of the West experiences Islam and its veil. Will the present era witness the unveiling of the West? In light of my arguments concerning the problematic of the feminine that lies at the origin of Islam, Claude Lévi-Strauss's statement might acquire a different nuance if we were to consider that it is from its own originary femininity that Islam has tried to sever itself.

## The *Nights'* Word

The first test of truth for Islam took place on a woman's lap. Although this statement seems unthinkable today within the Islamic order of discourse, there was a time when there was nothing shocking about it, for the scene of demonstration was transmitted and repeated by several generations of chroniclers, a chain that can be followed back to the seventh century.[49] No doubt this is one of the symptoms of the torment I referred to earlier, which made origin unavailable in a fictional mode. Research efforts in the humanities on Islam and "Islamic thought," as we have been accustomed to calling it for some time, have contributed more than a little to making the fiction of origin inaccessible. In conventional research such scenes of demonstration are considered to belong on the scrap heap of history and are "barely good enough for literature." According to this research, we should look for reason in the machinery of concepts, in the major theological constructs; that is where the system's gold is hidden, its pure originary truth.

## From the Angel's Greeting to Disrepute

Nonetheless, isn't the scene of the first, or initial, faith an important representation of a form of reason that refuses to hide its metaphysical side and accepts its power to affect us by presenting us with a scene of sharing and healing? Here, the founder, the man of the word of law, hallucinating, terrorized, repeatedly visited by an invisible being, wonders if he is possessed by a demon. Like someone comforting a child who suffers pain, a woman holds him on her lap to prove to him that the angel is an angel and to free him of his fear of madness. The scene clearly reveals that the representation of the origin of the Law in Islam needed the body of a woman to remove any doubt concerning man's reason and to help the angel place him on the path of the word. It is in this sense that we understand the angel's greeting to Khadija.

But what happened between this moment, when the woman mediates between man and the angel — in other words, when she assumes a posture of mediation between two mediators — and the moment when she becomes an auxiliary of the demon "whose wiles are great"; between the moment when she, through her unveiling, verifies the truth of the vision and the moment she must be veiled to protect the faithful from the sight of her charms; between the moment when she appears to possess a knowledge that predates the prophetic knowledge of the founder and the time when she will become the woman who "lacks reason and religion" (hadith); between the moment when she frees the Prophet from the suspicion of possession and the moment she becomes the troubling creature who must be possessed, appropriated, and monitored, and whose submission will be stringently organized; in short, between the angel's greeting and woman's disrepute in Islam? It is with this question in mind that we must scrutinize the future of women in Islam. This is necessary if we are to have any chance of understanding what transpired over a brief period of time (roughly twenty years) that determined women's destiny until today, perpetuating a position that can only be described as extreme. This excess, its origin and its many justifications, indeed the entire network of humiliating attitudes and assertions concerning women, must be analyzed without indulgence, with the greatest precision, for the mechanisms of alienation are far more complex than they appear.

This scene seems to accredit the notion that there was a time when woman was the witness of truth, in the twofold sense that she acknowledged what took place and was the proof and the test of the truth of vision. Then there was another time when woman became deceitful, a trap and a ruse, an artifice (this is the meaning of the word *kayd* in Koran 12:28) that had to be masked, unmasked, and controlled.

The approach that has been most popular until today has consisted in explaining this reversal in terms of the social and political context. The number of the Prophet's wives, for example, was due to the tactical necessity of allying himself with neighboring tribes in order to pacify them. However, a careful examination shows that this argument is not valid for many of those marriages. Reference is also made to the consequences of the battle of 'Uhud, during which the new community lost a great number of men, making polygamy "necessary," for it was vital to the group's survival. By itself this type of explanation, although it relies on important findings, cannot decipher the enigmatic change that occurred in the libidinal economy of the Prophet after the death of Khadija, who was about sixty years old at the time (Muhammad was around forty) and who remained his only wife until her death. Thus, the Prophet went from having a great attachment to a maternal figure to "feminine" figures of woman, from a strictly monogamous relationship to multiple relationships, which he adopted not only out of obligation or tactical considerations but out of desire, or pleasure, as indicated in this famous *hadith:* "Three things in your world were made worthy of love: women, perfume, and the prayer that refreshes my eyes." Although this change took place in the context of founding a new society, we can follow each episode through the legal and ethical statements found in the Koran. We have also seen how their roots are buried deep within the desire of the subject Muhammad himself. But the diachronic approach that considers the accumulation of wives and their historical circumstances sufficient to account for the regime of *jouissance* of Muhammad the man with respect to woman and the degradation of her situation has, for a long time, obscured a dimension that can't be reduced to political sociology.

## *The Question of* Jouissance

The hypothesis I want to test connects this change with a modification of the Prophet's relationship to the enigma of female *jouissance* in his own economy of *jouissance*. It starts with the observation that Muhammad's specific place in the prophetic chain of monotheism is characterized, from the point of view of the reception of the word, by striking, but unexamined, similarities with the position of the Virgin Mary (the most quoted woman in the Koran): the same angel Gabriel, the same sudden invasion, and the same subjugation of the body, which in one case welcomes the word and in the other receives the divine letter. Ibn Arabi's expression concerning Mary's virginal conception — "the breath was from Gabriel and the word from God"[50] — could easily apply to the transmission of Koranic speech described by the Prophet as being accompanied by intense physical pain. This operation of "the holy letter" was based on another kind of virginity, because the Prophet was assumed to be illiterate *(ummi)*, so that he received the text as if he were a blank page. This ignorance of the letter should be compared to what Pierre Legendre writes concerning the Virgin Mary in Christian tradition: "If we delve a bit further into the inventory of traditional exegesis, we find that the doctrine of innocent purity is, at the same time, a doctrine of ignorance.... The mother of God is ignorant, and exalted as being ignorant. This lack of knowledge, this being free of taint is specifically referred to as taking pleasure in God [*jouir de Dieu]*."[51] This posture is not limited to the imperative of acceptance commanded by the angel; for the injunction to read *('iqra)* that introduces the revelation and gave its name to the Koran contains, in Arabic, an entire range of meanings that are repeatedly mentioned in the *Lisān,* from which I excerpt the following: "a woman *'qara't'* when she has retained the male ... when her womb has gathered a fetus."[52] Receiving the letter would thus be a form of gestation in the womb. Reading would be connected with the transappropriation of the masculine toward the feminine. The object of the act of reading was a "letter-gesture" that, like the fetus, was able to cling to the shelter of the womb, only to be cast from its shelter into the world as finite gesture. And what more is there to say of the association that appears in the very first sura (sura 96 in current versions of the Koran) between the blood clot of the first sign of life ('*alaq*) in the womb and the quill?[53] If reading is a form of conception whose gesture is the letter, receiving it entails a position that can be qualified as feminine.

In the case of Muhammad the man, the letter was most certainly embodied. It took over the body and got caught in the body, which could signify that it remained within and issued forth through his voice. But for this he had to believe in this position of receptivity, of submission to the angel, and had to fully assume it; in other words, he had to believe in woman to receive the divine. That is why, in the scene of demonstration, where he is not yet assured of his position, he turns to Khadija to question her about what is happening to him, assuming, rightly, that as a woman she already knows what such a position entails. She answers with her body that this relationship is of a different kind. This is the background of the scene of demonstration, which is essentially an authentification of Muhammad's position and is directly connected to the enigma of female *jouissance* in its relationship to the Other.

We have approached what psychoanalysis since Lacan has identified as "Other *jouissance*" or "supplemental *jouissance*" to differentiate it from the phallic *jouissance* that both men and women share.[54] What we refer to by the word *phallus* is a so-called symbolic function, around which men's and women's desire is structured in terms of being and having — the one who has it isn't it and the one who is it doesn't have it — so that this function is the function of lack for both sexes. In the resulting radical asymmetry, although men and women share (differently) phallic *jouissance*, women experience a so-called Other *jouissance*, which escapes localization and knowledge. Freud was led to speak of the "dark continent" in relation to women and ask "What do women want?" because the enigma of this *jouissance* remained unresolved.

When speaking of *jouissance*, we are referring not to the recognition of the other that is implied by desire but, rather, to something that relates to the body proper as singular experience, one that is impossible to share and is always excessive. Recall that it was Hegel who introduced the notion of enjoyment (*jouissance*), exemplified in the contradiction between the enjoyment of the master and that of the slave. In his *Philosophical Propaedeutic* he writes, "When I say that something pleases me also, or when I give in to my enjoyment, I am only expressing that this thing has value for me. In this way I have suppressed the possible relation with others, which is based on understanding."[55] *Jouissance*, therefore, is at odds with understanding, which is why its fate has so many consequences for social bonds. Nor should *jouissance* be confused with pleasure, for pleasure and unpleasure are part of a system of regulation that imposes a limit on the body and achieves homeostasis through the discharge of pleasure. That is not the case with *jouissance*, which is always excessive ("consummation," as Georges Bataille put it) and which is not useful for physical survival. *Jouissance* is, in a sense, good for "nothing." Yet it is with this nothing that the most serious imbalances are created, that the law establishes its prohibitions, and that sovereignty fails. From there to what *jouissance* "condescends to desire," as Lacan put it, is a long road.

But if woman has access to *jouissance* and to a relationship that man can comprehend only through a remarkable prophetic dignity, through sanctity, through divine election, what, then, is the being of woman? If man needs an operation of the mind or letter, angels and demons, gods and devils — in short, the entire "spiritual fatum" that Nietzsche, in speaking of men, called "our nonsense" — to achieve what woman enjoys solely from the fact of being a woman, we can imagine the consequences such a finding will have for the theological order and its system, which relies upon phallic organization: consequences that affect truth, sovereignty, the difference between man and woman, the establishment of power and *jouissance* as models. Some of those consequences can be discerned through the scene of demonstration:

- Woman is presented as a (negative) power able to test the source of speech and distinguish what is true from what is false. The first would have its source outside man, the second within him, possessed and alienated by the demon. As a result woman appears to have the power to divide reason and unreason, or, as we might say today, a diagnostic ability.
- Woman's place is in the opening between man and the angel, so she fulfills the function of mediation between mediators, as if she inhabited not an interval or delimited region but a conjunction of edges.
- Woman possesses a knowledge that issues from the body and is not subject to the order of language. What's more, her body unveils the concealment of the origin of language, for the angel Gabriel,

the angel of speech, flees when Khadija removes her veil, as the narrative describes.

- If woman is between the angel and man, if she understands the boundaries between reason and unreason, and if her knowledge is not acquired by customary means, it is because her identity continually overflows identities. Each of these consequences taken in itself constitutes a danger for theological order and imperils sovereignty.

I want now to discuss the hypothesis toward which the preceding discussion has been leading up to: In its early stages, Islam, through the position of its founder's receiving the letter, was exposed to the enigma of Other *jouissance* in such a caustic manner that, once the turmoil and confusion of the initial experience was over, Islam had recourse to a stream of proscriptions to reduce, dismantle, then deny that Other *jouissance*, so as to gradually establish the sovereignty of a phallic, juridical, and ethical order congruent with the formation of the state. In short, Islam constructed an internal wall, which served as a forceful counter-feminine dam, one that was all the more powerful as the exposure to its abyss was so intense and central to its original focus.

Religions endure and acquire their strength only because they have anchored belief in some region of the abyss, which, through their founder, they have turned into some terrifying originary experience. During a second stage, they repress this experience and conceal the abyss. The founder of Islam proceeds no differently. He approaches the question of female *jouissance*, which has meandered through monotheism ever since Hagar, only to veil and eradicate its originary inscription, which can be read in the scene of demonstration. It is necessary, therefore, to read this eradication in terms of the specific position of the founder and his experience, where the enigma of female *jouissance* is tied to the fate of the Arabs through their ancestral mother, rather than to reduce the problem to his sexual behavior, to his wives, or to the political sociology of his matrimonial relationships, all of which fall within the jurisdiction of the veiling of the abyss and eradication.

In examining the movement from the angel's greeting to the ethical and juridical disgrace of woman, we need to follow the mechanisms of the eradication of female *jouissance* that came into being with the establishment of Islam's theological government. I want to briefly examine these mechanisms, which affect the three dimensions found in this scene: truth, the body, and Other *jouissance*.

## Eradication

Woman will become lying and deceitful. What's more, to the extent that she has the ability to test the truth and possesses an understanding of boundaries, she is capable of mixing true and false, as well as reason and unreason, and to conflate them. She can render the real imaginary and the imaginary real, cause symbolic barriers to collapse, ridicule emblems, and annul the effect of rituals. Situated between angel and man, she blurs differences and is endowed with the power to metamorphose visible and invisible identities. She has been said to have the ability to deprive beings of what is proper to them.

To the extent that woman's body possesses a knowledge that seems to predate that of the Prophet, along with the power to make language disappear (like the angel at the scene), it will become necessary to eradicate her in all her manifestations. This eradication is the screen thrown over her body, keeping it at a distance and making it opaque to society, to social relations, and sometimes even to intimacy, in order to eliminate the challenge she presents to the signifying organization of the phallic universe. Woman's body has the power of irresponsibility, of flight, and of the dispossession of language; her blindness imposes itself through the concept of *'awra* (the blind and obscene part), which has been generalized to include nearly the entirety of her anatomy.

But eradication is most effective against Other *jouissance* in woman. Its fundamental mechanism is the denial that encounters disavowal, which provokes an increased will to mastery that will fail. In failing, it finishes itself off in violence. As we have seen, woman seems to have a physical relationship with an Other *jouissance* that is not part of the economy of sexual enjoyment. Denial is directed toward this Other *jouissance* and the reduction of all *jouissance* in woman to phallic sexual enjoyment, according to the model of masculine sexuality. But because this model does not have the last word on woman's *jouissance*, and because denial fails to eliminate the experience of Other *jouissance*, the inadequacy of the model of phallic, masculine sexuality presents man with a positive balance of inexhaustible female *jouissance* that terrifies him. In his eyes it becomes the mark of woman's implacable lack of satisfaction. "Encore," which signifies the supplement, according to the title of Lacan's seminar, is synonymous in phallic reasoning with woman's insatiable demand and unlimited availability to receive other men: she still wants more! The denial of woman's Other *jouissance* — a denial I refer to as eradication — only increases man's uneasiness rather than relieving it. Worse yet, the object of his denial appears deformed to him, monstrous.

This unease before what appears as the "abyss of woman" drives masculine organization to seek greater control over her and attempt, using real and imaginary means, to control her *jouissance* — which culminates in the bolts and chains, the real locks and chests of the suras. But the tighter the rope, the more *jouissance* aspires to the impossible and tirelessly seeks the point of weakness. And it always finds it, because there is no form of organization that doesn't have a fault somewhere in its structure. At that point, woman's *jouissance* becomes, for the man who attempts to control it, the *jouissance* of the flaw in that control or, if you will, the *jouissance* of the flaw in man and, in some cases, the *jouissance* of the flawed man.

The preservation and capture of virginity crystallize the most radical challenges in this relation to female *jouissance*. As I have previously mentioned, Freud, when he encountered the "taboo of virginity," explained it, on the one hand, as man's castration anxiety before woman's sex and, on the other hand, in those societies where women must be virgins at the time of marriage, as men's desire to sexually mark women in order to continue to dominate them ("The Taboo of Virginity," *SE*, 11:191–208). To these developments we could add another interpretation, which sees, in the very strict tradition of keeping the hymen intact for the husband, a preventive attempt to control Other *jouissance* through the fantasy of absolute *jouissance*. Man believes that by this unique unveiling he can access woman once and for all, as if, by entering that intact depth and by removing the immaculate surface, he will succeed in "consuming" her entirely, with no remainder. By appropriating the unique loss, he makes a claim to being unique. Being the first and last to grasp that surface, he will seek to eliminate the possibility of other inscriptions. However, in claiming to become the master of that loss, he ends up freeing the woman from preserving the hymen, making her accessible to others. He unveils an unveiling that eliminates any control over the object he aspires to contain absolutely. The unique is lost the first time. Yet, as I will show, this loss is the fulcrum that tips into the violence and fury of the male fantasy of omnipotence, which attempts to respond to Other *jouissance* through the imaginary of an unlimited *jouissance* of the Other.

Eradication attempts to establish male sovereignty over the Other *jouissance* of woman, because this *jouissance* is related to a sovereignty that always seems to elude man, and eludes him all the more to the extent that he tries to control it and assure himself of his mastery over it. The theological order not only has sought to put the mechanisms of eradication into practice but has tried to shape them into a theory central to the system of laws, where the veil is the central element in a web of suspicion, control, confinement, and debasement that surrounds the female subject with an opaque circle of hypersexualized moral suspicion.

Nonetheless, attempts to remove the eradication have occurred even from within Islam. These have assumed either a poetic form, as during the period of courtly love and the idealization of the "Lady," corresponding to a desexualization of the woman; or an esoteric and allegorical dimension more durable than the first, based on the mystical experience whereby many sufis, such as Ibn Arabi and Bistami, saw themselves as "the wife of god."[56]

## *Speech,* Jouissance, *Death*

Now I want to turn my attention to a more common and more popular episode, one that appears in *The Arabian Nights*. I want to investigate the following claims: (1) *The Arabian Nights* can be read, from beginning to end, as the drama of the eradication of Other *jouissance* in woman and the attempt to eliminate that eradication; and (2) the inaugural scene of the narrative, which is also the central scene repeated night after night, reprises, although differently, the scene of demonstration: a man and a woman confronted with the question of Other *jouissance* and the logical confusion associated with that *jouissance*. Based on these premises, the initial scene of *The Arabian Nights* can be read as being that of the woman in whom Other *jouissance* is denied; in other words, the woman who becomes the lying, deceitful, dissatisfied creature whose sexuality is so anarchic that it destroys man's reason. The question revolves around determining the nature of the operation of removing the eradication and how this can be compared to the scene of demonstration.

Once upon a time there was a woman who drove a man crazy and another woman who brought him back to his senses. Reduced to this simple statement, *The Arabian Nights* is the story of a restitution, in a twofold sense: the narrative as therapy and the narrative that relates the therapy of the narrative. This background opens with the drama of a man who has been driven mad by his wife's infidelity — more exactly, by the sight of his wife giving herself to another man during an orgy. What the one woman undoes with her sex, the other restores through her speech. This is the outline of the story, which serves as another version of the "between-two-women": between the sexual *jouissance* of the first woman, who releases the man's murderous sexuality, and the heroism of speech embodied in the second. The story ranges from collapse to combat; it is simultaneously dramatic and epic. And Shahrazad embodies the figure of the epos of speech that calls upon reason from the night into which it was thrust by a devastating *jouissance.*

But this situation becomes extreme only because the man, having gone mad, is a white king whose queen gives herself to a black slave. It is not only the disorder brought about by the infidelity that is in question, but also the limitlessness of the disturbance of the master's *jouissance* in comparison with the slave's. The prologue of *The Arabian Nights* shows, in the most straightforward language, the queen being mounted by the slave and the humiliated king, the guarantor of the law, overcome by murderous sexual instincts. *The Arabian Nights* forms a narrative of the subversiveness of female *jouissance,* which wounds the man in his capacity as master while his queen, the mistress, does not hesitate to make use of a slave for her own *jouissance,* thus instilling madness into the heart of sovereignty.

But what point is there in risking sovereignty for the sexuality of the woman who defeats it, and then giving that sovereignty the opportunity of being rescued by the other woman? Why this insistence on seeing a *jouissance* challenged by language fall into the arms of love? For the nights are a trap of love, the love of the other woman, when the woman of the Other (the queen) has unleashed the king's murderous hatred — providing this love is not viewed as some naive sentiment or belief that assumes that all that is required for love to triumph over death and cast the veil of reason over the gaping abyss of *jouissance* is to narrate something or to speak. Speech alone has never been able to resolve any form of madness. It is necessary for speech to make sense, and for this to happen, a site, a mechanism, is necessary; otherwise speech escapes in all directions — it is pure loss. In short, we need to identify the way in which woman's speech delays death. What is the machinery of love in *The Arabian Nights* that seeks to get to the bottom of the madness of *jouissance*?

Here, we must limit ourselves to the intrinsic merits of the narrative. Why? Because a lengthy tradition of commentators denies to *The Arabian Nights* any understanding of unanswerable questions, seeing it as a work of amusement, a collection of stories in which the Orient gives free rein to its delightful fantasy and eroticism. It is, in particular, the prologue of the work, whose essential theme I have summarized, which has often been considered to be a "pretext" for the narration, the storyteller's way of introducing the tale.

This long tradition of orientalist anecdote has been interrupted, for several years, by analyses that attempt to read and question the content of the great narrative of the Arab world. Three texts are particularly significant. The first is *De la mille et troisième nuit,* by Abdelkébir Khatibi, which marked a turning point in this research.[57] Khatibi's reading subtly emphasizes the articulation between narrative, desire, and death. His interpretation revolves around what he sees, from the beginning of the story, as the principle of the succession of nights, that of an absolute constraint that can be crudely summarized as, "Tell me a story or I will kill you." At a single stroke, his analysis lifted the text out of a long period of syrupy glosses and showed the range of challenges it presents concerning speech and death. In pursuing this path, I will add that the problematic of desire cannot by itself be used to analyze madness and the extremity of violence; to account for this, we must isolate the dimension of *jouissance,* which is infinitely more abyssal. In other words, our triptych will be speech, death, and *jouissance.*

Gilbert Grandguillaume, using an anthropological approach that incorporates psychoanalysis, analyzes *The Arabian Nights* and its prologue in terms of jealousy and its two faces: the Oedipal paternal rivalry and the fraternal sexual rivalry between the central character of King Shahrayar and his brother.[58] His text supplies a close reading of the drama of alterity and sexuality for the masculine subject, the central element of the tale. Here too, significant insights give us a better idea of the importance of the tales in the ability of a culture to construct a site of metapsychological imagination. But the Oedipal interpretation, in spite of its relevance, reveals its limitations in the face of the originary composition that characterizes the opening of *The Arabian Nights,* which, according to my analysis, presents us with a figure of the "archaic father of the horde." Moreover, it as at this point — at the beginning of the narrative — that the question of *jouissance* makes its appearance.

The third text is an essay by Jamel Eddine Bencheikh, *Les mille et une nuits; ou, La parole prisonnière.*[59] Bencheikh is particularly interested in the questions raised by the tales' prologue, questions he does not necessarily try to answer. He writes:

> Why would a collection of the *Nights* need this fiction to exist and why would it need the one it decided to use?...The guilty queens do not even have names. Nothing explains how it came to pass that they gave themselves to their slaves during organized games that are bound to be seen by others....That is, nothing tells us why a queen would give herself to a slave....There is something genuinely astonishing about this: the prologue to the *Nights* abruptly concludes a drama no one seems to be concerned about, and the narrator [Shahrazad] responsible for seeking mercy from the scorned king hurriedly tells him stories that, logically, can only confirm his attitude toward women....There is no euphoric and simplistic vision of desire in the *Nights*. The tale is not about advancing the prospect of love.

Bencheikh is right: the tale is not about advancing the prospect of love; quite the opposite. But before seeing why this is the case, I want to return to the question Bencheikh poses: Why does a queen give herself to a slave? Why is this particular scenario used as the opening scene for *The Arabian Nights* and the motivation for the entire narrative?

Let's go back to that scene. A king leaves on a voyage to visit his brother. He forgets the gift he intended to bring him (forgetfulness is always the source of a discovery or a new point of view) and returns home. There he finds "his wife lying in the arms of one of the kitchen boys."[60] The answer to the question is obvious: *The Arabian Nights* intentionally begins with the defeat of the master and intends that this defeat have as its cause the spectacle of his wife's sexual pleasure with the lowest of his servants, one who is supposed to be deprived of any enjoyment as far as the master is concerned. Therefore, at the beginning of the story, there is no master of *jouissance*. A comparison with the story of paternity in Genesis is obvious, except that here we are faced with a reversal: the slave replaces not the mistress but the master, and the crux of the story is not the gift of the child but the gift of the imaginary and the text. To provide access to the imaginary, it is necessary that complete *jouissance* be withdrawn from the one assumed to possess sovereignty. It is true that

there is no absolute *jouissance*. The possibility of a thousand and one
nights – indeterminate duration and narrative time – begins not when
there is the gift of the imaginary but when the imaginary presents total
*jouissance* as impossible. For life to go on, an exercise of imagination is
needed, which expresses the possibility of the impossible. There is, therefore, an imaginary that makes a gift of the impossible. If we return to the
expression "There is there-is-not," we can now say that the "there is"
must necessarily be imaginary, an imaginary through which the real of
withdrawal ("there is not") can be presented. I suggest calling this imaginary the "necessary imaginary" to distinguish it from the imaginary of
narrative content. The necessary imaginary is the text exclusive of any
thematization, such as the interlacing, weaving, or intermingling of signifiers. That the withdrawal of a part of the master's *jouissance* leaves a
void in which the necessary imaginary relates the withdrawal that made
it possible is only another version of the father as gift of the impossible.
But the text of the necessary imaginary is once again narrated at the site
of the feminine. We are again confronted with the originary structure
previously described as the feminine divided between two women, the
woman of the Other (the queen) and the other woman (Shahrazad).

However, one can claim that, instead of the feminine in-between, in
this case there is a masculine in-between, where the queen as object of
*jouissance* is placed between the slave and his master. This "between" is
the point from which the narration of the story begins, but it gives rise to
a violent struggle that can result only in the neutralization of the slave
who negates sovereignty or in the collapse of the master's omnipotence.
Moreover, hasn't the slave already appropriated the master's sexual thing
for his own enjoyment? We are familiar with the dialectic of the relationship between these two men as described by Hegel: the space in which
that relationship occurs is like a battlefield, rather than the originary separation of withdrawal characteristic of the feminine in-between as the condition of possibility of the gift of the impossible.

Here, the narrative appears to employ a knowledge of psychic temporality, of the logic of trauma, of the narcissistic organization and emotional relationship to the other in all its states. It is not the king who
observes the scene of deception for the first time who goes mad and
swears "to marry for one night only and kill the woman the next morning."
Another term is needed, which the narrative introduces in the following
sequence. For, after the shock of the scene of debauchery, the king kills
the queen and her lover, then leaves his palace in a state of melancholic

despair to see his brother, the king of a neighboring country. There he discovers that the wife of his brother is also involved in orgies, just like his own wife. He feels relieved at not being the only one to experience this fate, and his melancholy lifts. But it is the second king, Shahrayar, who experiences the libidinal invasion, after his brother's revelations and his own observation, in his brother's presence, of his wife cheating on him with a black slave during an orgy. It is as if everything that happens to the mad king has been anticipated by his brother, who tells him what he has already seen. This anticipation, this narration of the other who has already seen in place of the ego (the subject), is the signature of the spec-ular nature of the libidinal drama. Pierre Fédida, in a short, dense text, has analyzed the scope of this in his recounting of an initial interview with an analysand: "Isn't discussion of jealousy always a means of turn-ing the story over to a rival, who is no other than the imaginary persecu-tory double?"[61] The subject is dispossessed of a story by the other, just as the rival has dispossessed him of his wife. It is the void created by the narrator (the double) that persecutes the ego, threatening it with destruc-tion, situated as it is before a real for which there is no solution other than to slip into the repetition of the other.

But before they trigger the deadly string of events, the two brothers decide to wander throughout the world in a desperate quest for love, with the hope of understanding what has happened to them. In their wander-ings together, they discover the scope of female perversity and formulate a plan for revenge against women, which the second king will enact upon his return to his kingdom.

Before reaching the point of deadly sexual violence, the narrative in-troduces, between the scene of trauma and madness, the repetition, the deviation that causes the subject to belatedly discover that the same scene has taken place at the home of another who is the same as him. The wan-dering of the two brothers, therefore, simply provides time for the hatred to ripen within a narcissistic duality that releases all its deadly potential-ity. This dimension of the narcissistic double is all the more striking for, once the sequence has fulfilled its function, the first king is cast into the background of the narrative, which then becomes the story of King Shahra-yar, who has lost his mind because of female *jouissance*. The mechanism of jealousy is certainly at work, noticeable in the presence of this "third brother" during the spectacle of the wife's sexual escapades, but this jeal-ousy is not directed at an identifiable rival, because the slave has been killed along with the queen. No, this is pure, unconscious jealousy, which, once the switchover to the double or his specular image has occurred within the narcissistic enclosure, becomes the absolute denial of *jouissance*, a void of the thing, which is highly destructive for the subject. As we saw with Ruqayya, this void appears once the phallus has been captured by an other (woman). Here, we can hypothesize that it is this "phallicity" of the man himself (in desiring his mother) that collapses; as if darkness, now lodged in every beloved image, his own and that of the other, and of any woman capable of being loved, reflected this intolerable dark stain onto his image. Consequently, he sees himself no longer as a lover but as a man annihilated by the absence of the gaze. It is this phallic void in place of his image that the king attempts to fill or erase by marrying a different woman every night and killing her at dawn. Here, the slave's *jouissance* serves as an unbearable phallic withdrawal, because it signifies castration for the master.

The woman whose *jouissance* is so devastating is none other than the figure of the eradicated woman. She has all the characteristics of the woman produced by denial of Other *jouissance* : unlimitedly available to men, insatiable, deceitful, uncontrollable. The best example is provided in the story of the young woman and the demon. This is the first informative encounter the two brothers have during their wanderings together. A young woman, held captive by a demon, forces them, under the threat of awakening her demonic husband, to make love to her. She then shows them ninety-eight rings of different shape and color strung on a necklace. "Do you know what these rings are?" she asks them. "All the owners of these rings slept with me, for whenever one of them made love to me, I took a ring from him. Since you two have slept with me, give me your rings, so that I may add them to the rest, and make a full hundred." By her own avowal, the woman avoids any possible control. The demon "carried [me] away on [my] wedding night . . . [and] has imprisoned me in this chest, locked it with four locks, and kept me in the middle of this raging, roaring sea. He has guarded me and tried to keep me pure and chaste, not realizing that nothing can prevent or alter what is predestined and that when a woman desires something, no one can stop her." The greater the constraint, the more *jouissance* seeks the impossible. Not only does the woman appear omnipotent and phallic in this story — doesn't she collect men like rings? — but the impossible becomes the goal of her *jouissance,* exactly where her seclusion is greatest. The poem the young woman then recites summarizes the reduction of Other *jouissance* to phallic sexual *jouissance:*

Never have faith in a woman! Never trust her oaths.
Whether satisfied or a fury, all depends on her vagina.
She feigns a lying love while cloaked in deceit.
Remember Joseph to save you from her cunning.
It is Eve's doing that Satan had Adam cast from heaven.

Like a dream, *The Arabian Nights* presents, from story to story, several faces, several versions that incorporate the same figure of the eradicated woman. We could even say that *The Arabian Nights* is an exhaustive clinical description of the suffering of the eradicated woman.

The most pathetic story, the one whose finesse reveals a sense of clinical observation, is the story of the king whose lower body is transformed into a stone by his wife. This story illustrates two other traits of the eradicated woman. One is her ability to expropriate the intrinsicness of beings, for this queen transforms the subjects of the kingdom into red, blue, or yellow fish, depending on whether they are Muslims, Christians, or Jews. The second trait relates to the horror of the *jouissance* of the eradicated woman, because the object of her passion is a monstrous black who subjects her to a variety of sadistic and degrading acts. The king having nearly killed him, the queen erects, in his honor, a chapel within the palace, which she calls "the house of sorrows" (in Arabic, *bayt al 'ahzan*). For years she openly preserves the living dead, the monstrous object of her *jouissance*, for her husband, the unhappy, impotent king.[62]

## Uneradicating

Although *The Arabian Nights* takes place in the between-two-women, Shahrazad embodies the other woman who will undo the effects of eradication on the *jouissance* of the woman of the Other (the ideal woman, the mistress), who has become perverse and traitorous in the eyes of the master. In this sense, Shahrazad addresses the mad king only to the extent that she also addresses the eradicated woman in him, the cause of the madness that affects man in his sovereignty. Deflowering hymens and killing wives assume a compulsive force through which the man, stripped of his sovereignty, tries to control his trauma, rediscover his omnipotence, and absolutely control the *jouissance* of any woman by suppressing her ability to obtain pleasure with someone else. *The unique wishes to preserve the first time.* It is only through repeated murders that the emergence of difference can be prevented. It is at this point that the narrative invents Shahrazad, to defer death and escape the originary scene in which

Shahrayar embodies the figure of the father of the horde, appropriating the *jouissance* of all women. It is a figure very close to the one Freud had in mind, except that here *The Arabian Nights* proposes a different scenario for escaping the omnipotence of the originary father: using speech to introduce an imaginary supplement into the real of sudden *jouissance*.

Man is sick from the eradication of female *jouissance*. This could be a kind of diagnosis, which the narrative continues to tell and retell, repeating the same theme from different angles. The tales in *The Arabian Nights* are the repetition, by Shahrazad, of the dramatic situation of the man who wants to be master and sovereign of the woman's *jouissance*. But although the man is a king and the husband a powerful demon, they are unable to confine this *jouissance,* which eludes omnipotence because it resides in the very absence of absolute *jouissance,* in the *"joui-absence"* as Lacan put it, or in the Nothing that characterizes sovereignty according to Georges Bataille. Frightened and upset, the woman appears to be more demoniacal than the demon. Therefore, he will seek to find someone — an other always being better than Nothing — and will vainly attempt to erase that someone's trace, at the cost of destroying the object of his passion. This sickness, the sickness of the jealousy of Nothing, stems from the inability of the masculine subject to support the impossible of Other *jouissance,* enclosed as he is in the phallic desire for the mother, which the story frequently portrays.[63] This results in the attempt to control the impossible through phallicism. This is the classic solution of monotheism, when we consider the radical solution found in Genesis, which brings about the divine birth of a male child in a woman who is more than seventy years old.

How should we understand Shahrazad's maneuver to undo the eradication of female *jouissance* and restore the lack of absolute *jouissance* (the impossible) in the king? Naturally, the man must be healed, but it's the eradication of the woman that needs to be undone. As I pointed out earlier, it's not enough simply to relate something in order for speech to triumph over the forces of madness and death. I would also suggest that a mechanism is necessary for speech to be operational. What, then, constitutes the machinery of love in *The Arabian Nights*?

Psychoanalysis tells us that whenever madness holds sway "between two," external reasoning is necessary for the torments to cease. In the scene of demonstration, there are indeed three parties: the man, the woman, and the angel. The suspicion of madness arises from the fact that there is doubt about the nature of the third: does it belong to the order of the drives (demon) or the order of language (angel)? The angel turns out to be the representative of the word of law. But who would constitute the third party, the bystander, between Shahrayar and Shahrazad? In other words, where is the angel?

The angel is the nonobviousness of the obvious. In *The Arabian Nights* he is convoked very rapidly:

> At nightfall the vizier [Shahrazad's father] took Shahrazad and went with her to the great King Shahrayar. But when Shahrayar took her to bed and began to fondle her, she wept, and when he asked her, "Why are you crying?" she replied, "I have a sister, and I wish to bid her goodbye before daybreak." Then the king sent for the sister, who came and went to sleep under the bed. When the night wore on, she woke up and waited until the king had satisfied himself with her sister Shahrazad and they were by now all fully awake. Then Dinarzad cleared her throat and said, "Sister, if you are not sleepy, tell us one of your lovely little tales to while away the night, before I bid you good-bye at daybreak, for I don't know what will happen to you tomorrow." Shahrazad turned to King Shahrayar and said, "May I have your permission to tell a story?" He replied, "Yes," and Shahrazad was very happy and said, "Listen."[64]

Dinarzad doesn't leave the couple, because the request is repeated nightly, until the younger sister is eventually replaced by the couple's child.

Introducing the young sister into the nuptial chamber was not a question of improvisation. Shahrazad had prepared the way. The narrative says, "She . . . went to her younger sister, Dinarzad, and said, 'Sister, listen well to what I am telling you. When I go to the king, I will send for you, and when you come and see that the king has finished with me, say, 'Sister, if you are not sleepy, tell us a story.'" This is Shahrazad's ruse according to the narrative: she will enter the bedroom with the third party!

But what makes this younger sister a third party? It is the fact that at the very place where the sexual act and the violence of deflowering will unfold, Shahrazad immediately introduces the "invocational voice" that instantiates infantile listening as close as possible to the sexual. This hearing is a creation of love in the service of the narrative and, therefore, in the service of life, for the story postpones death, or illuminates night. Ontotheology recognizes this as the foundation of existence and its preservation. Ibn Arabi sees the first signs of divine love in the "be" that man grasps through the sense of hearing while in the fetal state. And in Genesis (21:17), in reference to Ishmael, lost with his mother in the desert, we find "for God hath heard the voice of the lad where he *is*." The voice is also in the name of Ishmael ("god hears"), as if from this instance of infantile listening there might arise the possibility of transcendence of the third party who provides the time to live. We see how psychoanalysis recaptures the metaphysical utterance, translating its topology into the immanent scale of desire, because listening to the unconscious is listening to the infantile as original dimension of the subject of desire.

From this point on, the trap of love, or the device for deferring death, begins to function in *The Arabian Nights* no longer under the dictatorship of the sexual drives but between hymen and tympanum; that is, between the hymen, the penetrable surface of the woman who is given sexually to the man, and the tympanum of the sister, a surface that can be grazed only by words. If we consider the sister to be a figure of the double or helper, then Shahrazad, far from confronting the mad king directly, will have appealed to the impenetrable other of her self to represent that which cannot be taken sexually in woman, and she does so in the place where the sexual act occurs. In doing so, Shahrazad restores the Other *jouissance* of woman, sustaining the impenetrable part of herself night after night. Therefore, it is herself she sustains at the moment she speaks to the other, until the child of the ear (Dinarzad) is replaced by the couple's real child, who is the product of the love that, through the language of night, brings forth *jouissance* between hymen and tympanum until the day of survival arrives.

If we trust the intelligence of the narrative, we find that it isn't the delightful stories that heal the king's madness but the fact that the woman has become simultaneously penetrable and impenetrable; in other words, she has rediscovered her duplicate surface, which receives the man within her but leaves him to confront the infantile virginity of the understanding of speech. This is the prodigious device for undoing the eradication of woman found in *The Arabian Nights*, a narrative collected by the anonymous hands of language wishing to free men from the tyranny of absolute *jouissance* or the *jouissance* of the Other, whenever man claims to embody it.

The analogy with the scene of demonstration becomes clear, although it is not primarily between King Shahrayar and the Prophet, for the latter doubts and believes in the woman, whom he asks what is happening to him. Subsequently, when he receives the first Koranic fragment, he recognizes himself when named an orphan, that is, as the one who is related to the dead father, a naming from which arises the *jouissance* that in turn gives rise to a text endorsed by god, the Absent. The analogy arises, rather, from the woman's ability to distinguish between Other *jouissance* and the *jouissance* of the Other. The first is associated with the impossible as the defeat of total *jouissance* and its mastery; the second is a *jouissance* that lays claim to the absolute and the interrogation of the impossible. Woman not only seems to have access to a knowledge that can differentiate one from the other, but also offers to remotely reestablish their division and enable man to access sanctity and health. It is here that Shahrazad appears as an afterimage of Khadija in the scene of demonstration, the woman in whom Islam recognizes a relationship to the Other *jouissance* that releases the Prophet from the suspicion of madness. Shahrazad would be a remembrance of the woman who receives the angel's greeting, the woman before eradication, whose story is immemorial memory.

What a unique text is *The Arabian Nights*. It presents us with a problem, invents a woman to resolve it, who then invents a device in which a child appeals to a text, which gives the woman time to bear a child to the man who is the origin of the problem. As it unfolds, the text wraps itself around the initial problem of the suffering that takes the form of the madness of the omnipotent man. The text makes the child the medium through which it takes hold of this madness and, at the same time, its conclusion. The child in the text is both means and end, the knot of the story and its undoing. In a word, *The Arabian Nights* establishes an infantile solidarity between the gift of the text and the gift of sex.

The exploration of several figures of the destiny of the other woman has led us to a text that served to relieve a severe constraint, recognized as man's narcissistic madness in the presence of female *jouissance*. We must now investigate the relationship between masculine narcissism and the Islamic text.

# 4

# Within Himself

It is as in Grimm's fairytale *The Hedgehog and the Hare:*
"I'm here already!"

— MARTIN HEIDEGGER[1]

### *The Arabian Nights* as Clinic; or, Shahrazad's Tasks

## *The Enactment of Passion*

"Sister...tell us one of your lovely little tales to while away the night."
Of all the many repetitions scattered throughout *The Arabian Nights,* it is
this request by Shahrazad's little sister each night in the king's bedroom
that most disturbed the eighteenth-century French reading public. Antoine Galland, the book's translator, introduced the following warning
into volume 3 of the original edition: "The reader will no longer find the
following phrase, 'My dear sister, if you are not sleeping, please tell us ...
' repeated nightly; it has shocked many intelligent persons and I have
eliminated it to accommodate their sensibility."[2] In volume 15, the translator relates an even more radical decision: "Readers of the first two volumes of these tales grew weary of Dinarzad's interruption of their reading; this has been remedied in subsequent volumes."[3]

In this way the childish expression of the request for a story became
a "tiring interruption," and the child pretext of narration was cut out,
leaving behind only a "blank line," as if what was now most important
was the canvas separated from what the story had presented as its event,
the "pre-" of the text that turned it into speech that interrupted the king's
murderous rage.

What led readers to ask for this deletion? Was it the unbearable presence of the child in this supremely primitive scene, which combines observation of the parental sexual relationship with the immemorial violence of the figure of the father of the horde sexually enjoying all the women around him, then killing them to prevent other men from having access to them? Was this condensation of the two primal Freudian scenarios (on the individual and species levels) more unbearable because the child as subject is represented in it? Or, rather, was it the presence of written speech, which makes the role of the infantile request superfluous because another economy of the imaginary has taken its place with the technology of printing and publishing? From this point of view, the child pretext would be reduced to a silent space between the lines and margins of the page. Is this cleansing indicative of the gap between two civilizations, through the translation of their imaginary fields?

"Then the king sent for the sister, who came and went to sleep under the bed. When the night wore on, she woke up and waited until the king had satisfied himself with her sister Shahrazad and they were by now fully awake." The sequence is certainly abrupt, as if the story sought to impose the presence of the child at once, as witness and actor through whom a mutation of the sexual scene into the speech of the imaginary is brought about. The role this scene plays could not be eliminated without destroying the survival function of the narrative, in confronting the unleashed, sexualized death drive. It seems that the child-as-pretext constitutes the pivot of a therapeutic, ethical, and technical device that the story provides as a decisive element for initiating the process of deferring death. The structure of the scene, the three figures who compose it, the problem it formulates, in short, the entire clinical configuration of *The Arabian Nights* — and the term *clinical* is etymologically appropriate in discussing what takes place at the foot of the bed — appears as it does in this important work of Arabic literature only to the extent that history, politics, and society are deeply inscribed within it. In other words, although *The Arabian Nights* is both a healing and a liberation from the monarchical figure of the male whose *jouissance* becomes deadly, this figure is, all the same, a fundamental threat, a threat that can be confronted and overcome only through this use of imagination at the foot of the bed. *The Arabian Nights* thus bears the stigmata of excess in the Islamic edifice and the order constructed around masculine narcissism in its relationship to the desire of the Other. In this case we could add a third term to the relation

Gilles Deleuze established in his last book, between "the clinic and literature,"[4] to obtain a triptych: literature, the clinic, and politics.

In response to this hypothesis of masculine narcissism in the Islamic
edifice, one could object that the problem is the universal structure of
phallocentrism in general, and that the fictions of Islam merely reproduce elements shared by the entire patriarchal tradition of monotheism.
This objection, which one frequently encounters, often as part of a discourse on immediate conversion to universal reconciliation, should be
briefly discussed.

First, it is worth recalling Hegel's anecdote (reported by Heidegger),
used when he brought up the ontotheological problem of the universality of being. A man goes to a grocer to buy fruit. He is offered apples,
pears, peaches, and so on, but the buyer insists on buying "fruit." He
cannot resign himself to purchasing one kind of fruit and determines
that there is no "fruit" for sale. Heidegger comments on this as follows:
"There is Being only in this or that particular historical character,"[5] and
he goes on to emphasize that these figures of being are not arranged in
rows like apples and pears on historical shelves. Not only is there a different character each time, but each time difference cannot be given without
an effort to reveal it, through speech, in a language that offers and demands satisfaction.

Returning to an idea put forth by Georges Devereux, for whom the
difference between cultures is pathological,[6] I would emphasize the essential meaning of a "discourse of the passions." How can we conceive
of culture as a reasoned foundation if it does not arise from a foundation
of excess, surfeit, or anomaly, and how can we imagine a verbalization of
this foundation unless it articulates, at the same time, a challenge to the
"unreason" it wishes to overcome? Reason, in any institution, cannot
escape *différance,* that is, the exposure to death and the impossible, which
causes it to tremble in the very movement of its establishment.

In the grip of the passions that have marked their emergence, civilizations continue to struggle to free themselves of those passions and, in
doing so, unearth the resources for their inventions. Wishing to free themselves from their founding anomaly, in other words, to achieve immunity
and health, they produce works inspired by a powerful desire for sanctity — which is the desire to negotiate their passions and originary excesses.
These works they preserve as the focal point of the essence of what they
are. However successful they are in negotiating them, they repeat the

effort, return to it again and again, venerating and execrating the return and the overcoming. Here and there, they expose places for displaying the shadow of those passions in action and draw from them a deepening of their possibility.

The staging of the shadow of a passion, as found in *The Arabian Nights*, assumes the value of an act in order to challenge and overcome a kind of excess that is, a priori, that of neither Hamlet nor King Oedipus. The scenes of passion in a culture always indicate that some fundamental memorization has occurred, coextensive with the effect of the death drive, through which something memorable was recorded through the text as signifying reserve, psychically transmissible between generations. Therefore, we cannot limit either the specific approach of the motives of such scenes or their plastic strength, without which man's grasp on the field of the unconscious, as transindividual fact, would be incomprehensible in the political and historical space in which he lives. There is a "geography of metapsychologies" to be found, based on the impassioned *logia* of a people in their idioms.[7] This would be the end of the era of "ethnopsy" (ethnopsychiatry, ethnopsychology), an end toward which we patiently turn.

What I have attempted to focus on here is the idea that the disturbance of originary femininity, several important sequences of which I have analyzed, marks the metapsychological construction of Islam in a particular way. Islam appears to be haunted by a paroxysmal contradiction between a feminine that terrifies masculine identity and, at the same time, allows it to listen to reason, thus ensuring its openness to the wholly Other. The scope of Islamic mysticism, compared to other monotheistic religions, appears to correspond to the attempt to respond to this constraint with which masculine narcissism is confronted. It reflects the search by the "feminine-in-itself" as a means of access to this essence of absence that is the desire of the Other. Sufism has exposed the experience of the self to a vast desert where theological phallic *jouissance* exhausts its markers and encounters the linguistic exile of the lack in "Him" (god is referred to as "Him," *huwa*, in Islam), at the point where Islam's founding made woman responsible for this lack, which she translated into a fundamental defect of reason and religion.[8] It is a fact that the lack introduced by female *jouissance* subverts the relationship of identity *within Himself* — "He is who He is" *(huwa huwa)* being the formula of absolute identity — on which the masculine subject of theology is modeled. (See the section titled "Individuality, Islam, and Psychoanalysis" later in this chapter.)

I want to focus again on the scene of the two kings in *The Arabian Nights*. It is our best introduction, for both the problem it presents and the solution it offers, in confronting the impasse of masculine narcissism.

## The King and His Double

For both kings, the king and his double, or "the king and the king," the discovery of the queen's sexual pleasure with a slave is experienced as a form of illogic that suddenly sets a limit to sovereign omnipotence, provoking a loss of being that is signified by the two kings' melancholy and their decision to wander throughout the world.

The process of alienation that leads to madness is then triggered. This appears to reside in the dualistic relation between "Me and Me," which, because of the repetition of the same story in an identical manner, amounts to saying "You are Me." Note that here *The Arabian Nights* approximates the identification Lacan made in his discussion of the "vel of alienation," based on Hegel,[9] because the point of departure, which I have referred to as the withdrawal of absolute *jouissance,* introduces the king and the king to an experience of violent loss, whose terms are the positions of master and slave. But can we really speak of a struggle in this case? For the king suddenly discovers the slave in his place and realizes that he might be missing from the queen's desire. In principle, where the king is, the slave should not be; but his eviction from this exclusive place will expose the king and the king to the challenge of destitution, an irreparable wound to their narcissism as masters. Even when the slave has lost his life, he has won the thing, because not only has the master been dislodged from his place and forced to confront the lack in the desire of the Other but, additionally, by killing the queen, he suppresses this Other that is the object of her desire. The master finds himself cast into a process of catastrophic hollowing out, or voidance.

However, the void does not necesssarily lead to madness. The narrative shows this clearly. Although both are faced with the same situation, only one king goes mad. An additional condition of dispossession associated with language is needed. It is not the narrator king who goes mad but the second king, who is led to see through the story (sight) of the other what he will then see for himself. It is at this point that the specular captivation occurs that alienates the subject, who is absorbed by the narrator king (the ego). Before discovering that the slave has taken his queen, it is his fellow king who dispossesses him of speech about what has not yet occurred, so that, when the event does finally take place before him, the ego goes mad from effectively having been delighted in the repetition of the other. The mechanism of the fundamental experience of the destruction of woman is based on this, for it is the aggressive response to the expropriating intrusion of the peer, which precedes that of the slave. By marrying a virgin every night, whom he kills at dawn, the king attempts to erase the trace of the other (the other king and the other slave) from the object of his desire. But once the object is formed and he has access to it, the other springs into being through it. At this point, there is set in motion a pure objectless desire or a desire whose object would be the void. This is the fantasy of *jouissance* of what could be called the eternal virgin, namely, the sexual *jouissance* of pure destruction or death. The drive runs aground on the banks of this impossible, which gives rise to the repetition.

The fantasy of the eternal virgin is, in man, the effect of the aggressiveness of the imaginary relation to the other man, who takes the extreme step of attempting to obliterate the trace of the Other in the woman. Muslim authors have illustrated this by imagining those mythical women of paradise known as houris, assumed to compensate god's elect. "Every time you sleep with a houri," writes Suyūtī, "she is a virgin. What's more, the penis of the elect never bends. The erection is eternal."[10] Behind this paradisiacal promise hovers the radical originary fantasy of the unique phallic sex, which abolishes the lack introduced by the difference in *jouissance* between the sexes and their alterity.

This fantasy of absolute *jouissance* culminates in the emergence of the hyperoriginary scene preceding that of the "father of the horde," because it includes not only the appropriation of all women but an attempted regression to the originary object of the sexual drive from which the barrier of incest has separated the subject, putting substitutes in its place. "Psycho-analysis has shown us," Freud writes, "that when the original object of a wishful impulse has been lost as a result of repression, it is frequently represented by an endless series of substitutive objects none of which, however, brings full satisfaction. This may explain the inconstancy in object-choice, the 'craving for stimulation' which is so often a feature of the love of adults" ("On the Universal Tendency to Debasement in the Sphere of Love" [1912], *SE*, 11:177–90). Shahrayar is, in fact, the opposite of this, diametrically opposed to the figure of Don Juan. He does not escape the horror of the originary object by augmenting the series with *one more*; rather, he wants to reduce the series through murder: *one fewer* every night. The book is called *The Thousand and One Nights* (the alternate

title for *The Arabian Nights*), for this signifies the reestablishment of the
series, distancing us from the unique and the originary. Similarly, unlike
Don Juan, who seeks to save his desire, here we have something like a
desire for the end of desire, because the goal is to find an originary object
untouched by the Other. The desire not to desire is an extreme goal of
masculine desire, an expression of the death drive that wants to possess
woman's All and Nothing. The hollowing out of the series to reach the
first term provides the experience of the terrifying imminence of absolute *jouissance,* but results only in destruction. That is why we find in the
prologue to *The Arabian Nights* a hyperoriginary scene, in the sense that
this desire to abolish desire encounters the impossible. But isn't this the
phantasmic kernel of the figure of the virile warrior in the desert, as we
find him in Arabic poetry, whose most sublimated form appears in what
Nadia Tazi has called "an aristocratic, courtly and stoic virility"?[11] We
could also summarize the intent expressed in the extremity of this desire
as "a desire that aims for the desert."[12]

The fantasy of the eternal virgin or the furious desire of the desert is as
far as we can go in addressing the question of masculine *jouissance* that
confronts Shahrazad in *The Arabian Nights*. We see now what Shahrazad
must do to stop the destructive hollowing out: she must reinscribe the impossible access to the originary object by giving shape to the void through
language, by restoring the screen function of the imaginary.

### The Story of Jawdar

One of the significant examples of reinscribing the impossible in *The Arabian Nights* is the story of Jawdar, an adolescent who searches for buried
treasure, guided by a Moroccan sorcerer. The sorcerer burns incense and
recites secret formulas. He succeeds in drying a river, and beneath the
river, in a deep pit, the treasure lies buried. But Jawdar must open seven
doors to reach it. He must open the first six doors while reciting a formula.
And every time, at every door, he must undergo, without flinching and
with courage, his own death. He is murdered and brought back to life.
However, he will be brought back only if he shows courage in the face of
his trials. When he arrives at the seventh door, the sorcerer tells him this:

> You must knock on the door. Your mother will come out and will
> say to you "Welcome my son, come and greet me." But you will say
> to her "Stay away from me and remove your clothing." She will
> say to you "My son, I am your mother. I have rights over you for I

have fed and educated you. How can you expect me to expose my nakedness?" You will respond "Remove your clothing or I will kill you." Then look to the right, you will find a sword hanging from the wall. Take it, unsheathe it, and say to her: "Remove your clothing." She will again try a subterfuge, she will beg, but show her no pity. Each time she removes a piece of clothing, say "You must remove everything." Threaten her with death until she has removed all her clothes and appears entirely naked. Then you will have deciphered the symbols, undone the locks, and saved yourself.

The magician goes on to specify, "Do not be afraid, Jawdar, for she is only a ghost without a soul."

Quite clearly, the thing Jawdar must overcome is not his mother but her ghost (shabah). Although Jawdar succeeds in meeting the challenge of his own death, when faced with his mother's ghost he does not at first succeed; it takes him several successive tries to convince her: "Jawdar, having arrived before his mother, was unable to get her to remove the final piece of clothing hiding her sex. He was troubled by his mother, who continued to repeat: 'My son, you're turning out badly; my son, your heart is made of stone; do you wish to dishonor me, my son? Don't you know that it is forbidden [haram]?' Then Jawdar, hearing this word, abandoned his attempt and said to his mother, 'Keep the last piece of clothing' [a kind of G-string]. Radiant, his mother cried out, 'You have erred, and now you will be beaten.'" Jawdar is beaten nearly to death and thrown over the edge of a chasm. He and the magician must repeat the trials a second time, a year later. Jawdar begins the magical operations once more and this time succeeds in getting his mother to remove all her clothing. Once she is completely naked, she is changed into a "ghost without a soul."

The hero's solution, according to Shahrazad, is to confront incest with sword in hand. This is done not simply to kill the mother or carry out matricide, as is often said, but to conclude, through an act of bravery, that incest is impossible because crossing the threshold is resolved in the confrontation not so much with the mother's actual nakedness but with that of her ghost.[13] The finality of the initiatory path appears in an unveiling of the spectral in light of the real of the lack, through which the subject works out the withdrawal of the first object of his desire. "There is there-is-not" simultaneously evokes this original withdrawal and the subsistence of a remainder that endures, because of which we can say, "There is that there is not," as the gift of what is withdrawn. "There is" assumes the value of an appeal to the ghost, which we must at the same time dissipate, as if we were continuously encouraged to lose what we have already lost. To believe in the ghost is to believe in the remainder that supports the utterance of a "there is."

In Jean-Joseph Goux's fascinating *Oedipe philosophe*, the author shows how the Oedipus tragedy can be viewed as an anomaly among other myths with the same theme, this anomaly being that of a subject who retreats from the initiatory ritual of the ancient world (which is why we have the overcoming of the Sphinx) and thus finds himself involved in a radical transgression of human laws.[14] Similarly, Philippe Lacoue-Labarthe, in "Oedipe comme figure," provides a rigorous framework that targets the metaphysical foundation from which Freud turned the modern self-reflexive subject into a concept and a theory, referring to this anomaly as part of the *subjectum* of Western tradition.[15] Reading these works in parallel, we can advance the hypothesis that the modern psychological illusion has been to hide the impossible behind the forbidden, an impossible that tradition was able to preserve, up to a point, through its imaginary construction, as shown by the story of Jawdar.

In discovering that Oedipus is the proper (European) name of the subject of the unconscious, Freud, in his approach to maternal incest, favored the register of the forbidden, whereas after *The Project for a Scientific Psychology* he postulated the irremediable loss of the original object. The incestuous desire may occur; it is even desirable that it exist and that the prohibition should express this possibility, which will turn out to be impossible. We see how, in this story, Jawdar fails once he allows himself to get caught up in his mother's invocation of the prohibition ("You have erred, and now you will be beaten"). In this situation, the utterance of the prohibition appears to be complicit with the ghost's deceit. More specifically, although the prohibition might lead one to believe that the spectral is real, it doesn't allow us to distinguish, at this moment and in this "spectreal" state, between the spectral and the real, because the image invested with affect carries no index of reality, even when articulated in speech. The subject must, therefore, push his desire to cross the threshold as far as he can and discover the void as treasure, like someone who must continue to the end of his sentence to encounter the space of nonexistence of the object toward which the "I" has impelled him, and discover that it remains to be said.... The utterance is "spectreal," as is the language with which the unconscious is woven, but it is the remainder, the trace, Dinarzad's "while waiting for daybreak," that places the subject before the void, the inaccessible, the horizon of expectation. What "remains to be said" postpones death and introduces us into a possible relationship with the impossible or the real. This is what Francis Ponge called the "enduring impossible," which makes life so difficult. But, at the same time, it is through this that "we have everything to say... and can say nothing; which is why we begin again each day."[16]

I want to digress for a moment. Are we being asked to continue the surveillance of the impossible that tradition erected for the benefit of its subject? We know how pointless is the attempt to mend something. The Islamist movement has shown us where the illusion of restoration leads. The roadblock of the imaginary of tradition in the face of the reformulations dictated by science is obvious. For example, some versions of the story of Jawdar do not stop at the dissipation of the maternal ghost but have the subject access a treasure beyond the void, which reestablishes the imaginary of phallic fecundity and makes the impossible a simple transitional moment for accessing plenitude. This is where Genesis succeeds — with the birth of Isaac and not his adoption. We cannot subscribe to the mirage of the happy ending, even though the process of these texts is so close to what we today understand of the relationship between the subject and the law. Maintaining the challenge of the impossible as terminus, as transcendence of the void, is an essential but very difficult task for the modern subject, primarily because of the way technology and management have taken over the "spectreal." Literature, contemporary art, and psychoanalysis are trying to keep watch and open the necessary pathways. However, they can do this only if they are not isolated in cultural storehouses or temples of consumption. It is our job to invent the living mechanisms of transition for subjects from that point on. I would add that the question of the spectreal is a fundamental element in the problematic of becoming a psychoanalyst.

## Shahrazad's Second Task

I turn now to Shahrazad's second task. Alongside the inscription of the impossible access to the originary object, we have to ask how the child pretext constitutes a structural edge function in the hyperprimitive scene of *The Arabian Nights*.

In the classic interpretation, the child appears as a third term (which here makes an appeal to the child), namely, the phallus as universal signifier that limits *jouissance* between the sexes and leads it through speech

toward lack and desire. Its eruption onto the scene, following the deflowering and repeated supplication, leaves little doubt as to the function of
interruption (which so disturbed eighteenth-century readers). Addition-
ally, this phallus is associated with the father of the female narrator and
the fact that Shahrazad arrives with her sister, her father's child. This is a
profoundly important element in the narrative, for it forces a man who
cannot bear the trace of the Other in the object of his desire to be no more
than a substitute from the outset. Recall Freud's remark in his article "The
Taboo of Virginity" (SE, 11:191–208): "The husband is almost always so
to speak only a substitute, never the right man; it is another man — in
typical cases the father — who has first claim to a woman's love, the husband at most takes second place." The female narrator thus has a head
start; she is the virgin who signifies that she has always already been
invaded by the father's desire and that the king has arrived late, even if
her hymen is intact. The child pretext signifies, therefore, that originary
origin does not exist. Here, we could follow Hegel in saying that, generally, through the child, origin suppresses itself.[17]

A pretext is "a purpose or motive alleged or an appearance assumed
in order to cloak the real intention or state of affairs."[18] This is precisely
the simulacrum of the female narrator on which the text hinges and who,
through the child, transmits the plea, the hope placed in her for daybreak. The "pre-text" is, therefore, not outside the text (hors-texte), but in
its internal spacing — which is margin, reserve, "the making of the pre-,"
to quote the title of a collection by Francis Ponge — through the interplay of separation and reversal. The child is the gap-in-itself of the text,
through which it says to itself, "Come." Through the child, the text invites itself to the foot of the bed. Shahrazad does not say to the king,
"Sire, I'm going to tell you a story," or, "Sire, would you like me to tell
you a story?" She herself does not ask for herself. She does not place herself in a position of favorable address between "I and you," "you and
me." She chooses a child who is close to her and her sexual identity to
solicit the entrance of an other scene into the hyperprimitive scene. The
child enables an other to speak, introduces the speech of an Other through
the imaginary. The female narrator invents the third person. The supplication is this tipping point of the appeal addressed to the Other, to its
intercession, its substitution in the face of the interplay of life and death.
It is important to keep in mind the close relation between supplicate (sup-
plier) and substitute (suppléer), for these depend on the fact of a necessary
fold (supplicare literally means to bend the knees, to kneel down), which

leads to the introduction of the imaginary supplement in the heart of the sexual real.

Similarly, Shahrazad does not ask that the king stop killing women; she narrates, and what she narrates is used to dissimulate the real motive: to save life — her own and, at the same time, that of other women. This disposition is not factual in the presentation of the scene. The child and the imaginary are foregrounded with respect to a background question, which is the restitution of reason to preserve life. In this sense, the pretext introduces a gap, or play, between two planes. The play in question is not the story itself but the possibility of making things up, in the form of a childish demand that serves as the presumed cause or screen behind which the imaginary can play like a child.

It is this fold between front and back that establishes the conditions of a fundamental ambiguity, similar to the one Freud speaks of in *Delusions and Dreams in Jensen's "Gradiva"* (*SE*, 9:1–95), where he shows how, in order to cure Norbert, their discourse had to take on a double meaning. The first meaning follows the delusion in order to gain Norbert's confidence and penetrate his thought, and the second interprets the delusion using the language of unconscious truth. Some readers may recall Jamel Eddine Bencheikh's astonishment at this doubling of meaning: "The narrator [Shahrazad], charged with obtaining grace from the scorned sovereign, hurries to tell him stories, which, logically, can only confirm his attitude toward women." The ambiguity opens up the possibility of a *double entente* as play. While the child listens to a story, the imaginary plays where destructive *jouissance* is unleashed in an attempt to reason with it.

The concept of play must be dramatically emphasized here, because life is at stake. Recall that Shahrazad, against her father's advice, volunteers not to confront the king's madness with her so-called feminine wiles but to install play in the precincts of death and distract the master from her attractiveness. From this point on, it is not enough simply to say that this is "play" and not a "game," unless we also emphasize that it involves the play of dissimulation on the verge of death. However, this play of language and the imaginary with sex and death can only be the great Game we know as the Unconscious.

This implies that the unconscious is hidden in the so-called primitive or originary scene, without which "primitivity" or "originarity" would have wiped all else away, including the possibility of the scene itself. The unconscious is what has seen and heard for us since the dawn of time, ruled by the master of absolute *jouissance* who deals death and ensures that virginity is untouched by the trace of the Other.

The presence of story, narrative, or myth assumes concealment, simulacrum, and play. Every time survival allows us to see and hear its weft, the unconscious is already there, in the laying-in of life's intactness. The unconscious is always already there. The "there" is a separation preceding negation, a separation that appears in the guise of "dis-traction." Distraction is the opening of the place of the unconscious, an opening that precedes affirmation and negation. The unconscious could not be the point of view of a spectator outside the scene; it is found within as the condition of possibility of its opening as scene. It opens the scene from within through an "infantile imaginary supplement," where the murderous brutality of absolute *jouissance* reigns. I suggest radicalizing the theoretical position expressed by Jean Laplanche and Jean-Baptiste Pontalis in *Fantasme originaire, fantasmes des origines, origines du fantasme*. It is not only the subject who is part of the originary fantasy, it is the unconscious as play that introduces the possibility of "scenicness" and "originarity," where the subject can find shelter.[19] The murder of the imaginary father of the horde can have been committed only by purely imaginary means: the female narrator kills the father through the simulacrum of the child pretext, who strikes the blow of distraction, during which life is temporarily immunized by the fable. Returning to the expression of Abdelkebir Khatibi, who summarizes the constraint the terrible king has placed upon Shahrazad — "Tell me a story or I will kill you" — we could say that Shahrazad answered, "I will kill you in telling you a story." It has been little remarked upon, but the king in *The Arabian Nights* doesn't say a word once the female narrator begins to speak. He plays at being dead in an imaginary grave.

## *The Shahrazad-Sharayar Axis*

*The Arabian Nights* sets the scene for the axial encounter of the problematic of repressed femininity along with its avatars, and the most violent effects of the impasse of masculine narcissism on its other of the same sex. In this case, axial means that there is an orientation in the relations of alterity, where the confrontation between man and the other man (and the double) serves as the focal point for constructing a reference for masculine identity and its genealogical inscription, as perforation and performance.[20]

It appears that the spiritual inventions of monotheism were, to a large extent, constituted to resolve the problems of the destructiveness of the masculine subject in his narcissistic relations of disjunction-conjunction with the originary Other and captivation by the image of the semblable. The trouble begins once there are two men together or in an internal genealogical relationship. Different scenarios of violence then appear: sacrifice (father and son), the murder of one's fellow man (brothers), extermination (the child and the genocidal killer), forms of individuality (one, two, one), and community (the founder and his heir).

In the following sections, I want to look at the way Islam, heir to the monotheistic fictions that came before it, has dealt with certain fundamental figures of the relationship between two men. Obviously, the situations presented here do not exhaust all the possibilities. They are only examples of the manifestation of the impossible whose inscription the necessary imaginary seeks to acknowledge and around which it suggests detours, sometimes out of desperation.

## Sacrifice and Interpretation

Sacrifice in monotheism claims to be an interpretation of and solution to the problem of violence. It comes into being following a specific sequence that is composed within the configuration of the patriarchal family, between father and son. This configuration is haunted by the question of the interrelation of father and son, of their imaginary intermingling, at a point where their existence, their future, their salvation is presented in terms of the murder of one or the other.

Monotheism has sought to make the symbolization of this violence its foundation; it has raised this symbolization to the level of a model to resolve violence in general. It has chosen to present a dramatic scene in which the spectacle of the murder of the son by the father or the father's consent to the murder of the son is enacted. Since we know that other, nonmonotheistic traditions make use of the same situation in reverse — namely, the murder of the father by the son — the choice of one or the other of these versions modifies the interpretation of violence, its process, and its resolution, precisely where it concerns the origin of the murderous desire in the father or the son.

Biblical monotheism, although it chose to sacrifice the son, does not simply opt to locate sacrificial desire in the father. The father is, in effect, the subject of god, carrying out his will as part of a dreadful ordeal: the almighty's requirement to destroy what is most precious, or the desire of the One to destroy the unique. Sacrificial desire, therefore, is located in the Other, the Other who enacts the substitution that is simply the recompense for the father's absolute submission.

Judaism and Islam appear to agree in providing a solution wherein sacrificial desire is unrealized but finds a means of substitution, but the Christian solution opts, radically, for the actual enactment of the killing of the son. Islam, which is in the historical position of being familiar with the Judaic and Christian solutions, refuses to fulfill the son's sacrificial desire, as the Koran maintains in speaking of Jesus: "but they neither killed nor crucified him, though it so appeared to them" (4:157), because they substituted another (a double) in the place of Christ, which reestablished the substitution.[21]

Although Islam restores the biblical solution of substitution, it modifies some important points, a fact that allows us to speak of a Koranic version or interpretation of the sacrifice of the son. This interpretation is inscribed within a broad context, where the sacrifice of Abraham appears as one of the major genealogical intersections of the Koranic text with biblical monotheism. The ritual recitation during the annual feast of Eid ul-Adha, commemorating Abraham's gesture by the slaughter of a sheep is, in this sense, crucial, for it reactualizes the story of sacrificial substitution and gives it substance. Every year, every father of a family, by repeating the presumed gesture, engages in the subjectivization of the initial act. This coincides with the end of the pilgrimage to Mecca. It is impossible to conceptualize the subject in Islam without taking into account this domestic theatricality of sacrifice. The reactualization of Abraham's gesture within the family context was, as we shall see, present when the Islamic version of the sacrifice of the son first emerged.

## The Koranic Version of the Sacrifice

I want to start with the Koranic narrative (37:101–12). It begins with this invocation by Abraham: "O Lord, grant me a righteous son," and continues:

> So We gave him the good news of a clement son.
> When he was old enough to go about with him,
> he said: "O my son, I dreamt that I was sacrificing you.
> Consider, what you think?"
> He replied, "Father, do as you are commanded.

If God pleases you will find me firm."
When they submitted to the will of God,
and (Abraham) laid (his son) down prostrate on his temple,
We called out: "O Abraham,
You have fulfilled your dream."
Thus do We reward the good. —
That was indeed a trying test.
So We ransomed him
for a great sacrifice.
And left (his hallowed memory) for posterity.
Peace be on Abraham.
That is how We reward those
who do good.
He is truly among Our faithful creatures.
So We gave him the good news of Isaac,
apostle, who is among the righteous.

The passage merits commentary. "O my son, I dreamt that I was sacrificing you": This sentence, spoken by Abraham, indicates that, in the Koranic
version, god does not directly demand or order Abraham to kill his son.
Sacrificial desire is located in the dream. Abraham dreams and fulfills the
desire to sacrifice his son in the dream. Upon waking, and still under the
influence of his vision, he wants to put into practice what he saw himself
doing in his dream. It would seem that the interpretation of the sacrifice
occupies a different register once the desire to murder the son arises in
the father's (Abraham's) dream rather than from an order from god.

"Consider, what you think?": In Arabic, the two verbs that follow
one another — 'undhur ("look; consider") ma tara ("what you see") — should
be translated as "look and see," in the sense of "What do you advise?"
This indicates that Abraham is asking for his son's point of view of his
dream, as if, rather than seeking to impose his decision or obtain simple
agreement, Abraham is asking his son to confer a meaning on the dream.
Moreover, the verb meaning "to look" has given us, in Arabic, the notion
of "theory" (nadhariat), as well as the origin of Greek theoria.

"He replied, 'Father, do as you are commanded'": It is the son who
considers that his father has received an order.

"O Abraham, / You have fulfilled [believed in] your dream": This
sentence is stupefying. God refers to Abraham's belief in his dream and
not to a need that it might have imposed on him.

"So We gave him the good news of Isaac, / apostle, who is among the
righteous": Some Muslim commentators deduce from this passage that

the son in question is Ishmael, because the birth of Isaac is announced at the end of the act and Ishmael is the oldest of Abraham's sons. In fact, there is no clear-cut position in the Koran on the question of knowing which of the sons, Isaac or Ishmael, will be sacrificed. Commentators find arguments in this same passage for both positions. Some of them stop at the opening sentence — "So We gave him the good news of a clement son" — saying that the Koran speaks only of the news of Isaac: "So We gave him the good news of Isaac, / apostle" (37:112); and, in another passage, "We gave her [Sara] the good news of Isaac, and after Isaac of Jacob" (11:71). There is news of Isaac because he is the son who has come into being by miraculous means.

Those who opt for Ishmael base their choice on a saying by the prophet Muhammad in a *hadith* that reads, "I am the descendant of two victims" (or of two persons who were almost sacrificed). Commentators, such as Tabari, specify that the two victims are Ishmael, ancestor of the Arabs, and Abdullah, the father of the prophet Muhammad. Consequently, an entire tradition has maintained the uncertainty concerning the choice between the two sons.

Using this, we can refer to another sequence of the Islamic narrative of sacrifice, which this time concerns the genealogy of the prophet Muhammad and his family, briefly mentioned in chapter 3. Traditional historiography relates that during the pre-Islamic period, the Prophet's grandfather liked to sleep in the Kaaba, in Mecca (which was already a sacred spot at the time), in a place known as the *hijr* (a term that means "stone, step, hollow"), where sacrifices were made to the idols. In that place he had many dreams, in one of which a ghostly silhouette ordered him to dig up a buried treasure.

It seems that the Prophet's grandfather dug long enough to arouse the hostility of the members of the tribe, who considered the act sacrilegious. He eventually caused water to rise from the ground at the spot, which is, according to the Islamic narrative, the source of the water that god caused to spring forth beneath the heel of Ishmael to save him from death when he was with his mother. It was here that, with his father, he built the Islamic temple and the future city.

Muslim chroniclers say that at the moment when the Prophet's grandfather was exposed to the hostility of his tribe by digging a hole in the sacred place, having only his son with him during their confrontation, he vowed to sacrifice one of his children if he were to have ten. Therefore, it is when he discovers the biblical site of the child who is saved that the father vows to kill one of his sons, as if the question of place implied the sacrifice of the son. (It is also worth noting that it is in a dream that the Prophet's grandfather receives the order to rediscover the place of the Agareens — the Arabs as they were known to the ancients — and to re-open the spring. We need to bear in mind this antinomy of the child and the spring, which I pointed out earlier in the quotation from Hegel.)

Years later, when the Prophet's grandfather has had ten children, the vow begins to haunt him and he decides to carry it out. According to the same sources, his choice falls upon the youngest child, Abdallah, his favorite. When he is leading the chosen son to the place of sacrifice (the hollow), members of the tribe who have been alerted by the women — mothers, sisters, and aunts — stand between them. Faced with this general hostility, the grandfather was forced to redeem the son and to offer an animal sacrifice in expiation. He was so scrupulous that he decided upon a means of determining the purchase price that was based entirely on chance. He ended up having to pay a very high ransom of a hundred camels, which were offered in sacrifice.

In this way the Islamic narrative is established by reactualizing the sacrifice of the son within the genealogy of Muhammad. This reactualization takes place through the dream in which the desire to reopen the place occurs. Digging at the site and sacrificing the son appear to be joined in the paternal dream.

## The Desire for Sacrifice

It was the great Andalusian mystic Ibn Arabi (twelfth century) who provided the finest interpretation of the conjectured relationship between the dream and sacrifice in Islam. He incorporated it in his theory of the imagination, known as the imaginative presence *(hadrat al-khayal)*, which has been translated by Henry Corbin as "creative imagination."

Starting with the response "Oh, my father, do as you have been ordered," Ibn Arabi linked the entire question of sacrifice to the interpretation of the dream. He writes, "The child is the essence of his father. When Abraham sees in a dream that he kills his son, he sees he is sacrificing himself. And when he redeems his son by killing the ram, he sees the reality, which had been manifested in human form, now manifest itself in the form of the ram. In this way the essence of the father is manifest in the form of the child, or more accurately, in the relationship to the child."[22] The object of the privation the father experiences in his essence, through the intermediary of the son, is the child. Naturally, Ibn Arabi's interpretation is part of a long tradition of Sufism, which considers the "great sacrifice" to be the sacrifice of the Self. The Self is the *nafs*, or psyche, which is the animal and mortal part of the soul, represented by the peaceful lamb of sacrifice, for it is in this way that gnosis leads to extinction in the divine.

But Ibn Arabi's originality lies in the development, found in his *Bezels of Wisdom*, of one of the most elaborate and subtle theories regarding the dream of the desire to kill the child in the father and the transition from the act of the imagination to the real: "Know that Abraham, the friend of God, said to his son: 'In truth, I saw in a dream that I was killing you.' But the dream refers to the imaginative presence that Abraham has not interpreted. It was in fact a ram that appeared in the dream in the form of Abraham's son. God also redeemed the child of Abraham's fantasy *(wahm)* through the great immolation of the ram, which was the divine interpretation of the dream, of which Abraham was unaware *(la yach'ur)*."[23] There is no attempt in this translation to update Ibn Arabi for contemporary readers. Every term, every idea is part of the author's theory of "his dignity, the imagination," or "the imaginative presence"; not presence to the imagination, but the presence of the imagination as essence of the absence that is the desire of the Other.

In his theory, Ibn Arabi distinguishes two imaginary poles. On the one hand, there is an imaginary tied to the singular condition of the subject. "Every man creates through fantasy *(wahm)*, in his imaginative faculty, that which has no existence outside of itself. This is commonplace," he writes in *Bezels of Wisdom*. On the other hand, there is an unrestricted imaginary: "But the gnostic creates through spiritual imagination *(himma)* that which exists outside that faculty." The terms of this division are called imagination conjoined to the subject *(kahyal muttasil)* and imagination separated from the subject *(khayal munfasil)*. The last term includes, in my sense, what I have called the necessary imaginary, which does not make the impossible imaginary but indexes it as withdrawal, as a remainder to be said, as the "There is."

We see that, according to Ibn Arabi, Abraham was unable to interpret the fantasy of his dream, namely, the sacrifice of his son. He remained "not-conscious" *(bi lā chu'ūr)* of the true object of the desire for sacrifice. In fact it was the child that *he* was that he had to sacrifice, and not his son. Consequently, the scene of the sacrifice of the ram would be a reflection in the real (by god) of what, when expressed in the imagination, could not find the means for its transposition in the appropriate form.

What, then, is the appropriate form, and where do the means for its transposition come from? Ibn Arabi explains:

> The manifestation of forms in the imaginative presence (epiphany) requires another science to comprehend what God intended with this form.... When God called Abraham: "Oh Abraham, you believed in your dream" (37:104–5), he did not tell him that he believed that the dream to sacrifice his son was true, for Abraham did not interpret the dream, he apprehended it at the manifest level, but the dream requires interpretation.... To interpret is to transpose the perceived form to another order. If God praised Abraham for believing that what is manifest is true, he would have had to have really sacrificed his child. However, for God, this was *the great sacrifice through the form of the son* and not the sacrifice of the son. Therefore, the child was redeemed because of what was in Abraham's mind and not part of the divine order.[24]

In other words, Ibn Arabi leads us to believe that the sacrificial substitution of the ram would palliate a faulty interpretation by Abraham, who supposedly believed in the literalness of the dream images. Sacrificial substitution is a last-minute recovery from a faulty interpretation that would have led to infanticide. The sacrifice would serve as the interpretation. It was the sacrifice of the child in the father that was targeted through the son, more accurately, by the form of the sacrifice of the son and not by the murder of the son.

But if the sacrifice replaces a missing interpretation, substituting for it, then interpretation and sacrifice would be equivalent. If this were the case, the dream sacrifice would be the dream of fulfilling the desire for interpretation. And the sacrifice would be the desire to interpret, embodied in the real. What is at play in such interpretive desire, as we have just seen, is the killing of the child in the father. But the desire to kill the child in the father is the son's desire to become the father or, to put it somewhat differently, the becoming father of Abraham, who was at an impasse.

In this way, Ibn Arabi, a man of the Islamic Middle Ages, managed to extract the final consequences of the conjecture of sacrifice in Islam, namely, that sacrifice is an incorrect interpretation of the father's dream or the father's desire. In Ibn Arabi, a contemporary of Averroës, there is an attempt, found throughout his work, to separate the spirituality of

Islamic monotheism from the obscure god who demands the badge of flesh and requires the blood of the son to calm the guilt of the fathers. He relates Abraham to his desire for the Other, to the imaginary child, that is, to a god lying in his nonconsciouness. We can see why Islamists ban his books and burn them as the work of an apostate.

## The Son as Lack

In *The Generalities,* Al-Kafaoui (seventeenth century) writes, "It is necessary to mention the son to define the father, for it is impossible to represent the father as father without representing the son, as when we say that blindness is the absence of sight. It is necessary to mention blindness when speaking of sight, even though one arises from the quiddity of the other, as the son arises from the quiddity of the father."[25] The father is an essence that can be determined only from the lack it brings about. According to the author's reasoning, a blind Oedipus would finally have become the son of Laius. But it is highly unlikely that Al-Kafaoui read the Greek tragedies, which, unlike the philosophical and scientific legacy of Greece, were not translated by the Arabs. The use of the Jewish and Christian monotheistic heritage by Islamic thinkers and the advanced interpretation of the great biblical myths from the dualistic point of view we find in many authors (explanation of a fact by the divine, which then entails an explanation by purely human laws, without the one negating the other) have given rise to subtle formulations of the foundations of the human psyche.

The son as the effect of a lack at the heart of the essence that engendered it and without which that essence could not be determined — in other words, which would remain unsettled — articulates the principal challenge of one of the figures of the infantile in Islam, through the question of sacrifice. This brings us back to the quotation from Hegel mentioned previously: "For the child, the parents are the self-suppressing origin."

## The Child People

### Moses in the Koran

The story of Moses is undoubtedly one of the longest and richest of the Koranic narratives. His name is, without contest, the most frequently cited in the sacred book of Islam. It appears in a collection of prodigious deeds spanning four hundred verses spread across twenty-seven suras, which incorporate episodes from the Bible along with other material. The commentators amplify Moses's acts and distinguish him with the title "interlocutor of God" *(kalim Allah)*, based on the episode in which Moses speaks with god and receives the Law directly from him. This partiality is matched by the fact that the Koran refers to the Law of Moses as the *furqan* (difference), which is one of the major names of the Koran itself. Even at the beginning of Islamic revelation, the tradition mentions that a Christian monk, Waraqa, had compared the prophetic manifestations of Muhammad to the *nomos* received by Moses.

Moses's importance is comparable to no other individual in the Islamic text. This explains why, when in May 1939 the well-known Egyptian daily *Al-Ahram* published an article by its London correspondent on Freud's *Moses and Monotheism*, there were numerous protests and responses from the academic community, arguing against Freud's construction of Moses's Egyptian origin. One Egyptian academic wrote, "Professor Freud is the only one to distinguish himself among scholars and historians with this strange and unorthodox thesis. The historical books and the books of revelation support the belief, held for thousands of years, that Moses had a Jewish father and ancestry, even though he was raised in the Egyptian palace. He rose up with his brother Aaron to defend his Jewish brothers against the Pharaoh, then led them out of Egypt."[26] All the reactions that appeared in *Al-Ahram* were similar, supported by Koranic and biblical quotes; which shows that there was little sympathy for the anti-Semitic spirit shown in Europe in numerous so-called scientific works of the period. In Islam there was great attachment to the epic and heroic figure of Moses as a child of the people, a savior of his own people, and sometimes even the adversary of a people subjected to the tyranny of the pharaoh, and this attachment harbored a crucial concern.

The popular books on this topic, known as "yellow books" because of the color of their paper, clearly emphasized this aspect of the Mosaic deed. Something similar occurs in books on the interpretation of dreams, like those of Ibn Sirin and Nābulūsī (seventeenth century). Seeing Moses in a dream is essentially interpreted as an indication of a forthcoming deliverance from a tyrant and/or a sign of the trial of a child's separation from his family. Other themes are certainly present (disturbances of speech, crossing the sea), but those concerning the child and the hero are clearly predominant.[27]

Many stories repeat scenes from the history of Moses: a poor family abandons a threatened child to the care of a royal family, and the child ends up assuming power by freeing his people from oppression and destruction. This figure of the child passing from one family to another, from one mother to another (between mother and nurse) is also repeated. It becomes a basic narrative element in the stories of insurrection that relate the rescue of an individual, a group, or a people from annihilation, and the perpetuation of the memory of that individual, group, or people — in this case, the spiritual memory of monotheism — as if memory depended for its survival on the family to which one did not belong or, worse still, to the family that threatened one's own.

The Arab historiographer Tabari (ninth century) relates the story of Moses by reminding the reader that the Jews were nearly eliminated by Pharaoh after he had a dream that was interpreted by his astrologers as the announcement that he would be made destitute by a child of Israel: "Yet, while the Pharaoh killed a great number of Israelite children, the Israelites themselves were struck dead. The Egyptians went to Pharaoh and said to him: All the Israelites who are made men are dying and all the children born to them have been put to death. In a few years, the children of Israel will all be destroyed and the terrible deeds they do, we will be forced to do, and that will be hard for us."[28] According to Tabari, Pharaoh responded to this request by suspending the massacre for a year, during which time Moses was conceived. When the massacre resumed, he was thrown into the Nile so he would be saved.

Consequently, in the tragedy of imminent destruction, the emergence of the figure of the child savior is due not to the uprising of a downtrodden people but to a discontinuity at the core of evil. It is a twofold discontinuity: that of the momentary interruption of the massacre, and that which occurred at the hands of a woman in Pharaoh's family (Asiya is Pharaoh's wife, according to Islamic tradition) who took the child in and protected it. Consequently, there is no absolute evil, yet without it the tragic tale itself (memory) would be impossible. The infant savior came into being from this impossibility of absolute evil, as the possibility out of which arises the salvation of being, of a people.

Asiya, the other woman, the wife of the terrible tyrant (or his sister, according to the story in Exodus), by hiring Moses's mother as nurse, separates the maternal into two positions: procreative and nourishing. This split, with the help of the sister as middle term,[29] was salutary for the infant.

## A Sum of Lives

The most beautiful and profound Islamic text on Moses is, again, one by the great Sufi Ibn Arabi (twelfth century). In *The Bezels of Wisdom,* he opens the chapter devoted to the "sublime word of Moses" as follows:

> According to its spiritual meaning, the murder of the male infants occurred so that the life of each infant killed with that intention should flow to Moses; for it was in assuming that he was Moses that each of the infants was killed; however, there is no ignorance in the cosmic order, so that life, that is the vital spirit of each of those victims, necessarily had to return to Moses. It was pure life, primordial, unsoiled by egotistical instincts. Therefore, Moses was, through his psychic make-up, the sum of the lives of those who had been killed with the intent of destroying him. From then on, everything that was prefigured in the mental disposition of each murdered infant was found in Moses, which represents a divine favor that no one before him had received.[30]

Ibn Arabi seems to interpret the figure of Moses not only from the point of view of the infant, but as a summation; in other words, as a community of murdered children, which will become, in him, the place of assembly of the "murdered infantile." It is here that the principle of choice and the insurrectional power that saves the people from destruction will reside. The infantile is the memorial potentiality of the dead children; in other words, the power of something that has remained without memory, with Moses as the power of foundation.

A few paragraphs later Ibn Arabi explains the power of infantile potentiality:

> ...for the infant acts in the adult. Do you not see how the small child acts specifically on the adult, so that he abandons his position to play and babble with him and appear to him through his childish intelligence? It is because the adult is unconsciously (*bi-la chu 'ur,* "without awareness") under the domination of the child. He takes care of him, educates him, protects him, humanizes him so that he experiences no anxiety. All of this is the result of the child's action on the adult, because of the power of the child's station (*maqam*); for the child's relationship with God is newer, because he is recently formed, while the adult is far removed from Him.[31]

Consequently, for Ibn Arabi, Moses embodies in himself alone all the murdered children of his people, assembled into an insurrectional power; a power that, as infantile potentiality, has an actual bond of attachment to the divine. In short, Moses is the child who joins god and the people; he is a place for the mediation of speech from one side to the other.

Ibn Arabi concludes "The Bezel of the Wisdom of Moses" with these words:

> The wisdom of the appearance of God in the form of fire [referring to the episode of the burning bush, when god spoke to Moses] resides in the fact that, Moses being in search of fire, God appeared to him in the object of his desire [his demand]; for if God had revealed himself to him in a form other than the one he desired, he would have turned away because of his fixation on a particular object and God, in turn, would have gone away from him. But Moses was the chosen one and close to God. But if God brings someone close to him, he reveals himself to him in the object of his desire [of his demand], without his knowing it.

In his own way, Ibn Arabi informs us that desire is desire of the Other.

This is neither the first nor the last time that the theory of the imagination in Ibn Arabi, within the context of the mysticism he practiced, clears a path of intelligibility through psychic processes that often recalls that of psychoanalysis in another context. But what is remarkable here is to see Ibn Arabi approach a concept of the infantile with Freudian overtones while discussing Moses. For the figure of Moses, at periods that are quite distant from one another, where the contexts of knowledge and civilization are so different, offers those who question him, who seek the secret of his transhistorical construction, the same response: the indestructible infantile as desire of the Other, as the heterogeneous power of insurrection against the tyrant.

Is it an accident that we again encounter the theme of the woman introducing the child into the abode of the tyrant as a survival maneuver? Moses and Pharaoh, Dinarzad and Shahrayar — they represent the installation of the infantile in the heart of danger. By extending Ibn Arabi's meditation on the figure of Moses, we can isolate the difference between the unconscious as the reservoir of fantasy and the unconscious as a function of the necessary imaginary, that is, as infantile power or potential. The necessary imaginary is a fracture of the impossible that establishes the impossible as impossible.

It remains that the Mosaic upheaval was supported, as Ibn Arabi tells us, by the devastation of lives at their roots, forcing us to confront the enigma of creation from the vantage point of the death impulse.[32] But why is it the masculine that embodies this deadly potential to destroy the other man who represents destruction? Death against death? Himself against Himself? Are we on the eve of the deconstruction of that performance?

**Fratricide**

I now want to review certain aspects of Cain's murder of Abel as it appears in the Koran and in Islamic tradition. I have always been struck by the drama of this first murder, which has been, in my opinion, inadequately addressed, presumably because it is so difficult to symbolize.

In the fifth sura (5:27–32), the Koran recognizes Abel's murder by Cain as the foundation of human violence.[33] It places the two brothers in the midst of a dialogue where violence and speech are wrapped around the question of law and responsibility in a way that allows us to approach the act of murder as a decisive element arising from a strange structure of altercation.

*The Story of the Murder*

"Tell them truthfully the story of the two sons of Adam." Abel and Cain will never be called by their names. They are referred to anonymously as the two sons of Adam, two sons and two brothers, or one or the other.

"When each of them offered a sacrifice (to God), that of one was accepted and that of the other was not." The Muslim commentators say that the sacrifice originated in a conflict. At the dawn of humanity, Eve regularly gave birth to twins, a boy and a girl. Abel and Cain are the first two sons, each of whom was born with a twin sister. Adam decided to give Abel in marriage to Cain's sister, and Cain to Abel's sister. This was the introduction of a minimal principle of exogamy, the basic prohibition against incest, founded on the separation of the androgynous unit.[34] However, according to the commentators, Cain refused and wanted to keep his sister for himself. But Abel insisted on respecting the paternal law. Adam suggested that they make a sacrifice to god together. Abel's sacrifice was accepted, but Cain's was rejected. Abel had offered a lamb, Cain had offered grass. Just then, Adam was called by god to make a pilgrimage to Mecca. (Adam's being called to the house of god may signify that he was dead.) It was in his absence that the murder was committed.

The text continues: "Said (the one): 'I will murder you,' and the other replied: 'God only accepts from those who are upright and preserve themselves from evil. If you raise your hand to kill me, I will raise not mine to kill you, for I fear God, the Lord of all the worlds.'" In this dialogue, one of the two brothers indicates that he wishes to kill the other, but the other responds, You can kill me, I won't do anything to stop you.

As the text continues, it is assumed that it is Abel who is speaking: "I would rather you suffered the punishment for sinning against me, and for your own sin, and became an inmate of Hell." What is striking in this response is that Abel speaks as if he is already dead. Cain's desire to kill him, still limited to speech, becomes an act for Abel. Abel dies in speech, that is, he anticipates the other's desire and introduces the word of the law as the anticipation of murder. Abel speaks from beyond his death, so that the murder is seen as the future of the language of that law. In short, Abel responds to Cain's murderous desire with the desire that the murder take place, so that, through it, the law will triumph and Cain will go to hell.

## The Two Hatreds

We do not have Cain's hatred on one side and Abel's innocence on the other; we also find in Abel a fearsome will to push Cain toward the extremity of the act. He endorses the murder, even anticipates it, so that Cain will receive the supreme punishment of hell. In a way, Abel says, Since you wish to kill me, then I am already dead, and from the point where I am assumed dead, I will allow myself to be killed so that you go to hell. Where does the responsibility lie: in the brother who manifests the desire to kill, or in the one who lends himself to the realization of the murder so that the other brother is punished for all eternity? Abel supports the possibility of his own murder so that Cain will be found guilty and damned. Abel is ready to pay for Cain's responsibility with his life.

On this account, the situation appears disastrous. Evil is not only on the side of the brother who rejects the law of exchange but also on the side of the brother whose speech, in clinging to the law, supports Cain's wish to kill and situates it at the point where he responds to the desire for murder by anticipating it. The situation assumes the subject of the law is already dead or, at least, is someone who accepts murder to ensure that the law triumphs through his own death.

The situation is aggravated when the one who is supposed to be Abel says, "I would rather you suffered . . . for sinning against me, and for your own sin." The anticipation of the murder makes Cain responsible for something that does not belong to him. Cain's crime is obvious: he wants to keep his twin sister for himself, to remain united with her in twinship, denying the original division of the difference between the sexes and of alterity. But what is Abel's sin, other than to have desired Cain's sister, and to have desired death for this desire? In fact, what Abel causes Cain to assume responsibility for is not only the rejection of the law of exchange, and not only his wish to kill him, but also his own faults. Abel's goal here is that through his own murder he will be relieved of his sins; he will become pure, totally innocent, because the murderous brother will, through his act, assume complete responsibility for everything. It seems to me that, at this moment, the altercation reaches a degree of hatred that is more disastrous than the murderous intent itself.

"Then the other was induced by his passion *(tawwa'at lahu nafsuhu)* to murder his brother, and he killed him, and became one of the damned." The word *induced* is not entirely correct in this translation. *Taww'a* means "to obey," "to take part in," "to comply with"; and the word *nafs*, here translated as "passion" (or sometimes "soul"), is really the psyche, the vital breath that withstands corruption and death. The *De Anima* of Avicenna or Averroës is not the book of the soul *(kitāb arrūh)* but the book of the psyche *(kitāb an-nafs)*. In other words, Cain did not obey his passion (or soul) but gave in to the libidinal forces of his psyche.

"Then God sent a raven which scratched the ground in order to show him how to hide the nakedness of his brother. 'Alas, the woe,' said he, 'that I could not be even like the raven and hide the nakedness of my brother,' and was filled with remorse." Note that the text places the time of remorse at the moment of the preparation of the corpse; Cain reflects upon his act and recognizes his guilt.

The text of the murder concludes, "That is why We decreed for the children of Israel that whosoever kills a human being, except (as punishment) for murder or for spreading corruption in the land, it shall be like killing all humanity; and whosoever saves a life, saves the entire human race." According to this passage, we will all die, and if we return to life, it will be through that death. Cain's crime is total, absolute. We have all been murdered by Cain, we are all Abels, we are the "substitutes" of the word of the law that tends to anticipate the murder, so that the law can be made manifest. The principle of this responsibility is as follows: we are assumed to be dead so that the word can manifest the law. Ever since this first crime, humanity's moral condition has been martyrological.

This is the basic outline of the founding murder in Islam. I now want to reevaluate the mechanics of its logic. In the beginning, Adam-Father promulgated a law prohibiting incest. We should note that this prohibition affected not the mother but the marriage between twins, which I will refer to as the prohibition against sibling incest. This law entailed a minimal degree of exchange, the first rule governing exogamic union between siblings. Cain rejects it. He rejects the division and the lack of the other, wishing to remain within the narcissistic wholeness of the couple. Cain's refusal to swap is the rejection of the so-called symbolic law; that is, as the Greek prefix *syn-* indicates, that which separates and joins. Was this enough to trigger the murderous fraternal rivalry? No. Another significant occurrence was needed: Adam does not appear to pay any special attention to the law. He issued it but does not appear to require its application, for, when confronted with the conflict between his two sons, the father refers them to his own father, to god. And he does so in a very specific way, which is a competition through gift giving, vis-à-vis a third party. The violence arises from the incorrect orientation of the dialectic of desire and the law. Apparently, Adam vacated the law of its prohibition, which is based on the logic of division and distance *(syn)*, and replaced it with a logic of oblation and sacrifice that seeks to overwhelm the Other, the Other, in this case, being a third party that is more carnivore than vegetarian.

What happens next? Cain's refusal to give up his sister encounters god's refusal to accept him. Perhaps Cain practiced the religion of flowers and did not understand the demands of the religion of herders or animals, to recapitulate Hegel's distinction; a religion of animals with which "the quiescence and impotence of contemplative individuality [of the religion of flowers] pass into the destructive activity of separate self-existence."[35] But it is intimated that it is Abel's generosity that paid off. Many commentators have written that the lamb offered by Abel is the one god sent as a substitute for Ishmael (or Isaac) when Abraham went to sacrifice his son. In the genealogy of sacrifice and the divine economy of murder, the murder of the brother would have served to ransom the son or, rather, the gift of Abel's death would have served to avoid the murder of the son.

What is apparently being said is that the law — the good law — is the one on the side of death, in other words, the law of speech and of the father who utters the prohibition. However, here we have a father who believes he is legislating the narcissistic involvement of the son with his other by overwhelming the Other; he then leaves on a voyage to his Father. Is there really a good ending for this story? Desire in agreement with the law leads to death (Abel); desire in disagreement with the law leads to murder (Cain). Which side wins in this game, between the murder of one brother and the crime of the other?

But isn't the good son identified with the absent or dead father (Adam being with his father) so that he will become the spokesman of his law, the law that the father was unable to interpret or defend correctly? If Abel is a substitute for the father, this could mean that he was killed in his place. Abel would be sacrificed to take the place of a father who abandoned his children, who abandoned them to a world filled with a faulty interpretation of his own law.

Identification and substitution would engage another logic, that of the son who takes the place of a failing father to embody an ideal father who will not yield to the narcissism of the other son. The brother would become, for his brother, a righteous ideal father, which introduces the terrifying position of the innocent martyr.

These elements lead to a clear-cut demarcation with respect to the interpretation of the founding murder that tradition accredits, namely, the enactment of a crime resulting from the refusal to give, of an envious and hateful brother and a generous, nonviolent brother who allows himself to be killed as the innocent lamb of sacrifice. The psychoanalytic position congruent with this point of view — which is often found in interpretations of this crime — is to consider Cain as the representative of the primordial hatred of the narcissism that rejects the division of the ideal unity of identity and wishes to keep its femininity, seeing the brother, or equal, as a persecutor who dispossesses him of the specular other or the other of himself. In short, the crime would be one of paranoid jealousy.

But the structure of the altercation that the Islamic text transmits enables us to provide a reading that differs from the traditional one, including the traditional Islamic reading. Naturally, Cain's narcissistic logic, which coincides with that of the ideal ego, is obvious, but the mechanism of the crime is not found in this single disposition operating alone. There exists another kind of confrontation, with another kind of logic — that of the father substitute and identification with the ideal father. Here, the law assumes a melancholy posture, whereby the subject remains unresponsive and desires martyrdom so he can be cleansed, so he can become the pure Other of the law. Isn't this another form of narcissism, that of the ego ideal that gets satisfaction not in sexuality, as Cain does, but in death?

In this case, the narcissism of the righteous can only be the complement that instigates the criminal's narcissistic act. In the structure of altercation, there exists, in contrast to the primordial hatred of indifferentiation
and the imaginary ideal ego, another hatred, the ideal hatred of the glorious symbolic that is so easy to glorify. If we turn to current events, we see
that this structure of fraternal altercation persists. In other words, the period of the first phase of the text that reads "Tell them truthfully the story
of the two sons of Adam" has not yet come into being. Will it arrive? Will
there be a time when the sons will be placed, in their altercations, before
the law according to the impossible?

## He Is He

In his treatise on ethics, the tenth-century philosopher Miskawayh wrote:

> For the carpenter, the jeweler, and all the artisans hold in their
> mind only the basic laws and principles of their art. The carpenter
> knows the shape of the door and the bed; the jeweler the shape of
> the ring and the crown, in general. As for individual realizations
> ('ishkhās) of what is in their mind, they produce them from those
> laws but cannot know the individualities (al-'ashkhās) because these
> are infinite in number. For every door and every ring is made ac
> cording to the desired dimension, according to need and the nature
> of the material. The skill [the art] uniquely guarantees only the
> knowledge of basic principles.[36]

This passage occurs when the author attempts to explain why it is impossible to predict the behavior of "each individual" singularly (fardin
fardin) in terms of good and evil. Although the example he provides makes
use of objects, all the terms used are part of the Arabic lexicon concerning human beings. Consequently, it harbors a highly elaborate theory of
individuality. What does Miskawayh tell us? First, that individuality is
the realization of a universal form that is made singular in matter. The
individual is nothing less than a figure of the universal. Second, that this
realization resides in the encounter of two universals: that of the identity
of matter (wood, gold) and the universal of formal skill (laws and basic
principles). The individual would thus be the link between nature and
culture, the fruit of their union, as the child is between its mother and
father.

Implicitly, this theory relies on a metaphysics of the creation of
forms, according to which culture would be the Father of individualities

whose function is to transmit culture's form to human matter. Mother nature, as receptacle and mold, provides a setting for this shapeless matter, makes the figures visible in herself, and brings them into the world. The myth of the *chora* in Plato uses this same concept of generation but connects it to a political theory.[37]

## A Transference of Form

When, near the end of his treatise, Miskawayh establishes his typology of love, at the center of which he places a particular kind of love whose cause, known as the *'uns*,[38] founds society, he begins by evoking the love of father and son: "If, between the father's love for the son and the son's for the father, there exists, in one sense, a certain difference, they have one essential point in common. By essential I mean that the father sees in his son another self *(huwa huwa)*. He believes he has naturally reproduced his own *(al-khāsati)* human form *(suratahu al-insāniya)* in the individuality *(shakhsi)* of his son and has really transferred *(naqala)* his essence into his own."[39]

Paternal love would be the love of the transfer of the father's human form individualized again in the son. Note that Miskawayh is very careful with his formulation; he does not claim that this is the way things are; it is the father who "sees," who "thinks." He then supports the father's claims by stating that they are, in truth, consistent with the divine directive of "a natural policy" *(siyāsa tabī'yya)*. One of the key concepts in this development is that of *huwa huwa*, initially translated as "another self." This is a philosophical concept that is, approximately, equivalent to the term *identical*,[40] except that here the identical is reflected in the doubling of the same word: "He is he" *(lui lui)*. (Later I will describe the reasons for this doubling.) The translation that most accurately reflects the meaning of the text would then be: "The father sees that his son is identical to him[self]."

What is it about the identical that is so important? In Islam it is one of the principal names of god. God is, in fact, called *huwa huwa*, which literally means "He He," or "He is Himself." Often, in Arabic calligraphy, we find the word *identical* represented by the mirror form of the word *huwa* (see Figures 1 and 2).

*Huwa* is both the third-person-singular personal pronoun that designates the absent referent, and the copula that takes the place of the verb "to be" in Arabic. In his study "Functions of 'To Be' and 'To Have,'" Émile

Figure 1. The pronoun "He" *(huwa)* in Arabic calligraphy.

Benveniste mentions this use of *huwa* and quotes the following Arabic sentence: "God he (= is) the living *[Allahu huwa 'lhayyu]*."[41] We have many examples where the two terms *huwa huwa* are interlaced in a mirror image and appear in their correct location in a mosque, often decorating the center wall, immediately above the head of the imam and opposite the faithful in prayer. Absolute sovereignty is represented by the depiction of the interlaced mirror figure; it is the love of Self for Self unique to god, which not only does man not have access to but which also he must venerate as the inaccessible figure of the Wholly Other. But once the doubled letter *huwa* is interlaced, the mirror is cancelled, because in principle the mirror separates confusion.

Ibn Arabi, in his essay on the word *seth,* has a remarkable commentary where he indicates that, when someone looks into a mirror, he cannot, at the same time, see his own image in the mirror, and when he sees his own image, he cannot contemplate the mirror. Either his own image comes between the self and the mirror, or the mirror comes between the self and its own image. His formulation is comparable to Heisenberg's uncertainty principle. The principle of human identity is to be separated in two. However, through the son, the father is confronted with something like the possibility of identifying with the impossible. Ibn Arabi indicates, in the same essay, that this question is the "highest in the domain of spiritual knowledge."[42]

Arab philosophers have also considered identity, unity, and being in terms of the notion of doubling. For example, Avicenna writes, "*Huwa huwa* is the union of two, which are two in one position."[43] According to Al-Farabi, "*huwa huwa* means oneness and being."[44] And for Averroës, "the *huwa huwa* ... is similar to when you say: you are me in humanity."[45]

Figure 2. The pronoun "He" interlaced as a mirror image, the representation of absolute identity.

Therefore, by "God's natural policy," Miskawayh refers to the making of an identical copy, which man carries out at one remove: "It is He [God] who has helped man in the genesis of the child, by making him the second cause of existentiation and the transfer of his human form to the child." We should note that the father becomes Man *(al-insān)*, which tends to connote "son" *(walad)* in the more general sense of child.[46] But what is most important is that this assistance from god consists in enabling the Man-Father to imitate the identity of god through the child-son. The Man-Father becomes *huwa huwa* through his child-son, as god is *huwa huwa* in himself. In this way, through the child-son, the Man-Father assures his identification with god. In other words, access of the Man-Father to the model of god's identity takes place through the child-son. And just as every man was once a child (son or daughter, which is the general sense of the word *walad*), every individuality represented for its genitor (its father) this element identifying the self with the divine identity. The relation god-man becomes a double game of doubling, thanks to the child, because god's *huwa huwa* is doubled by the *huwa huwa* of the Man-Father once he engenders a child-son, and this child becomes the mediating factor — the unitary characteristic *(einziger Zug)*, to use the Freudian concept — that makes the two sides of the equation similar.

This recalls Freud's comment about our early identifications with our parents. In *The Ego and the Id* *(SE, 19:1–66)*, he writes, "This leads us back to the origin of the ego ideal; for behind it there lies hidden an individual's first and most important identification, his identification with the father in his own personal prehistory. This is apparently not in the first instance the consequence or outcome of an object-cathexis; it is a direct and immediate identification and takes place earlier than any object-cathexis." This obviously means that the father of personal prehistory is not the concrete father. In a footnote, Freud returns to this idea in the following terms: "Perhaps it would be safer to say 'with the parents'; for before a child has arrived at definite knowledge of the difference between the sexes, the lack of a penis, it does not distinguish in value between its father and its mother." This remark is corroborated in the Arab tradition by the fact that, genealogically, the mother is considered the "father" and the two parents are reunited in the expression "the two fathers" *(abawayn)*. In fact, in Arab metaphysics, the mother *becomes* father once there is a transfer of form, for her initial status is associated with matter.

I want to make two provisional comments about these metaphysical considerations of individuality in Islam. (1) Islamic thinkers, in terms of their own environment and using different means, have examined the same space concerning the relation between human individuality and god as Christianity, which is reputed to be an individualizing or individualist religion. (2) This metaphysics has made every Man (son or daughter) the element of identification with god for his genitor, who served the same function previously for his own parent. For every member of society, humanity is genealogically constituted as a chain of "unary traits." Filiation is that system wherein the descendant is a "marker" for the ascendant. Man identifies with Man only to the extent that this identification is directed at the model of divine identity.

The questions present themselves as follows: What happens if this system of identification with god ceases to be, as was the case in western European societies? What does mankind identify with — with itself? What does this "itself" imply, and what are the consequences of such an identification? There is little doubt that god's redundancy in the European tradition necessitated the reinvention of a Wholly Other, from which god is absent. But what happens to narcissism when identification means identifying with the absence of an absence?

## The Double

The dualistic system intrinsic to human individuality is also reflected in the Islamic social sphere. When Miskawayh evokes the *'uns* as the cause of love, which is the basis of society, he reminds us that the word *'insān,* which in Arabic refers to mankind as a species, is derived from the term *'ins.* According to the dictionaries, *'ins* refers to what is familiar, close, intimate, as well as to what is seen and, by extension, to the pupil of the eye.[47] Ibn Arabi, in his essay on Adam, says that man was called *'insān* because "man is to God what the pupil is to the eye."[48] In the great thirteenth-century lexical encyclopedia the *Lisān,* mankind is defined as a visibility that sees as often as it is defined as something familiar, and sometimes the two senses overlap.[49] This is the case, for example, in the opposition between *'ins* (mankind) and *jin* (djinn), the latter being, by definition, a strange and invisible being. This visible familiarity or familiar visibility is doubled in the name of man, since the word *'insān* is composed of *'ins* plus *an,* the latter being the sign of duality.

Perhaps it would be simpler to say that Man is a dualistic species, or a species whose essence is doubling, and that the double would be his essential familiarity. The Koran says as much: "For Man *('insān),* He (God) created two sexes, male and female" (75:39). Originally, there was the "Human," an androgynous species from which the genders were drawn. But sexual difference did not put an end to duality, for, once we had the couple, man and woman, everyone in turn became part of a pair: "That He created pairs *(zawjayn),* male and female" (53:45). The couple is a couple of pairs, the male pair *(zawj)* and the female pair *(zawja),* as if the equation with four terms *(huwa huwa* and *huwa huwa)* examined earlier had been reconstituted. Whenever we have the human, there is duality; where there are two humans, there is a quaternary.

## The Exposed and the Singular

In the example of the artisan, Miskawayh uses the term *tashkhīs* for "individualization" and *shakhs* for "individuality." Both words are derived from the root *shkhs,* which has given us the terminology of individuality as it applies to the person. The three principal axes of meaning it exposes are erection (standing, verticality), causing to appear and opening the eyes, and fixing something through the gaze. Obviously, the question is one of the distinction of individuality, to the extent that it makes the individual a being "exposed." In the Arabic tradition, there are three aspects to *shaks:* (1) the *'ird:* that which exposes someone to the influence of others; virtue, respectability, honor, personal dignity, and an individual sacredness known as *hurma,* which constitutes the kernel of dignity of the human person; (2) the *hasab:* that which counts, representing the individual value acquired or inherited from the person, his social rank, his resources; and (3) the *nasab:* filiation; enrollment in existence through genealogical rules, lineage, heredity, family, or clan affiliation. The rights of persons in Islam are organized around these three distinct elements of individuality, making the exponents of the person inviolable: life, assets, honor.

To address the level where individuality is seen as absolute difference, we need to return to Miskawayh's idea that it is impossible to predict the behavior of "each individual singularly." On this occasion he uses the word *fard*. This concept is central to the notion of individuality among Islamic philosophers and mystics. It would seem that it was by translating this concept in the work of Avicenna that the Latin authors of the Middle Ages had recourse to the term *individualitas*, which subsequently became a philosophical concept.[50] What, exactly, does it refer to?

The fifteenth-century philosopher Jurjani defines *fard* as "that which comprises but a single thing, without any other."[51] Therefore, this would be an individuality that was intrinsically not marred by any form of alterity. To better isolate the concept, the linguistic and philosophical dictionaries rely on its opposition with the even numbers *(shaf')*, as if *fard* were a synonym for the English "odd" *(watr)*. But it is with Ibn Arabi that this concept becomes a theory of the genesis of being as singularity. It is this that leads me to translate *fard* as "singular."

What does Ibn Arabi say? That the singular, if it has distinguished itself from something, is distinguished only in distinction to the pair. This distinction is obtained through resemblance to "oneness." Therefore, there must be two, and the One must be postulated for singularity to occur. The first singularity occurs only when there are three or more. "The first singular is three, for the One is not singular." It is the One that confers upon two the possibility of producing singularity. Singularity occurs in fourth place. Every structure of production and creation arises only from the ternary structure (2 and 1), and everything that is produced or created can come into being, as singularity, only as an emanation of the three. Ibn Arabi writes, "The male and the female could not procreate unless the act of copulation was between them. That act is singularization."[52] Therefore, the sexual relationship divides. "There is no sexual relationship" is a very old story that Jacques Lacan reinvented for our era, which failed to understand or forgot that which withdraws and separates in the *jouissance* of difference, or "there is there-is-not." But isn't this always the case? Ibn Arabi's theory of singularity is, contrary to what we have seen earlier, a theory of the absence of the pair, which occurs through identification with the One. In support of his ternary theory, Ibn Arabi has recourse to a Koranic quotation to demonstrate that, in the process of formation of the fetus, the soul is instilled at the end of the third phase of development. Therefore, the soul coincides with the principle of singularization, or with *différance*. Moreover, this approach is consistent with the Koranic view that ties singularity, soul, and responsibility together, as in the following sura: "Each soul earns (what it earns) for itself, and no man shall bear another's burden" (6:164).

At this point we have examined three planes, or levels, from which the problem of individuality in Islam can be approached: The first is the plane in which it is related to the Wholly Other, to absolute identity and to the identification of Man with god, or the child as the unary trait for its genitor, with respect to god. Second is the plane in which individuality interacts with sociability, in the sense of a personal individuality. This plane, along with the first, appears to be governed by a binary system. The third plane is that in which individuality is related to absolute difference and in which the concept of the singular is part of a ternary system.

## The Subject

I now want to examine a fourth plane of individuality in Islam, that of the subject. There is the philosophical subject known as *al-mawdhū*, the by-product of the culture of the Middle Ages, which has exactly the same meaning as the concept of the "subject" in Europe, that is, what is assumed, placed under, the Latin *suppositum* and Greek *hypokeimenon*. There is also a theological subject, which is not unrelated to the first, since it still involves subjection to the Other, but which clearly identifies that subject as a subaltern, a serf, subjected, bound by adoration to god. In fact, that is the very meaning of the word *'abd*.

In the fifteenth century, Jurjani proposed, with his usual conciseness, the following definition of *subjection ('ubūdiya):* "fidelity to commitments, the observation of prohibitions, consent to existence, or resignation before a lack."[53] Each of those four forms of loyalty is also given a definition. Their internal consistency is determined by the principle of *adoration ('ibāda or religion)*, which the author defines as "the act of someone who is solicited by the passion for an Other than himself with respect to his God."

If we examine the four loyalties that define this subjection, apart from the "observation of prohibitions" (which assumes adhesion to the penalties of theological law, including its physical punishments), all the others could be acceptable maxims for a modern subject. Besides, is it an accident that the concept of the "subject" is still found in European thought today, in spite of the considerable upheavals that the world has undergone? Certainly, I am aware of the criticism of subjectivity, as well as the internal transformations the concept has undergone. But the relationship of subjection to alterity cannot be easily erased. Inventions such as citizenship can displace, modify, even subvert the forces and lines of subjection.[54]

It would not be out of place, here, to quote the philosophical definition of the subject *(al-mawdhū)* provided by Avicenna: "The subject is any arriver [carrier] that holds itself and causes what comes within it to be held."[55] By connecting the subject to the concept of *hulūl,* that is, to that which happens, is embodied, takes up space, settles in, and takes up residence, he is already suggesting that we think of the subject as "the one who arrives."[56]

## Individuality, Islam, and Psychoanalysis

These considerations reveal just how highly developed the problem of individuality was in early Islamic thought and its complexity, free of the reductivism and trivialization we see today. This arises either from an ideological prejudice in which modern liberal Western individualism appears as the summit of civilization's accomplishments and hopes, a model for humanity's future; or as a result of a cultural essentialism that, for some, idealizes Islamic integration of the individual in his environment but results in the opposite, and for others, produces the kind of humiliation that turns Islam into a powerful system for the dissolution of the individual in the community. Over the past few years, we have seen psychoanalysts and psychiatrists express themselves accordingly, presenting "the Muslim" as being inaccessible to psychoanalysis, or as someone insufficiently differentiated from his group to present the kind of individuality that can be analyzed. Such remarks are characterized by ignorance and irresponsibility. The debate on the figure of psychoanalysis in Muslim countries has gotten off to a bad start, and has been based on false premises. At the same time, we associate the existence and spread of psychoanalysis with the rise of an individual whose individuality will be most fully realized when it comes into being in Western societies.

However, the above developments show that Islam makes use of an extremely powerful dimension of individuality and considerable conceptual richness. This dimension could not have developed without being consistent with the reality of the culture. It is indeed a culture of individuality, but one essentially governed by identification with god. To correctly state the question of the role of psychoanalysis in such a culture might consist in asking whether the identification with god in the working of the system is contrary to the fundamental principles of psychoanalytic practice and thought, or, more specifically, whether being raised in such a system prohibits access to the psychoanalytic experience. But is this really the most relevant formulation of the problem?

In her work on the growth of psychoanalysis around the world, the historian Élisabeth Roudinesco has developed an approach that breaks with speculation about the individual's "mentality" or the "psychology of a people" that are often raised when discussing Islam. She identifies three factors that promote the establishment of psychoanalysis in a given country or cultural region: (1) the existence of concentrated psychiatric knowledge, involving a scientific approach to madness that isolates it from demonological and sacred approaches; (2) the integration of psychoanalysis with general intellectual endeavors, especially through literature and philosophy; and (3) the existence of a state of law, even in the case of a dictatorial government, which is not the case with totalitarian regimes.[57]

Let's return to the obstacles faced by psychoanalysis in the structure of the traditional subject. The following remarks intersect Roudinesco's three conditions:

The traditional subject ('abd), although possessing all the prerogatives of a subject of law (and divine law is a law and not an arbitrary power), remains subject to a theological-political structure whose goal is to harmonize the human identification of individuality with god and the political space. That structure attempts to govern the psyche and society at the same time. But the modern subject addressed by psychoanalysis appears in societies where the separation between the birth community and the political community has taken place through a civil revolution backed by a powerful government apparatus. We should not forget that, in the traditional world, the patriarchal structure made the father both a paterfamilias and a political leader, since the space of the group and that of society were nearly the same. Filiation determined power. In the gap that opened up in the modern world, spaces for freedom guaranteed by the state as third party led to the appearance of civil society (between the state and the family, according to Hegel), which is the real environment for psychoanalysis. Moreover, psychoanalysis is a Western invention not because the West produced a more accomplished human individuality, one better suited to exist, experience pleasure, and die, but because the modern West has segmented the spaces of politics and the family in a new way and, let us not forget, has also fashioned a type of subject whose alienation necessitated the introduction of psychoanalysis.[58]

## Sharing the Impossible

How can a community represent its possibility? How can it answer the question, How is it that separate individuals can work in common? I am not asking, "Why community?" which would be a pointless question because the answer has, for a long time, been known: "There exists a principle of insufficiency at the root of each being," wrote Georges Bataille.[59] I would add that, nowhere, except in a certain form of biological discourse, is insufficiency reduced to a question of need. What, then, is held in common by a community for a community?[60] The question is related to what Freud referred to as the "riddle of the libidinal constitution of groups" (*Group Psychology and the Analysis of the Ego, SE*, 18:65–143), a riddle that touches the most incandescent point in the discourse of the passions concerning the origin of a people.

*Common:* To undertake, unify, contaminate, lead toward a single destination for the purpose of assembly, to hold together in a place; "as if" — Kant's heuristic regulator, or fiction, or possibly hallucination — everyone, in accepting the withdrawal of something essential, or proper, were to sacrifice it for the sake of a trait shared by others: a "unary trait" *(einziger Zug)*, as Freud called it. "The trait is withdrawal *[retrait]*," wrote Jacques Derrida.[61] The unary trait would necessarily be an erasure, a captivation of the self by the other at the very site where its trace is made. According to the mystic tradition, god had to partially withdraw to leave room for his creation, and in the void of "Himself" he left behind through his work, he produced the trait of his community with his creation — He is Himself. So, we can say that the trait of his community with himself is, at the same time, the separation of his identity.

## *The Community and the Impossible*

Freud described the trait-withdrawal that lies at the base of the common quite clearly for the individual in the group, as the point where "the notion of the impossible disappears" (*Group Psychology, SE*, 18:65–143). This is followed by what he called the "libidinal constitution of groups": a certain number of individuals make someone their guide, leader, or mentor in place of their ego ideal. We could add to this another formula, that of the psychoanalytic theory of the subject's introduction to collective identities: the transition from the ideal ego to the ego ideal. This is where the community of Cain and Abel became impossible. The fact that the foundational crime of monotheism arose from the impossibility of a minimal community of two clearly shows the nature of the failure on which any fraternal community is based.

Before publishing his ideas, Freud, as was sometimes the case, shared his doubts about his theory — in this case, the model of hypnosis and love that would explain group psychology. He begins *Group Psychology and the Analysis of the Ego* by writing, "But on the other hand we may also say that the hypnotic relation is (if the expression is permissible) a group formation with two members. Hypnosis is not a good object for comparison with a group formation, because it is truer to say that it is identical with it." A few lines later, he continues:

> Hypnosis would solve the riddle of the libidinal constitution of groups for us straight away, if it were not that it itself exhibits some features which are not met by the rational explanation we have hitherto given of it as a state of being in love with the directly sexual trends excluded. There is still a great deal in it which we must recognize as unexplained and *mysterious* [my emphasis]. It contains an additional element of paralysis derived from the relation between someone with superior power and someone who is without power and in *distress*[62] — which may afford a transition to the hypnosis of fright which occurs in animals.

Freud's difficulty in this text is not that of extending to group psychology concepts that relate to individual psychology. That problem is taken care of for him, given that the other is always present in the ego. Rather, it is the problem of transferring the model of what transpires "between two," primarily when in love, to the many. There is, in the model of the between-two, something similar to what transpires in the group, but which is at the same time difficult to export as such — on the one hand, because of the number of individuals in the group, which is obvious; and, on the other, because this eliminates "directly sexual trends." We know that Wilhelm Reich wrote one of his best books, *The Mass Psychology of Fascism*,[63] on this question, theorizing a deflection of sexual drives from their goals, their sadistic transformation, and their projection onto figures of the inner stranger.

If we attempt to provide a formulation of the problem as a function of the elements discussed earlier, we could say that exporting the model of love "between two" turns out to be problematic, because the commonality of community is not sexual. If, in the love relationship between two, sexuality consists in physically juxtaposing two lacks, then this would be what was missing from the commonality of community. What would be missing from "being together" is this relationship to a lack, which individuals experience as physical pleasure in the love relationship, as sexual beings. The commonality of community has no body to experience or enjoy the lack. Note that the great collective delusions, which have engendered the worst forms of mass violence, physicalize and sexualize the commonality of community to encourage the purification of this body, often represented as a female or feminized body. What, then, is the nature of the lack by which the community should be sufficiently affected in order to live without an excess of madness?

## An Allegory of the Community

In what follows, I want to analyze an allegory of the "libidinal constitution of a group" that intersects all the problems that have been raised. I have intentionally set aside the theological-political concept of community in Islam ('umma), whose literature is extensive,[64] as well as a number of psychologizing considerations that take advantage of the fact that the word 'umma is associated with the root that has given us the term meaning "mother." This has led to ethnocentric statements that border on racism concerning the inadequacy of the "symbolic" in Islam. However, if community is possible and necessary, it is because the mother's body is lacking and because this originary bodily lack does not resolve the question of lack, in any community.

During my lexicographical research into the root that has given us the word "rumor" in Arabic (shaya'a), I encountered a constellation of words whose meaning reminded me of an enigmatic story I read long ago.

The story has the characteristics of myth, a scene that illustrates the primal nature of the secret, its revelation, and its propagation; of the rumor as an intimate test at the foundation of a community. More specifically, it is the secret of the mystery, or how the sense of mystery can unite men and divide them in a communion outside themselves.

The story is told by Rumi, a Sufi poet who lived in the twelfth century in Konya, Turkey:[65]

The prophet Muhammad had revealed to his son-in-law Ali secrets
that he forbid him to repeat. For forty days Ali struggled to control himself. Then, no longer able to do so, he went into the desert,
stuck his head into the opening of a well, and began to tell those
mysteries. A drop of saliva fell into the well. Shortly thereafter, a
reed sprung up in that well and grew, day by day. A shepherd cut
it, made holes in it, and began to play on it while he grazed his
flock. His flute playing became celebrated, multitudes came to listen
to him with delight. Even the camels made a circle around him.
From mouth to mouth this story reached the ears of the Prophet,
who had the shepherd come to him and asked him to play. When
he began to play, all those present fell into a state of ecstasy. "Those
melodies," said the Prophet, "are the commentary on the mysteries
that I told Ali in secret."

In what sense does this story have to do with rumors, given that the
word never appears? The Arabic root that has given us the word rumor
(shaya'a) is a verb whose primary meaning is to disseminate publicly and
to reveal a secret.[66]

What led me to Rumi's story was the presentation, in the great
thirteenth-century lexical encyclopedia, the Lisān, of a constellation of
nouns derived from the verb shaya'a, meaning: the sound of the flute in
which the shepherd blows, the call of the shepherd's flute to gather the
flock, the shepherd's bringing together the camels by the voice of the flute.
It is not simply a question of saying that the sound of the flute (shiyā') is
referred to by the word rumor. The indication is much more precise and
accurately incorporates one of the important scenes in the story: the
voice of the shepherd's flute, which creates an assembly of men, including their camels. It is this voice that will be designated at the end of the
story as a "commentary on the mysteries communicated . . . in secret."
I say "voice" rather than "sound" because the Arabic term used (sawt) is
closer to English "voice" than it is to "sound," although it can be used for
the latter.

In fact, there are so many coincidences between Rumi's story and
the Lisān, between the mythical scene and the etymology, that we may
wonder whether the story did not introduce the word to the language;
and whether the allegory of community, or the enigma of the libidinal
constitution of a group, is not the place where semiotics and semantics
intersect, introducing the possibility of an irrepressible enchantment.

There is another group of words generated from the verb shaya'a, for
which the Lisān gives the following meanings: "the call to assembly,"

"the fact of forming a flock," "a gathering," "to lead a flock before oneself," "to agglomerate," and so on. The meanings focus on creating a compact mass of individuals that must be kept together by a call. One of the terms means to call to join the last and the first.

However, the story explicitly narrates this call to assembly: "multitudes came together," "the camels formed a circle," "those present." One of the properties of *shaya'a* is to attract the crowd, to agglomerate units, and to encourage them to form a group.

The *Lisān* also contains a number of terms, derived from the same verb, that refer to a type of individual one might call a "gossip." These are individuals who are unable to keep a secret *(mishyā')*; they reveal it and spread it wherever they go. In the story, this might occasionally refer to Ali, the Prophet's son-in-law, for whom the revealed mysteries became too important to conceal. For forty days (the standard period of mourning in Islam) Ali struggled to conceal them and revealed them only to the bottom of a well, presumed to be without ears, in the desert. The shepherd reveals them as well, but without realizing it, and these are only commentaries on the mysteries. His mouth and breath are his, but the commentaries are those of the instrument. But who is the instrument of whom? And what is the instrument of rumor?

The *Lisān* distinguishes another axis of meaning in the verb *shaya'a*, referring to the many names and actions that signify "to fill a recipient until it overflows" *(shi'tuhu)*, "what is outside of," "what exceeds the limit," and "excess" *(sha'ān)*. In this sense, the gossipers, who cannot keep a secret, do so from excess and not from any failure. It isn't that they are incapable of withholding the information; rather, they are overwhelmed by what they receive. However, the Arabic word for "ecstasy," in the mystical sense, is *shath*, which means "to overflow." Consequently, *shaya'a* would contain an ecstatic condition.

The story recounts two scenes of overflow: Ali's ecstatic overflow in the well and the ecstasy of the crowd listening to the commentaries on the mysteries revealed by the flute. Better yet, the flute is represented as the stalk of the seed that issued from the overflow (of saliva). The instrument of rumor is, therefore, created by the overflow it in turn creates.

The scene of the story represents an entire system of rumoring: the voice, the call to assembly, the overflowing and overwhelmed crowd, the overflow. Conversely, we could say that what is represented in the scene has already been named by the signifiers of language. What, then, is this thing in *shaya'a* that is so narrowly divided between word and representation?

We now need to focus on the point where the myth of the rumor reaches the dimension of an originary myth of community and communion, of sharing understood in both senses: "to have in common" and "to divide." The division is the internal one between Sunni and Shia in Islam. As we know, this division is the source of major conflicts and civil wars resulting from a twofold problem of political legitimacy and textual interpretation. The Shia consider Ali, Muhammad's son-in-law, to be his successor, not only because of their kinship but also because of the transmission of mysteries and secrets from one to the other. The Shia confer upon Ali the status of first imam, whose function is to provide the esoteric sense to the exoteric revelation of the prophet Muhammad. While one accepts the Koranic revelation around which the Islamic community is founded, the other would be the revelation of this revelation; which is indeed its position in Rumi's story.

Yet, the terms Shiism and Shiite derive from this same verb *shaya'a*. In the dictionary, it is at the center of a constellation of words meaning "to adhere to," "to follow someone," "a meeting of men around a man," "to become a follower or partisan," or "to take part in." In short, *shaya'a* harbors a sectarian effect, the consequence of the secret, of its transmission, and of its sharing around one individual.

## Sharing and the Passion for Sharing

The scene can be read as one of investiture and legitimation based on the sharing of the secret between founder and successor. It is a scene of transmission, which contains in its folds the division of the community (schism), but at the same time culminates in the group of men brought together in ecstasy by the melody of the flute *(nay)*.

A man invested with a mystery shares the secret with another, who divulges it to a hole in the desert; a third produces the commentary without realizing it; and it is around this commentary, as rumor of the secret of a mystery, that the community of ecstatic men is formed.

While the scope of *shaya'a* seems narrowly tied to the political question of the legitimacy and power of a man who wants to share with another man, nevertheless all the others are still excluded: they receive only the melody (the commentary), which is what eventually brings them together. They are gathered around a sharing that cannot be shared. It is a community of sharing to the extent that sharing is impossible. The rumor is the emanation that magnetizes men, the melody of a mystery that brings them together outside themselves. If we consider that the ecstatic state is part of the essential condition of existing, which is to have one's enduring outside the self, the myth simply says, A mysterious melody brings the existents together.

To share what is not shareable, therefore, to share nonsharing — we encounter these words as is in the lexicon, words also derived from *shaya'a:* "to leave a portion without sharing it" *(sahmun shā'i'un);* "to not share what is not yet shared," "what is still held in common among the rightful owners"; "the situation of someone who owns a thing jointly with another, given that the sharing has not yet taken place," and so on. *Shaya'a* contains a form of joint tenancy, that is, an asset in which everyone shares, without being able to withdraw their share and make use of it for themselves alone. To share an asset that is impossible to share is the condition of the community and of any community of existents united by rumor.

Here, we begin to get an idea of the nature of the rumor. The author of the *Lisān,* Ibn Manzūr, indicates this concisely when he writes, "To *shaya'a* something is to lose oneself in its passion."[67] The form of the verb used here is *tashaya'a fī,* in the sense of adopting an extreme position about a cause (or thing), disclosing it to others, and overflowing in it. We see that the thing in question is the impossible sharing, that is, the commonality of community. Rumor is the passion of the community. That is why the air of mystery magnetizes the men who gather together outside themselves in the community of existents. In an ancient sense, this is rumor according to myth — rumor as emanation of the impossible.

I want to try to examine this interpretation of the mythic speech of rumor from two different aspects. First, no matter who the man is — and this man may even be divine — the secret of the founding of the community cannot be retained, it must be transmitted. But the secret of the founder cannot be carried by the heir. At the conclusion of the ritual period of mourning, the heir spits out the secret and buries it, as if it were the dead founder or the ingested portion of the dead (even though he is still living, for isn't he already dead when transmitting it?). Try as he may to rid himself of the secret in a well in the desert, away from the listening ear and out of range of all hearing, the secret reemerges. It returns in the form of the instrument of the rumor, here the flute. We can call this instrument of rumor the "ghost." Prior to this sequence of events, the problem treated by the myth had been that of the secret shared by two people, of the unbearable secret between-two.

But once the ghost returns and is absorbed by the shepherd, the impossible sharing begins, that is to say, the time of the community of existents. The existents are cut off from the secret and, because they are cut off from it, they gather around its commentary, ready to lose themselves in its passion. However, the commentary is the voice of the ghost of the secret. The rumor is the voice of the ghost. The voice of the ghost magnetizes the men who are gathered in the community of existents outside themselves. In a psychoanalytic sense, the rumor is the voice of the originary repressed around which the community is established. What the flute sang, what enchanted those who heard it, is the voice that belongs to the originary region of the founder who died with his secret, which gives rise to the ghost.

The ghost is in the hands of the shepherd (rā'ī), which in Arabic refers to the khalif, the sovereign, the political leader. The sovereign calls men to form a community by mimicking the voice of the ghost, the product of the overflowing that provokes the overflow of men outside themselves. Just as rumor is the passion of the community, it is essentially political power. It is the voice through which those who use the secret of the ghost address those who have access to neither the ghost nor its secret, but who remain together in the jouissance of listening. Rumor is the expression of power through the voice of the ghost.

This political interpretation of the voice of myth encourages us to return to the enigma of the ghost — the buried secret that is revealed. The tale leads us to believe that this secret could be the secret of the dead or the dead as secret that returns at the end of the period of mourning (forty days). It arises from the substance that overflows, the saliva that becomes the instrument of excess. It receives the breath and produces the melody that steals men from themselves. It is voice. . . . What then is this secret-of-the-dead-ghost-breath-voice-instrument, other than language itself? It returns embodied in an empty body (the reed), calling the existents to assemble. Through language returned to existence an air of mystery is played, which magnetizes those gathered in the community of existents, outside themselves.

Second, something impossible to say is said without being said. To turn this into an enigmatic question, we might ask, What does the man do who overflows into a well, leaving behind a drop of his substance, which becomes the seed from which grows a branch that produces the voice?

The enigma cannot resist the last of the line of Oedipus — the last, the one who, here or elsewhere, attempts to isolate this impossible-to-say rather than leaving, to isolate it in its function of founding the human community. Man makes love, but there is no sexual relationship. This much is obvious. It was an allegory, *allos agoreuein,* so it said something other than what it was about. A man transmits the secret of the seed of the Other to another, who impregnates the Earth that engenders the phallic instrument of enchantment, which brings men together. Therefore, it was love that the founder transmitted to his heir, who made love without doing so in order to give it to others, to draw them to him, and to bring them together.

The love, without the sexual relationship, that is spoken when it becomes *allos agoreuein* (therefore without becoming), is the impossible or the "as if," which the simple formula "There is there-is-not" expresses more concisely, that is, without seeking the effects of rumor. Rumor is love as emanation of the impossible. What drives men outside themselves, drives them to ecstasy (the mystical, says Freud), is the love they experience in the relationship to the impossible that rumor allows them to hear through the phallus. What do they hear? Certainly not the content of the secret; they are not privy to that. Rather, the melody, the voice, the music — therefore, nothing signified. The secret of the Other, as well as the sexual relationship, is lacking in the love that brings about the community. In other words, the commonality of the community has always been impossible, and it is only when this impossible disappears or is made imaginary in certain circumstances that men cease to be a community. They are then given over to a kind of embodiment of the sexual, a sexualization of the common, to signifieds that become flesh. In this case, language itself is absent, for language contains detours of the impossible, through which mankind can give itself speech and remain silent.

# Epilogue

In this book I have tried to clarify the underlying structures of Islam, beginning with its contemporary crisis. Throughout, my approach has been to use the psychoanalytic method as applied to historical events. One of the characteristics of the method is to question the ways men make history, by examining what they say. It enables us to situate their experience in permanent confrontation with libidinal forces, feelings of guilt, and the threat of dislocating established connections. Such an experience is neither totally nor definitively controllable, and the language that attempts to circumscribe it within the limits of reason is itself likely to fail. This failure is structural, certainly, turning man into the being "who follows his path in the midst of ruin," to quote a line from Sophocles' *Antigone*. But there are also circumstances where catastrophic failures occur, which release the destructive energies of delusion and destruction.

What has been going on in Islam for the past twenty years is part of this situation. It derives from a caesura that divides its history and exposes another historical possibility within it. The notion of "crisis" is, for all that, unsuitable for referring to the rush toward the unknown and the unthinkable that has been driven by modern events. This is experienced by the masses as a transgression of the fundamental Law of Islam, a fault that is all the more forgivable because it is, to a large extent, unknown and desirable, born of a desire that belongs to an elite that has been incapable of translating the modern for the commonality or of implementing the interpretive and political possibilities appropriate to its excess. Modernity was, therefore, only a simulacrum of the modern. It drove people into a pact that can only be referred to as a "group perversion": a game of genealogical delegitimation, of de-identification with constitutive references, under the cover of pretenses that are assumed to embody "the modern intellect" but that are in reality a form of devastation of hitherto unknown savagery. Modernity provided a kind of forced entry into a "fetishized modernity," a trap dissimulating the modern real.

This condition resulted in pushing powerless individuals toward a process of "subjective revocation." By this I mean a mode of massive destitution of the human self that is produced when the real can no longer be apprehended through the signposts of subjectivity, and when the living being finds itself fully exposed, threatened in the continuation of its being. Islamism (a concept that has been erased, struck out) is motivated by a sense of identificatory despair, which relies on the most archaic elements of identification in order to ward off this situation. Herein lies the appeal to the veil of origin.

By demonstrating how the discourse of Islamism reveals a profound disturbance in the ever-precarious relation between the Real and symbolic structures, I have tried to lay out problems that have gone unnoticed by the political sociology that dominates current thinking on such matters. One of the elements it has ignored, no doubt considering it to be negligible, is the "torment of origin," the radiant core of the myth of identity in Islamism. This controls the entirety of its ideology, where origin appears as simultaneously a place threatened in its generative potential and the place of salvation toward which its adherents must return. This is not the metaphorical return of tradition, but a return that causes the spectral to erupt in the Real, producing the triumph of the law in the destruction of interpretation, and arranging the communion of the community around the martyr's corpse.

We cannot absolve Islam of this ideology. Certain dispositions are found in the avatars of its formation, and throughout its history. This is the case for the situation that allowed theology to hobble the emancipation of philosophy and restrict it to its orbit, which began somewhere between the twelfth and thirteenth centuries. It is this that characterizes the pathetic struggle of Averroës in a text such as *The Book of the Decisive Treatise*.[1] Dostoyevsky's saying, "What happens to us, resembles us," is fitting here.

Of course Islamism is not all of Islam, nor is it fatal, but we cannot dismiss it as a simple aberration. Analysis of the devastating effects of caesura should not, however, succumb to an essentialist process, which would conceal the historical and contemporary material forces that have caused Islam to become unhinged. To paraphrase Shakespeare's *Hamlet*, Islam is out of joint. No substantial effort has been made within Islamic civilization to anticipate and reveal the dissimulated and sudden exit from the time of eternal origin, of which ~~Islamism~~ is the boisterous symptom. The work of culture struggles with conceptualizing this alienation. This voiceless transgression has determined the psychoanalyst's task.

The bulk of this book has been devoted to translating Islamic origin into the language of Freudian deconstruction. To translate is not to apply or annex but, by means of a signifying displacement, to reread a tradition within the framework of its language and its images in order to provide access to what is secretly thought within it. However, psychoanalytic deconstruction considers the fecundity of this access to be conditioned by the intelligibility of the logic of repression that underlies the foundation of a symbolic organization.

In my research I have identified female alterity as the central nerve of the repression characteristic of monotheistic repetition in Islam. By picking up the thread of the story from the figure of Hagar in the first monotheistic text (Genesis), by following the subsequent effects of her dismissal in the founding of the new religion, and by analyzing the repressive consequences of female *jouissance* that threatened control of the structure after having accredited it, the process of deconstruction has provided access to places deprived of meaning in the institution of Islam.

One of those places harbors the Islamic enigma of the father in his nonrelation to god. This analysis has, in effect, enabled me to raise the most decisive question in conceptualizing the symbolic structure of Islam and, certainly, the most incisive with respect to the assumed continuum of the monotheistic field, because it is at this crucial point that Islam separates from the other two religions.

The problem, as we have seen, arises from the radical Koranic claim that god is not the father and could not, in any way, be compared to the father's representation, function, or metaphor. Indeed, there is in Islam a prohibition against approaching god from the perspective of paternity. It leaves man to confront a genealogical desert between himself and god — a desert that is impossible to cross, not because it cannot be crossed but because beyond it lies the impossible. However, this objection, whose provenance I have examined with respect to Judaism and Christianity, is transported de facto into psychoanalysis, where the god-father relationship lies at the heart of constructions relative to the fields of symbolism, ideality, and spirituality through their hold on the subject. How can we integrate the Islamic objection into the theoretical complexity of psychoanalysis, which is already considerable? Perhaps we should consider the theory of god-the-father by examining the genealogical desert. Life in the desert exposes men to wandering; it forces them to remain united and to take care of the oases where they find refuge, so they do not dry up. In other words, the desert between god and the father is the site where politics is instituted. This could be one of the guiding questions for psychoanalysis: to conceptualize the space between god and the father, not only in terms of murder, of the symbolic, of the name, of the void, and so on — all of these modalities being obviously relevant — but also, and more resolutely, in terms of the aridity in which the construction of politics takes place. The threat that haunts men in the desert is either the "There is nothing" of nihilism or the abundance of the totalitarian mirage.

It would be appropriate, then, to leave my final remarks to Nietzsche, the modern thinker of the desert, with the following two quotations. The first speaks to what is taking place today in Islam: "We know that the destruction of an illusion does not produce truth but only one more piece of ignorance, an extension of our 'empty space,' an increase of our desert."[2] The second, from Nietzsche's notebooks, relates to my concluding remarks: "I looked into origins. I became estranged from worship in all its forms — all became strange around me, and solitary. But the veneration itself within me secretly burst forth; and there arose in me a tree, in whose shade I sit, the tree of the future."

# Notes

**Preface**

1. Two psychoanalytic societies have already been established: la Société libanaise de psychanalyse (1980) and l'Association psychanalytique marocaine (2001).

2. All English translations of Freud's work are taken from *The Standard Edition of the Complete Psychological Works of Sigmund Freud* (abbreviated *SE* and cited throughout the text), translated from the German under the general editorship of James Strachey, in collaboration with Anna Freud, assisted by Alix Strachey and Alan Tyson (London: Hogarth Press and Institute of Psycho-Analysis, 1986). The terms cited here are from the *Psychopathology of Everyday Life* (1901), *SE*, 6:276.

## 1. The Torment of Origin

1. Aboul Kacem Chebbi (1909–1934) was Tunisia's best-known modern poet and one of the authors of the country's national anthem.

2. Habib Bourguiba (1903–2000) led the struggle for Tunisian liberation against colonialism. Having become president in 1965, he implemented a set of modern social reforms based on secularism and the equality of men and women under the law. Because of this he held a unique place in the Arab world. His views on the international scene were no less advanced. In 1965 he introduced a proposal to settle the Israeli-Arab conflict, which included the recognition of Israel. However, he ran up against the hostility of the majority of Arab leaders at the time, especially Nasser.

3. Islamic law forbids the form of adoption, known as "full adoption" in France, that alters the child's filiation. However, in the pre-Islamic code it was possible to adopt while maintaining the child's initial filiation. The real issue, however, was incest.

4. After the death of the Prophet, in 632, the Islamic community went through a period of civil war while also undergoing considerable expansion. See Hichem Djaït, *La grande discorde* (Paris: Gallimard, 1989).

5. Søren Kierkegaard, *The Sickness unto Death,* ed. and trans. Howard V. Hong and Edna H. Hong (Princeton, N.J.: Princeton University Press, 1980), 47.

6. When, in 1990, I created *Cahiers Intersignes* as a way of examining the interrelations between Europe and Islam through psychoanalysis, I did not think the project would ever address events of this nature. With the help of psychoanalysts and writers, some of whom belonged to the Groupe de recherches maghrébines de l'université Paris VII (created in 1978), it became our school of thought. The contributors to one or both of those groups regularly included Zhor Benchemsi, Olivier Douville, Khélifa Harzallah, Jean-Michel Hirt, Abdelwahab Meddeb, Michel Muselli, Okba Natahi, and Nadia Tazi.

7. The conference took place on May 15 and 16, 1987, in central Paris, and was organized by the writer Abdelkébir Khatibi as part of a program titled "Raison et déraison en islam" that ran between 1986 and 1989. The proceedings were published in the first issue of *Cahiers Intersignes* in 1990, in Paris.

8. The expression was inspired by a text by Jacques Derrida, "Qual Quelle: Valéry's Sources," in *Margins of Philosophy,* trans. Alan Bass (Chicago: University of Chicago Press, 1985). These two terms, which mean "torment" *(Qual)* and "origin" *(Quelle)* in German, are taken from a text by Hegel, where he claims that actual awareness of the self constitutes itself as separation from the source. I'll return to this idea later.

9. Friedrich Nietzsche, "On the Utility and Liability of History for Life" (originally published 1874), in *Unfashionable Observations,* trans. Richard T. Gray (Stanford, Calif.: Stanford University Press, 1998).

10. Pierre Fédida, *Le site de l'étranger* (Paris: Presses Universitaires de France, 1995).

11. Fethi Benslama, *La nuit brisée: Muhammad et l'énonciation islamique* (Paris: Ramsay, 1988).

12. What in Islam is known as "the mother of the book" is the "guarded tablet" kept near god for all eternity, of which the monotheistic books are said to be an emanation. In short, it is the womb of the text.

13. The word *intruder* can no longer be written without reference to a recent book by Jean-Luc Nancy on organ grafting in medicine: *L'intrus* (Paris: Galilée, 2000).

14. That is why, fundamentally, it can be claimed that there is no humanism in Islam, assuming we understand this to mean the philosophy that postulates that man finds his essence in his humanity and that invites him to live up to it. Man as the measure of man — an expression Nietzsche ridiculed — is based on an Oedipal presumption that can end only in blindness.

15. See, for example, 26:224–26: "As for the poets, only those who go astray follow them. Have you not seen that they wander distracted in every valley, and they say what they do not do." In the following passage, the accusation concerning the Prophet is made explicit: "Yet they say: 'These are only

confused dreams,' or rather; 'He has invented them'; or: 'He is only a poet'"
(21:5). These and subsequent quotations from the Koran are from the English
translation by Ahmed Ali (Princeton, N.J.: Princeton University Press, 1993).

16. Tabari, *At-tarikh* (tenth century), translated by H. Zotenberg as *Mohamed, sceau des prophètes* (Paris: Sindbad, 1980).

17. Salman Rushdie, *The Satanic Verses* (New York: Viking, 1989).

18. I refer readers to my *Une fiction troublante* (Paris: Éditions de l'Aube,
1994).

19. Salman Rushdie, "One Thousand Days in a Balloon," from a speech
given at Columbia University and published in the *New York Times*, Decem-
ber 12, 1991.

20. Jacques Lacan, *Le séminaire des noms du père* (1963), partially reprinted
in *L'Excommunication*, a supplement to *Ornicar?* 8 (1977): 110–11.

21. This is reported by Jean Bottéro in *Naissance de Dieu* (Paris: Gallimard,
1986), 21.

22. The distinction I am proposing between the position of the Prophet
and that of the institution of Islam is necessary, even if Muhammad contributed directly to the creation of this institution. We could say that the man
associated with the revelation of the Koranic word was, at the same time, the
founder of Islam, that is, the equivalent of both Jesus and Saint Paul for Christianity. More accurately, we find in the Prophet of Islam a first, Christic phase
and a second, Pauline phase.

23. See the commentary and analysis by Philippe Lacoue-Labarthe in *The
Subject of Philosophy*, ed. Thomas Trezise, Theory and History of Literature 83
(Minneapolis: University of Minnesota Press, 1993). The quotation is from
Nietzsche's *The Will to Power*.

24. What Guy Debord called the "society of the spectacle" is not, therefore, the cause of the disintegration of the relationship to truth, as he claimed.
If there has been any disintegration, it arises rather from the *fictionalization* of
being and truth; and it is this that results in the generalized "spectacle," and
not the reverse. But can the metaphysical conception of truth and its restoration, as it appears in Debord's text, be interpreted in this sense? Guy Debord,
*The Society of the Spectacle*, trans. Donald Nicholson-Smith (New York: Zone
Books, 1994).

25. Here, I rely upon the position I took immediately following the condem-
nation of Salman Rushdie in a text that appeared in the French newspaper
*Libération* on February 16, 1989. See also the collection of essays to which Anouar
Abdallah and more than a hundred other Arab and Muslim intellectuals con-
tributed, at the request of Nadia Tazi and Eglal Errera, *For Rushdie: Essays by
Arab and Muslim Writers in Defense of Free Speech* (New York: Braziller, 1994).

26. Lacoue-Labarthe, *Subject of Philosophy*, 14.

27. Acharif Al-Jurjani, *Kitāb atta'rifāt* (Beirut: Dar Al-kutub al-'ilmyya,
1988), 50–51.

28. The following Koranic passage on the cycle of existence indicates this clearly: "He gave you life when you were dead. He will make you die again then bring you back to life: to Him then you will return" (2:28).

29. The Arabic phrase is "'asala 'achchy'a: qatalahu 'ilman fa 'arafa aslahu." Ibn Manzūr, Lisān al-'Arab (Beirut: Dar Lisān al-'Arab, n.d.), 68–69. (This encyclopedic dictionary, written in the thirteenth century in southern Tunisia, is a monument of the Arab language and a respected reference work. I will refer to it repeatedly.) Hachem Foda has pointed out to me that "to kill something by knowing it" metaphorically signifies examining something exhaustively. Nevertheless, "killing the thing" literally stipulates murdering the thing.

30. My ideas in this section were initially developed during a presentation given to the Groupe de Cordoue, created following the 1992 meeting that took place in that city at the initiative of the International Freudian Association. Since then, over a period of several difficult years, there has been a shared effort among Jewish, Christian, Muslim, and secular thinkers to evaluate the texts of the three monotheistic religions. This effort has given rise to a series of high-level debates and meetings. Being an external member, as my way of thanking the participants, I would like to mention the importance this group has assumed in my work. I especially thank Denise Sainte Far Garnot and Pierre-Christophe Cathelineau for their efforts in sustaining the group.

31. This thesis has been formulated primarily in Sayyid Qutb, Fi dhilali al-qur'an (Beirut: Dar Achuruq, 1968). See Olivier Carré, Mystique et politique: Lectures révolutionnaires du Coran par Sayyid Qutb (Paris: Presses de la FNSP/ Éditions du Cerf, 1984).

32. I had direct access to this type of statement.

33. Christian Jambet, La grande résurrection d'Alamût (Paris: Verdier, 1990).

34. It was Henry Corbin, in France, who demonstrated the scope of this theory, although in Jungian terms, in L'imagination créatrice dans le soufisme d'Ibn Arabî (Paris: Flammarion, 1958). Jacques Lacan mentions Corbin's book in his seminar The Ethics of Psychoanalysis, 1959–1960, trans. Dennis Porter (repr., New York: Norton, 1997), with reference to courtly love, given that Ibn Arabi's theory is also a theory of love in the face of the Other in the imaginal world. On at least one other occasion, Lacan returned to Ibn Arabi. This took place at a 1960 conference at the Facultés universitaires Saint-Louis (Brussels), to which he was invited by J.-P. Gilson. In the typed transcript that was sent to us, Lacan recalls the episode of the meeting of and dialogue between Averroës and Ibn Arabi in Andalusia, and affirms that his position as a psychoanalyst is aligned with Ibn Arabi rather than the philosopher. Cahiers du Collège de Médecine 12 (1966): 459.

35. Ni'mat Sidqī, al-Tabarruj (Tunis: Éditions Bouslama, 1985), 53.

36. Jacques Derrida, "Foi et savoir," in La religion (Paris: Seuil, 1996), 9–86. See "Faith and Knowledge," in Religion, ed. Jacques Derrida and Gianni

Vattimo, trans. David Webb, Cultural Memory in the Present series (Stanford, Calif.: Stanford University Press, 1998), 2.

37. Jacques Lacan wrote, "Sacrifice signifies that, in the object of our desires, we try to find a witness of the presence of the desire of that Other I call the obscure God." *The Four Fundamental Concepts of Psychoanalysis*, trans. Alan Sheridan (New York: Norton, 1998). The obscure god is an old problem in the tradition of biblical commentary, as Thomas Römer reminds us in *Dieu obscur* (Paris: Labor et Fides, 1998).

38. Manzūr, *Lisān al-'Arab*, 1:165.

39. See Pierre Ginésy, "Trépan," and my response, both of which texts appeared in *Césure* 13 (1998): 10–39.

40. In the religions of India, it is man himself who is the debt. See Charles Malamoud, "Psychanalyse et sciences des religions," in *L'apport freudien* (Paris: Bordas, 1993), 587–91.

41. Jean-Michel Hirt, in *Le miroir du prophète* (Paris: Grasset, 1993), has tried to show how the Koran makes use of the paradigm of the mirror for the believer. This interpretation is the opposite of tradition, which makes the subject the mirror of the Koran and of god.

42. In an informative essay, François Balmès distinguishes two forms of god in Freud: the sublime god of Moses found in *Moses and Monotheism*, and the god of *Totem and Taboo*, the product of the father of absolute pleasure. See *Freud et Moïse: Écriture du père*, vol. 1 (Toulouse: Érès, 1997).

43. *Webster's Third New International Dictionary*, ed. Philip Gove (Springfield, Mass.: Merriam, 1971), s.v. "abstraction."

44. See the article "din" in Manzūr, *Lisān al-'Arab*, 1:757–59.

45. Freud introduced the thing *(das Ding)* in *Project for a Scientific Psychology* (1895), *SE*, 1:281–387. Jacques Lacan, in Seminar 7, takes up the problem and gives it greater scope and relief, which have made it one of the central questions in psychoanalysis, falling as it does at the intersection of the unconscious, *jouissance*, language, and law. See *The Ethics of Psychoanalysis*, trans. Dennis Porter (New York: Norton, 1992).

46. Names are nostalgic for things, Ibn Arabi says somewhere. Freud, in *Civilization and Its Discontents* (1929; *SE*, 21:57–145), sees writing as the language of the absent, a substitute for the maternal body, whose "longing always remains."

47. Derrida, "Foi et savoir," 59. Derrida's thoughts on the subject are complex, and I do not wish to comment on or summarize them here. I feel that my remarks on Islamism intersect the author's philosophical arguments concerning the relationship between religion and science from the viewpoint of the logic of the "unscathed."

48. Averroës, *The Book of the Decisive Treatise Determining the Connection between the Law and Wisdom; and, The Epistle Dedicatory*, trans. Charles E.

Butterworth, in English and Arabic (Provo, Utah: Brigham Young University Press, 2001). Elsewhere, I have shown how the pseudoattempt to reconcile religion and science attributed to Averroës turned into a cross-examination of religion by science. See "La décision d'Averroès," in Colloque de Cordoue, *Ibn Rochd, Maïmonide, saint Thomas* (Paris: Climats, 1994).

49. *Ceci est la vérité,* videocassette (Paris: Édition Ramou, n.d.). On the cover, we read: "The inimitable sign of the times is revealed in a scientific dialogue with fourteen renowned thinkers. The living wonder of the Koran, tangible and radiant beyond the centuries, astonishes us today by its scientific relevance in various fields." There are thousands of documents of this kind in the Muslim world.

50. Concerning this question of martyrdom, see the following articles published in "Penser l'Algérie," special issue, *Cahiers Intersignes* 10 (1995): Fethi Benslama, "La cause identitaire"; Yassine Chaïb, "Les martyrs des uns et des autres"; Ramdane Babadji, "Le martyr, l'état, et le droit"; and Khaled Ouadah, "Les temoins."

51. The platform was published in the *Tribune d'Octobre,* July 25, 1989, and reprinted in France in the review *Crises* 1 (January 1994).

52. Mohamed Talbi, "Islam et modernité," *Nouveaux Cahiers du Sud* 1 (1995): 59ff.

53. Hannah Arendt, *The Origins of Totalitarianism* (New York: Schocken, 2004).

54. Olivier Roy, *Vers un Islam européen* (Paris: Éditions Esprit, 1999), 10.

55. Hamza Mohamed El-Hachimi, *Les cinq valeurs universelles et les quatre superbombes,* vol. 1 (Tunis, 1996). The author is introduced on the back cover of his book. A graduate of the Sorbonne in natural science, geology, and micropaleontology, he is head of research at the Department of Agricultural Research and Training in Tunisia and an engineer at the École nationale des eaux et forêts in Nancy, France.

56. In Islam, the prohibition against incest between blood relations applies also to those who have been nourished at the same breast, known literally as "milk brothers and sisters."

57. Émile Poulat, "Intégrisme," in *Encyclopédie universalis* (1995), 12:416.

58. El-Hachimi's proposed arrangement is as follows. The sacred and transcendent sense in the Koran is twofold: to adore god ("I have not created the jinns and men but to worship me" [51:56]) and to undergo testing (god "who created death and life in order to try you to see who of you are best of deed" [67:2]; "Every soul will know the taste of death. We tempt you with evil and with good as a trial; and to Us you will return" [21:35]). There is also the absurd sense: "Yet they say 'there is nothing but the life of this world. We die and we live, and only time annihilates us.' Yet they have no knowledge of this; they only speculate" (45:24).

59. This is the title of a book by Jean-Luc Nancy, which helped me to de-

velop this argument: Jean-Luc Nancy, *The Sense of the World,* trans. Jeffrey S. Librett (Minneapolis: University of Minnesota Press, 1998).

60. I discuss this hypothesis in "La dépropriation," *Lignes* 24 (1995), and "L'oubli de l'éthique," *Che Vuoi* 7 (1998). Here, I simply point out the elements of this vacillation between the discourse of religion and that of science.

61. The four superbombs that free death from the hold of meaning are, according to El-Hachimi, "the DPM bomb," which affects the population explosion; "the C bomb," or excess consumption; "the SST bomb," which combines sex, AIDS, and drug addiction; and "the IF bomb," arising from the false information that promotes an uncontrollable planetary imaginary. El-Hachimi, *Les cinq valeurs universelles,* 6.

62. Ahmad Hilal, *La vérité au service de la vérité* [Al-haq fi khidmati al-haq] (Cairo: Dar al-islamiyat, n.d.), 3.

63. Gilles Deleuze, *Critique et clinique* (Paris: Éditions de Minuit, 1993), 42–43.

64. Everything Freud wrote about culture is based on this foundation, without which psychoanalysis adds nothing new to the subject. More recently, Nathalie Zaltzman has helped to rework this theory by examining it in light of eyewitness accounts of the Nazi camps. Specifically, Zaltzman looked at accounts of the extermination of the inmates and their survival under extreme conditions, when the individual-collective anchorages of *Kulturarbeit* were swept away. Nathalie Zaltzman, *De la guérison psychanalytique* (Paris: Presses Universitaires de France, 1998).

65. Alice Cherki's *Frantz Fanon, Portrait* (Paris: Éditions du Seuil, 2000) illustrates the scope of this violence for the psyche.

66. Cf. Philippe Lacoue-Labarthe, *L'imitation des modernes* (Paris: Galilée, 1986), 67–68.

67. Benslama, "Le dépropriation," 34–62.

68. See Ghyslain Lévy, *Au-delà du malaise* (Paris: Érès, 2000).

69. Jacques Derrida, *États d'âme de la psychanalyse: L'impossible au-delà d'une souveraine cruauté* (Paris: Galilée, 2000), an address given to the États généraux de la psychanalyse.

70. The États généraux de la psychanalyse, organized by René Major (July 8–11, 2000, in Paris), was, in this sense, one of the significant efforts to address these problems on an appropriate scale, that is, globally. Not only that, but the attendees went so far as to question the very rationale for psychoanalysis, as Élisabeth Roudinesco does in *Why Psychoanalysis?* (New York: Columbia University Press, 2002).

71. Abdelmajid Charfi, "Les islamistes sont-ils les ennemis de la modernisation ou ses victimes?" *Labinat* (Sud-Édition, 1994): 95.

72. Michel Foucault, "Le chah a cent ans de retard," in *Dits et écrits, 1954–1988* (Paris: Gallimard, 1994), 3:679–83. See Janet Afary and Kevin B. Anderson,

*Foucault and the Iranian Revolution: Gender and the Seductions of Islamism* (Chicago: University of Chicago Press, 2005).

73. Miskawayh, tenth-century philosopher. See the section titled "He Is He" in chapter 4.

74. The phrase is taken from the title of a book by Jacques Lacan, *Les complexes familiaux* (1938; repr., Paris: Navarin, 1984). However, Lacan doesn't discuss the role of the state, although it is essential for a causal understanding of what he has referred to as "the social decline of the parental imago" in the West.

75. Jacques Taminiaux, *Naissance de la philosophie hégélienne de l'etat: Commentaire et traduction de la Realphilosophie d'Iéna (1805–1806)* (Paris: Payot, 1984), introduction.

76. Étienne Balibar, *La crainte des masses* (Paris: Galilée, 1997), 49.

77. Friedrich Nietzsche, *The Will to Power*, trans. Walter Kaufmann and R. J. Hollingdale (New York: Vintage, 1968), 13.

78. See, for example, the article by Pierre Hassner in *Le Monde*, September 23–24, 2001.

79. *Le Monde*, September 24, 2001.

## 2. The Repudiation of Origin

1. G. W. F. Hegel, *La raison dans l'histoire* (Paris: 10/18, 1965), 293; repr., *Lectures on the Philosophy of World History*, trans. H. B. Nisbet (Cambridge: Cambridge University Press, 1975).

2. "Entête" is the title André Chouraqui gave to his translation of the book of Genesis. See André Chouraqui, *La Bible: Traduite et commentée*, vol. 1, *Entête (la Genèse)* (Paris: J.-C. Lattès, 1992).

3. I am referring here to Jean-Luc Nancy's splendid "L'être abandonné," in *L'impératif catégorique* (Paris: Flammarion, 1983), 143–53.

4. Henri Meschonnic proposes the following translation of this passage: "Mon Dieu mon dieu à quoi m'as-tu abandoné?" (My God, my God, to what have you abandoned me?). This "to what" completely alters the meaning of the abandonment, for it is no longer a request to the father to supply a reason, but a question about the uncertainty of the destination. Program for *Jeanne d'Arc au bûcher*, by Arthur Honegger, libretto by Paul Claudel, Opéra de Paris-Bastille, November 1992.

5. This idea lies at the center of Jacques Derrida's idea of deconstruction. See *Glas*, trans. John P. Leavey Jr. and Richard Rand (Lincoln: University of Nebraska Press, 1990).

6. Jahiz, *Rasa'il al-Jahiz* (Cairo: Al-Sandubi, 1933), 292.

7. This is what Okba Natahi has referred to as the "Ishmael effect" on Muhammad. "Ismaël ou le retrait de la lettre," *Intersignes* 1 (1990): 38.

8. This first chapter of *Moses and Monotheism* was the first article to appear in the review *Imago,* in 1937.

9. See Jacques Félician, *L'orient du psychanalyste* (Paris: L'Harmattan, 1995).

10. Here, I am following the title of Antoine Berman's book on translation, *L'épreuve de l'étranger* (Paris: Gallimard, 1984). See *The Experience of the Foreign: Culture and Translation in Romantic Germany,* trans. S. Heyvaert (Albany: State University of New York Press, 1992).

11. We could read Abdelkébir Khatibi's beautiful novel *Amour bilingue* (Montpellier, France: Fata Morgana, 1983) in this light — the son abandoned in the bilingual death of the father. See *Love in Two Languages,* trans. Richard Howard (Minneapolis: University of Minnesota Press, 1990).

12. See chapter 1, "Luther: Translation as Foundation," of Berman, *Experience of the Foreign.*

13. Jacques Derrida developed the concept of the archive as being closely linked with psychoanalysis and, especially, with Freud's *Moses and Monotheism.* See Jacques Derrida, *Archive Fever,* trans. Eric Prenowitz (Chicago: University of Chicago Press, 1998).

14. *Midrach Rabba* (fifth century), trans. B. Maruani and A. Cohen-Arazi (Paris: Verdier, 1987), 1:414–17; Louis Pirot and Albert Clamer, *La Sainte Bible: Traduction, commentaires exégétiques et théologiques* (Paris: Letouzey et Ané Éditeurs, 1953), 1:269.

15. Sarai was said to be Abram's half sister through his father (Genesis 20: 1–12).

16. In his close translation of the Hebrew text, André Chouraqui translates the last phrase of Genesis 16:2 as: "Peut-être serai-je construite d'elle" (Chouraqui, *Entête,* 169). Biblical citations throughout the text refer to the King James Version unless noted otherwise.

17. The Code of Hammurabi stipulates that the sterile woman must provide a *sugetum* (concubine) so her husband may have children. Pirot and Clamer, *La Sainte Bible.*

18. The expression "the lack of god in her" is nearly identical to the one used by Lacan to define love, as well as hatred and ignorance, when the appeal to receive from the Other that which fulfills forgets that, for the Other, being is also lacking. Jacques Lacan, *Écrits* (Paris: Seuil, 1966), 627. See *Écrits: The First Complete Edition in English,* trans. Bruce Fink (New York: Norton, 2006), 524.

19. "And she called the name of the Lord that spake unto her, Thou God seest me; for she said, Have I also here looked after him that seeth me?" (Genesis 16:13).

20. "Heman, Calcol, and Dara, though men of great talent, were not prophets, whereas uneducated countrymen, nay, even women, such as Hagar,

Abraham's handmaid, were thus gifted." Benedict de Spinoza, *Theological-Political Treatise*, trans. R. H. M. Elwes (New York: Dover, 1951). For a more recent translation, see Baruch Spinoza, *Theological-Political Treatise*, trans. Samuel Shirley, 2nd ed. (Indianapolis: Hackett, 2001). In contrast, in his *Guide for the Perplexed* (twelfth century), Maimonides, referring to an old tradition, arrives at the completely opposite conclusion, writing, "Hagar the Egyptian, was not a prophetess." Because she was not prepared for that role, her vision was based on a heightened and deceptive imagination. Moses Maimonides, *The Guide for the Perplexed*, trans. M. Friedlander, 2nd ed. (New York: Dover, 1956).

21. Pirot and Clamer, *La Sainte Bible*.

22. Catherine Chaliez, *Les matriarches* (Paris: Cerf, 1985), 41.

23. Chouraqui's translation, in *Entête*, reads, "Sa patronne s'allège à ses yeux" (Her mistress was lessened in her eyes).

24. The *Midrach Rabba* translates Sarai as "my Mistress" (1:489).

25. Marie Balmary, *Le sacrifice interdit* (Paris: Grasset, 1986). See the chapter titled "La guérison de Sarah."

26. The *Midrach Rabba* indicates the sharing this way: the numerical value of the letter *yod* is 10, whereas the value of the letter *hey* is 5. The commentary also points out that Sarai was her husband's mistress and that Abraham had to obey her, according to god's commandment: "In all that Sarah hath said unto thee, hearken unto her voice" (Genesis 21:12). Bernard This considers the letter *yod* to have a phallic character. See *Naître et sourire* (Paris: Champs-Flammarion, 1983), 112.

27. *Midrach Rabba*, 1:490.

28. Jacques Lacan, "La signification du Phallus," *Écrits*, 685–95. See "The Signification of the Phallus," in *Écrits: The First Complete Edition in English*.

29. Sigmund Freud, "On the Sexual Theories of Children," SE 9:205–26.

30. *Midrach Rabba*, 1:545–52.

31. Chouraqui, *Entête*.

32. In an early address to Muhammad in the Koran, god refers to him as an orphan. This is a significant piece of biographical information, for the Prophet was orphaned first by his father and mother, then by those who had sheltered him, his grandfather and his uncle. I refer readers to my *La nuit brisée* (Paris: Ramsay, 1989), 172–77. As for the prohibition of appearing as the father of members of his community, that is, the prohibition against full adoption, it is clearly stated in the Koran, "Muhammad is not the father of any man among you, but a messenger of God" (33:40).

33. This is confirmed by the important sura known as the "Pure Faith" (112): "Say: 'HE IS God, / the one, the most unique, / God the immanently indispensable. / He has begotten no one, / and is begotten of none. / There is no one comparable to Him.'"

34. Jacques Derrida, *Given Time,* vol. 1, *Counterfeit Money,* trans. Peggy Kamuf (Chicago: University of Chicago Press, 1992), 7.

35. *Midrach Rabba,* 1:473.

36. See Chouraqui, *Entête;* and Pirot and Clamer, *La Sainte Bible,* vol. 1.

37. See also *Midrach Rabba,* 1:563.

38. Pirot and Clamer, *La Sainte Bible,* 1:306; Chouraqui, *La Bible,* 1:213.

39. Derrida, *Archive Fever.*

40. Aristotle, *The Eudemian Ethics,* trans. H. Rackham, Loeb Classical Library (Cambridge, Mass.: Harvard University Press; London: Heinemann, 1981), 1.1241b.

41. René Dagorn, *La geste d'Ismaël d'après l'onomastique et la tradition arabe,* with a preface by Maxime Rodinson (Geneva: Librairie Droz, 1981).

42. Ibid., 377.

43. Ibid., 47.

44. Ibid., 49.

45. Ibid., 377.

46. Rodinson, preface, xviii.

47. I refer readers to my *La nuit brisée,* 81ff.

48. This quotation is based upon the French translation of the Koran by André Chouraqui, who translates this opening phrase as, "Au Nom de Dieu le matriciel le matriciant." The conventional English translation is, "In the name of Allah, most benevolent, ever-merciful," or something quite close. [See, for example, *The Koran,* trans. Ahmed Ali (Princeton, N.J.: Princeton University Press, 1993), which is the edition used in this book. — Trans.]

49. "Read in the name of your Lord who created, Created man from an embryo; Read, for your Lord is most beneficent, Who taught by the pen, Taught man what he did not know" (96:1–5).

50. Régis Blachère, trans., *Le Coran* (Paris: Maisonneuve & Larose, 1980), 46.

51. Benslama, *La nuit brisée,* 172ff.

52. Dagorn, *La geste d'Ismaël,* 202.

53. Ibn Qutayba, "Kitāb al-'arab," in *Rasā'il al-bulagā* (Cairo: Lajmat al-Ta'līf wa-al-Tarjamah wa-al-Nashr, 1954), 536.

54. Ibn Garsiya, quoted in Dagorn, *La geste d'Ismaël,* 229.

55. Tabari, *De la création à David,* in *La chronique: Histoire des prophètes et des rois,* trans. Hermann Zotenberg (Arles, France: Actes Sud-Sindbad, 1984), 144.

56. Ibid., 148–49.


## 3. Destinies of the Other Woman

1. "Disavowal" *(désaveu)* is one of the possible translations of Freud's *Verleugnung.* I base my reading on a text by Claude Rabant, which shows the complexity of the concept and distinguishes four different senses: denial *(le*

*démenti*), disavowal *(le désaveu)*, abjuration/refusal *(le déni)*, and repudiation *(la répudiation)*. Rabant offers the following definition of *désaveu:* "Failure to recognize as one's own, to claim one did not say or do something." Claude Rabant, *Inventer le réel* (Paris: Denoël, 1992), 79ff.

2. Philippe Lévy correctly notes that disavowal concerns genealogical attachment. See "Le ban du lieu," in *Y a-t-il une psychopathologie des banlieues?* ed. Jean-Jacques Rassial (Ramonville Saint-Agne, France: Érès, 1998).

3. *Référence* is a concept that Pierre Legendre developed to designate the mythical place of the provenance of the law, a place generally presented by a name. This place harbors a treasury of signifiers, images, emblems, and so on. See *L'inestimable objet de la transmission* (Paris: Fayard, 1985), 178ff. The implications of *Référence* with respect to the foundations of reason are examined in *La 901ᵉ conclusion* (Paris: Fayard, 1998).

4. This reflects Hegel's schema in *Phenomenology of Spirit,* according to which it is the slave who mediates the master's *jouissance.* The latter is related to the thing only through the intermediary of the slave, who "behaves negatively with respect to the thing and suppresses it." But the thing is independent and cannot be eliminated, just as the slave can only transform it into an object of desire. However, the structure of the between-two-women, as a structure of originary difference, goes beyond this schema. I'll return to this idea later. G. W. F. Hegel, *Phenomenology of Spirit,* trans. A. V. Miller (London: Oxford University Press, 1979).

5. I discuss this episode in *La nuit brisée: Muhammad et l'énonciation islamique* (Paris: Ramsay, 1988), 184. I have borrowed several ideas from it, which I have used to illustrate the hypothesis of the other woman.

6. These authors, considered to be the principal biographical sources for the Prophet, are Muhammad Ibn Ishaq, *Sirat Ibn Ishaq* (seventh century), based on several manuscripts (Maison d'édition et de diffusion de Konya, Turkey, 1981); Ibn Hicham, *Assayrat an-nabawyya* (Beirut: Dar al-ma'rifa, n.d.), vol. 2; and Tabari, *Tarikh ar-rusul wa al-muluk,* translated as *Muhammad sceau des prophètes* (Paris: Sindbad, 1980).

7. This story is told in nearly the same terms by Ibn Ishaq, in *Sirat Ibn Ishaq,* 23; and by Ibn Hicham, in *Assayrat an-nabawyya,* 1:164. According to tradition, Waraqa was a learned Christian who was the first to recognize in Muhammad the *nomos* revealed to Moses.

8. Tabari, *Tarikh ar-rusul wa al-muluk,* 56.

9. Freud's approach incorporates the analysis found in "Family Romances," *SE,* 9:235–41 (1908–1909), also published in Otto Rank's *The Myth of the Birth of the Hero: A Psychological Interpretation of Mythology,* trans. F. Robbins and Smith Ely Jelliffe (New York: Brunner, 1952), and originally published as "Der Familienroman der Neurotiker," in Rank's *Der Mythus von der Geburt des Helden: Versuch einer psychologischen Mythendeutung* (Leipzig: F. Deuticke, 1909), 64–68.

10. Jacques Lacan, "The Signification of the Phallus," in *Écrits: The First Complete Edition in English*, trans. Bruce Fink (New York: Norton, 2006), 583.

11. Jacques Derrida indicates that this expression is not Lacan's. He apparently borrowed it from Heidegger, who took it from Plotinus, without either of them citing the source. "Fidélité à plus d'un," *Cahiers Intersignes* 13 (1998): 237.

12. The word *economy* is a borrowing from the Greek *oikonomos*, which is derived from *oikos*, "house," and *nomos*, "rule, custom, law."

13. Jacques Berque, trans., *Le Coran* (Paris: Albin Michel, 1990), 705. Youssef Seddik has examined this question in his doctoral thesis in anthropology, "L'enfance grecque du Coran" (École des hautes études en sciences sociales, 1995).

14. Michèle Montrelay, *L'ombre et le nom* (Paris: Éditions de Minuit, 1977).

15. Michèle Montrelay, "Entretien avec Madeleine Chapsal," in *La jalousie*, by Madeleine Chapsal (Paris: Gallimard, 1977), 142–73.

16. From the point of view of the genesis of the subject, 1 precedes 0. Pierre Legendre considers this binary function and the position of the void as the very foundation of reason. A binary relation is not the same as a "dual" one, and for good reason, given that the bar of the Third is present. See *La 901ᵉ conclusion*, 209ff.

17. Recall that with Hagar, there is a knowledge of alterity through sight and through naming. The other woman would, in a sense, be the starting point for the formation of a speculative theory, a metaphysics, our witch of metapsychology.

18. This idea of interval as temporality is found in a text by Pierre Fédida, appropriately titled "Le vide de la métaphore et le temps de l'intervalle," in *L'absence* (Paris: Gallimard, 1978), 197–238.

19. Concerning these lines by Apollinaire, see Claude Lévi-Strauss, "Une petite énigme mythico-littéraire," *Le Temps de la Réflexion* 1 (1980): 133–41.

20. François Bayrou: "Depending on whether we will have defended our ideal or abandoned it, in ten, twenty years, the face of France, the place of Islam, of Muslim women, will no longer be the same." Interview in the newspaper *Libération*, October 10, 1994.

21. The reference is to Bayrou's decree banning the ostentatious display of religious symbols in French schools: ". . . the minister of education, François Bayrou, decreed on September 20, 1994, that 'ostentatious' signs of religious affiliation would henceforth be prohibited in all schools." See Joan Wallach Scott, *The Politics of the Veil* (Princeton: Princeton University Press, 2007), 27.

22. Concerning the sign and the hand, and the relation between monstration and monstrosity, see Jacques Derrida, "La main de Heidegger," in *Psyché* (Paris: Galilée, 1987), 415–51.

23. Jean-Jacques Delfour, "François Bayrou, censeur sémiologique," *Libération*, October 20, 1994, 7.

24. Mohamed H. Benkheira, in *L'amour de la loi* (Paris: Presses Universitaires de France, 1977), has begun to trace the entire theological corpus associated with the veil and shows how it is an institution.

25. See, for example, the entry "hajaba" in the encyclopedic dictionary by Ibn Manzūr, *Lisān al-'Arab* (Beirut: Dar Lisān al-'Arab), 1:567; and in Acharif Al-Jurjani, *Le livre des définitions* (Beirut, 1977), 82, where we read, "*Al-hajb,* in contemporary use, that which is forbidden."

26. Abdelwahab Bouhdiba, *La sexualité en Islam* (Paris: Presses Universitaires de France, 1975), 50.

27. Quoted in ibid., 45.

28. Jacques Lacan, in Seminar 11, refers to a crushing gaze that reduces one to shame: "not a gaze that has been seen, but a gaze imagined by me in the field of the Other." *The Four Fundamental Concepts of Psychoanalysis,* trans. Alan Sheridan (New York: Norton, 1998).

29. See Serge Tisseron and Mounira Khémir, *Gaëtan Gatian de Clérambault: Psychiatre et photographe* (Paris: Les Empecheurs de penser en rond, 1990).

30. Ayyam Wassef, "L'oeil et la nuit," *Cahiers Intersignes* 6–7 (1993): 217–24.

31. Ibn Hazm (994–1014), *Tawq al-hamama* (Beirut: Dar maktabat al-hayat, 1982), 210. See *The Ring of the Dove,* trans. A. J. Arberry (London: Luzac Oriental, 1997).

32. In the French translation of the *Ring of the Dove,* L. Bercher emphasizes this when he writes, "They play with the pupil." Quoted in Bouhdiba, *La sexualité en Islam.*

33. Asma Gmati, a student in Paris, letter in *Libération,* November 18, 1994.

34. Annie Jaubert, "Les femmes dans l'écriture," *Revue Chrétienne* 219:2–16.

35. Georges Bataille, "The Pineal Eye," reprinted in *Visions of Excess: Selected Writings, 1927–1939,* Theory and History of Literature 14 (Minneapolis: University of Minnesota Press, 1985).

36. Michel Surya, in his *Georges Bataille, la mort à l'oeuvre* (Paris: Gallimard, 1970), 137–41, has shown how the fantasy of the eye, which has a sinister biographical provenance, was at work in the author's psychoanalysis and in his writing.

37. All these meanings are found in Manzūr's *Lisān al-'Arab,* in the entry for "baraja," 1:184–85.

38. Ibn Arabi, *Les gemmes de la sagesse* [Fusus al-Hikam], translated as *La sagesse des prophètes* by Titus Burckhardt (Paris: Albin Michel, 1974), 27. See *The Bezels of Wisdom,* trans. R. W. J. Austin (New York: Paulist Press, 1980).

39. I wrote about this scene for the first time in *La nuit brisée.* Because of its significance, I return to it here, together with some additional material.

40. Tabari, *Muhammad sceau des prophètes,* 65–66. There are many versions of this scene, but all of them preserve the basic structure given here.

41. Ibn Hicham, *Assayrat an-nabawyya,* 3:309–16; and Tabari, ibid., 237–42.

42. Tabari, ibid., 221–23.

43. Ibid., 78–79.

44. Zhor Benchemsi and Okba Natahi comment on this in "Le féminin et la question du savoir dans la civilisation arabo-islamique," *Psychanalystes* 40 (1991): 73.

45. It is not only theological discourse that illustrates man's unease; the same can be found in philosophy, Nietzsche being one example. See Jacques Derrida, *Spurs: Nietzsche's Style,* trans. Barbara Harlow (Chicago: University of Chicago Press, 1981). Psychoanalytic discourse is equally culpable, as characterized by Freud and his well-known remark about the "dark continent." See "Female Sexuality," *SE,* 21:221–43; and "Femininity," in *New Introductory Lectures on Psychoanalysis, SE,* 22:1–182.

46. Martin Heidegger, "De l'essence de la vérité" (1954), trans. A. de Waelhens and W. Biemel, in *Question I* (Paris: Gallimard, 1968).

47. Pierre Legendre points out this idea in *Les enfants du texte* (Paris: Fayard, 1993).

48. Claude Lévi-Strauss, *Tristes tropiques,* trans. John Weightman and Doreen Weightman (London: Penguin, 1992), 408–9.

49. See Ibn Ishaq, *Sirat Ibn Ishaq.*

50. Ibn Arabi, *Fusus al-Hikam,* 139. See *Bezels of Wisdom.*

51. Pierre Legendre, "La phalla-cieuse," in *La jouissance et la loi* (Paris: UGE, 10/18, 1976), 9–31.

52. This expression is only one of many examples of the analogy between reading and conception. See the entry "qara'" in Manzūr, *Lisān al-'Arab,* 3:42–44.

53. On the verb "to read," see my analysis in *La nuit brisée,* 83–92. But there I had not yet made use of the concept of feminine *jouissance* in formulating my arguments.

54. Jacques Lacan, *On Feminine Sexuality: The Limits of Love and Knowledge,* trans. Bruce Fink, Seminar of Jacques Lacan 20 (New York: Norton, 1998). Although Lacan specifically addresses the question in this essay, from this point on the problem of *jouissance* takes center stage in Lacan's work. See Nestor Braunstein, *La jouissance* (Paris: Point Hors Ligne, 1992).

55. G. W. F. Hegel, *The Philosophical Propaedeutic,* trans. A. V. Miller (Oxford: Blackwell, 1986).

56. See Abdelwahab Meddeb, "Épiphanie et jouissance," *Cahiers Intersignes* 6–7 (1992).

57. Abdelkébir Khatibi, *De la mille et troisième nuit* (Paris: Éditions Mazarine, 1979).

58. Gilbert Grandguillaume, "Jalousie et envie dans *Les mille et une nuits,"* *Che Vuoi* 6 (1997): 53–67. This article is the culmination of an inquiry that involved several researchers: see Gilbert Grandguillaume and François Villa, "*Les mille et une nuits:* La parole délivrée par le conte," *Psychanalyses* 33 (1989); and Jacqueline Guy-Heineman, "Les nuits parlent aux hommes de leur destin," *Corps Écrit* 31 (1989).

59. Jamel Eddine Bencheikh, *Les mille et une nuits; ou, La parole prisonnière* (Paris: Gallimard, 1989), 25–27.

60. Husain Haddawy, trans., *The Arabian Nights* (New York: Everyman's Library, 1992), 3.

61. Pierre Fédida, "Le narrateur mis à mort par son récit," in *L'absence*, 49.

62. This sequence corresponds to what Lacan has written concerning female *jouissance:* "If there is no virility that castration does not consecrate, it is a castrated lover or dead man (or the two in one) who, for woman, hides behind the veil in order to call her adoration to it." See Jacques Lacan, "Guiding Remarks for a Convention on Female Sexuality," in *Écrits,* 617, translated from "Pour un congrès sur la sexualité féminine," in *Écrits* (Paris: Seuil, 1966), 733.

63. René Major insightfully notes, "From this point on, the masculine should be considered from the feminine point of view." See "Le non-lieu de la femme," preface to *Le désir et le feminine,* by Wladmir Granoff and François Perrier (Paris: Aubier, 1991), 13.

64. Haddawy, *Arabian Nights,* 16.

## 4. Within Himself

1. In his race with the hare, the hedgehog devises a stratagem whereby he hides his wife, who is indistinguishable from the husband as far as the hare is concerned, near the finish line. The hedgehog only pretends to run the race, however, and remains at the starting line. No matter in which direction he runs, the hare always finds a hedgehog waiting for him at the finish line crying, "I'm here already!" Martin Heidegger, "The Onto-theological Constitution of Metaphysics," in *Identity and Difference,* trans. Joan Stambaugh (Chicago: University of Chicago Press, 2002), 63.

2. Antoine Galland, trans., *Les mille et une nuits* (Paris: GF-Flammarion, 1965), 1:255.

3. Ibid., 2:256.

4. Gilles Deleuze, *Essays Critical and Clinical,* trans. Daniel W. Smith and Michael A. Greco (Minneapolis: University of Minnesota Press, 1997).

5. Martin Heidegger, "Es gibt Sein nur je und je in dieser und jener geschicklichen Prägung..." See "Onto-theological Constitution of Metaphysics," 66.

6. Georges Devereux, *Essais d'ethnopsychiatrie générale* (Paris: Gallimard, 1970). The pathological is the subject of his article "Normal et anormal."

7. I borrow the term *logia* from Heidegger. It appears in the text cited earlier, "Onto-theological Constitution of Metaphysics," where he uses the term to avoid confusion with the logic of scientific knowledge and to designate a set of rational foundational relationships.

8. I would like to remind readers of the *hadith* "Women lack reason and religion."

9. Jacques Lacan, *Les quatre concepts fondamentaux de la psychanalyse* (Paris: Seuil, 1973), 185–208. See *The Four Fundamental Concepts of Psychoanalysis*, trans. Alan Sheridan, Seminar of Jacques Lacan 11 (New York: Norton, 1998).

10. Quoted by Abdelwahab Bouhdiba, *La sexualité en Islam* (Paris: Presses Universitaires de France, 1975), 96.

11. Nadia Tazi, "Le désert perpétuel, visage de la virilité au Maghreb," "La virilité en Islam," special issue, *Cahiers Intersignes* 11–12 (1998): 25–57.

12. We could also analyze from this point of view the (certainly unwarlike) figure of virginal love *('udrite)* that has assumed considerable importance in Arab poetry.

13. See my discussion with Jean-Joseph Goux, Lucien Mélèse, Georg Garner, and Philippe Réfabert, whom I wish to thank for their comments, in *Les travaux d'Oedipe,* ed. Claude Dubarry and Jean-Joseph Goux (Paris: L'Harmattan, 1997), 55–64.

14. Jean-Joseph Goux, *Oedipe philosophe* (Paris: Aubier, 1990).

15. Philippe Lacoue-Labarthe, "Oedipe comme figure," in *L'imitation des modernes* (Paris: Galilee, 1986).

16. Francis Ponge, *Méthodes* (Paris: Gallimard, 1961), 164–65.

17. To be more specific, the sentence rendered by Jean Hyppolite is: "For the child the parents are: *'der sich aufhebende Ursprung,'* the self-suppressing origin." G. W. F. Hegel, *Phénoménologie de l'esprit,* trans. Jean Hyppolite (Paris: Aubier, 1941), 2:24.

18. *Webster's Ninth New Collegiate Dictionary,* s.v. "pretext."

19. Jean Laplanche and Jean-Baptiste Pontalis, *Fantasme originaire, fantasmes des origines, origines du fantasme* (1964; repr., Paris: Hachette, 1985).

20. See the recent work done by Monique Schneider, *Généalogie du masculin* (Paris: Aubier, 2000), which intersects certain aspects of my argument. The book appeared too late for me to make use of her research, however.

21. It seems that, concerning this point, the Koran refers, for its own purposes, to the version of one of the Arabic Judeo-Christian communities extant at the time of revelation, which maintained the thesis of substitution by someone resembling Jesus. The apocryphal gospel of Barnabas makes use of this idea, putting Judas in the place of Jesus.

22. Ibn Arabi, "De la sagesse sainte dans le verbe d'Enoch" [The Wisdom of Holiness in the Word of Enoch], in *The Bezels of Wisdom,* trans. R. W. J. Austin (New York: Paulist Press, 1980), 82.

23. Ibid., 87–88.

24. Ibid.

25. Al-Kafaoui (Abi Al-Baka), *Al-Kulliyat* [The Generalities] (seventeenth century) (Damascus, 1981), 1:15.

26. Quoted by Annajar Abdelwahab, *Qasas al-anbiya* [The Stories of the Prophets] (Cairo: Dar al-ilm, n.d.), 156–57.

27. Nābulūsī Abd al-Ghanī, *Ta'tīr al-anām fi ta'bīr al-manām* [The Perfume of Creatures in the Interpretation of Dreams] (Beirut: Grande librairie commerciale, n.d.), 218.

28. Tabari, *Extrait de la chronique: De la création à David,* trans. Hermann Zotenberg (Paris: Sindbad, 1984), 250.

29. According to the Koran, Moses's sister follows and monitors the movement along the Nile of Moses's ark, and then suggests to the Pharaoh's wife that she take in Moses's mother as nurse. "[Moses's mother] said to the sister [of Moses]: Follow him. She stayed out of sight and observed him and no one saw her" (20:39). "[His sister] said: can I show you a family that will take care of him for you and be devoted to him?" [The translation by Ahmed Ali at 20:39, reads, "We bestowed Our love on you that you may be reared under Our eyes." The text at 20:40 reads, "Then your sister followed you, and said (to the people who had retrieved the child), 'Should I guide you to a person who can nurse him?'" — Trans.]

30. Ibn Arabi, *Les gemmes de la sagesse,* 163. My French translation differs slightly from Burckhardt's text. See *The Bezels of Wisdom,* trans. R. W. J. Austin, ed. Titus Burckhardt (Paulist Press, 1980).

31. Ibid. My translation.

32. See René Major's comments in *Au commencement: La vie la mort* (Paris: Galilée, 1999).

33. I am referring to the translation of the Koran by Régis Blachère (Paris: Maisonneuve & Larose, 1980). [Please note that the English translations of the Koran presented here are by Ahmed Ali (Princeton, N.J.: Princeton University Press, 1993). — Trans.]

34. This calls to mind the primordial couple imagined by Plato in *The Banquet,* found in numerous myths throughout the world, such as those of the Dogons. See Geneviève Calame-Griaule, *La parole chez les Dogons* (Paris: Gallimard, NRF, 1965), 94ff.

35. "The innocence of the *flower religions,* which is merely the selfless idea of self, gives place to the earnestness of warring life, to the guilt of *animal religions* ; the passivity and impotence of contemplative individuality pass into destructive being-for-self." G. W. F. Hegel, *Phenomenology of Spirit,* trans. A. V. Miller (Oxford: Oxford University Press, 1977), 420.

36. Abou Ali Ibn Miskawayh (944–1020), *Thadīb al-akhlāq wa-tathīr al-a'rāq,* translated as *Traité d'éthique* by Mohamed Arkoun (Damascus: Éditions de l'Institut français de Damas, 1969). The translation of the passage quoted in the text is my own.

37. Plato, *Timaeus,* 49c–53c.

38. On the *'uns,* see Hachem Foda, "En compagnie," *Cahiers Intersignes* 13 (1998): 15–39.

39. Miskawayh, *Traité d'éthique,* 224.

40. Djemil Saliba, *Al-mu'jam al-falsfī* [Arabic Philosophical Dictionary] (Beirut: Dar al-Kitāb, 1972), 2:527.

41. Émile Benveniste, *Problèmes de linguistique générale* (Paris: Gallimard, 1966), 1:190. See *Problems in General Linguistics*, trans. Mary Elizabeth Meek (Coral Gables, Fla.: University of Miami Press, 1971), 165.

42. Ibn Arabi, *Bezels of Wisdom*.

43. Avicenna, *Métaphysique de la Najat* (Cairo: Librairie arabe, 1975), 365.

44. Al-Farabi, quoted in Saliba, *Al-mu'jam al-falsfī*, 2:527.

45. See Averroës, *Tafasīr mā ba'da at-tabī'a* (Cairo: Librairie arabe, 1969), a commentary on Aristotle's *Metaphysics*.

46. *Walad* has two possible meanings: a first, general meaning, "the engendered," or "child"; and a second meaning, "son" of "Wālid," who can be the genitor, or father. Here, I have followed Mohamed Arkoun (in his translation of Miskawayh, *Traité d'éthique*), in using "son" and "father," but it is also possible to translate these as "engendered" and "genitor," respectively.

47. See Foda, "En compagnie."

48. Ibn Arabi, *Bezels of Wisdom*.

49. Ibn Manzūr, *Lisān al-'Arab* (Beirut: Dar Lisān al-'Arab), 1:114.

50. Saliba, *Al-mu'jam al-falsfī*, 2:9139.

51. Al-Jurjani (Acharif), *Kitāb at-a'rifāt* [The Book of Definitions] (Beirut, 1977), 166.

52. These developments are remarkably summarized by Souad Alhakīm, in *Lexique du soufisme* (Beirut: Dandra, 1981), 873–75.

53. Al-Jurjani, *Kitāb at-a'rifāt*, 146.

54. I am referring to the work of Étienne Balibar, especially to an essay that touches upon this very point, namely, his "Sujétions et libérations," *Cahiers Intersignes* 8–9 (1994): 79–90.

55. Avicenna, *Risala fī al-hudūd* (Cairo: Éditions du Caire, n.d.), 83.

56. "Après le sujet qui vient" was the title of a wonderful collection of essays in a special issue of the review *Confrontation*, no. 20 (1989), under the editorial direction of Jean-Luc Nancy.

57. Élisabeth Roudinesco, *Généalogie* (Paris: Fayard, 1994), 82–85.

58. I have begun to address these issues in the following two articles: "La dépropriation," *Lignes* 24 (1995): 34–83; and "L'oubli de l'éthique," *Che Vuoi* 10 (1998): 121–43.

59. The quotation from Georges Bataille appears in Maurice Blanchot's *The Unavowable Community*, trans. Pierre Joris (Barrytown, N.Y.: Station Hill Press, 1988), 5. But Michel Surya, who checked the context of the sentence, realized that it was incorrect. "There exists a principle of insufficiency at the root of human life," wrote Bataille, in his *Oeuvres complètes*. All the same, I quote the sentence the way it appears in Blanchot.

60. Bataille's and Blanchot's arguments have been developed with the help of Jean-Luc Nancy's *La communauté désoeuvrée* (Paris: Christian Bourgois, 1985).

61. Jacques Derrida, "Le retrait de la métaphore," in *Psyché: Inventions de l'autre* (Paris: Galilée, 1987), 63–93. See *Psyche: Inventions of the Other*, vol. 1,

ed. Peggy Kamuf and Elizabeth Rottenberg (Stanford, Calif.: Stanford University Press, 2007).

62. I am using "distress" rather than the "helpless" given by the standard translation.

63. Wilhelm Reich, *The Mass Psychology of Fascism*, trans. Theodore P. Wolfe, 3rd ed. (New York: Orgone Institute Press, 1946).

64. See Salim Daccache, "La notion d'umma dans le Coran," *Annales de Philosophie* (Tunis) 3 (1982): 1038.

65. Jalal-uddin Rumi was one of the great masters of Sufism. He created a path known as the "al-mawlawya," which incorporated music and dance, including the famous cosmic dance known as the dance of the whirling dervishes. Rumi's work focuses on three key terms: *love, secrecy,* and *speech.* That is why he developed a method of treating mental illness that consisted in asking the subject to lie down, holding his hand, and having him free-associate, using words chosen from his speech. See Éva de Vitray-Meyrovitch, *Rumi et le soufisme* (Paris: Seuil, 1977).

66. Arab-speaking readers can consult the entry on *shaya'a* in Ibn Manzūr, *Lisān al-'Arab,* 2:393–95. In French, the etymology can be found in Albert de Biberstein-Kazimirski, *Dictionnaire arabe-français* (Paris: Maison-neuve et cie, 1860), vol. 1.

67. "Wa tashaya'a fī ash-shay'i: istahlaka fī hawā'ihi."


### Epilogue

1. I refer readers to my commentary on this text, "La décision d'Averroès," in Colloque de Cordoue, *Ibn Rochd, Maïmonide, saint Thomas* (Paris: Climats, 1994), 65–74.

2. Friedrich Nietzsche, *The Will to Power,* trans. Walter Kaufmann (Vintage, 1968), 327.

# Index

abandonment: from the abandoned (woman) to, 104–5; capacity for illusion based on infantile despair of, 22; gift and, 73–75, 105; Muhammad's experiences of, 12, 19, 105

Abdallah, Anouar, 219n25

Abdelwahab, Annajar, 233n26

abduction: in Freud, 11–12

Abdullah (Prophet's father), 112–15, 117, 180; glow (signifier) on face of, 112, 113, 114–15, 118, 119, 120–21

Abel, Cain's murder of, 189–94; psychoanalytic view of, 193; two hatreds involved in, 190–94

Abimelech, King, 86

Abraham, 79–98; abandonment of Hagar and Ishmael, 73–74; change of name from Abram to Abraham, 83; as "Father-of-Genesis," 72–75, 78; nostalgia for father organized into doctrine of return to religious and paternal origin of, 104; reconciliation with Ishmael, 103–4, 107–8; repudiation of Ishmael's wife by, 107–8; return to, 69; sacrifice of, 178–80; split between two principles of origin in family of, 89–91

abrogation of origin, 23–29, 49; comparing abolition of the Law in Alamut to, 27–28; return and interpretation, 24–25; return, theory, and delusion, 25–29

absolute *jouissance*, 151–52, 169, 176

abstraction, 34

absurd sense in Koran, 46–47, 222n58

actuality of religion, 22–23

Adam: Islamic version of Adam and Eve, 138–39; response to Cain-Abel conflict, 189, 192–93

adoption: in Islamic law, 217n3, 226n32

adoration (*'ibāda* or religion): principle of, 201

Afary, Janet, 223n72

*Ahram, Al-* (Egyptian daily), 185

Aisha (Muhammad's favorite wife), 137

Alamut: abolition of the Law proclaimed in (1164), 27–28

Algeria: FIS (Front islamique du salut, or Islamic Salvation Front), 39; FLN regime in, 38–39; GIA (Armed Islamic Group), 71

Alhakīm, Souad, 235n52

Ali (Prophet's son-in-law): in allegory of community, 207–8; Sunni-Shia difference over status of, 209

Ali, Imam, 128

alienation, 215; leading to madness, process of, 168–96; of mankind from the essence of his being, 53

allegory of community, 206–9, 211

*al-mawlawya*, 236n65

ambiguity, fundamental, 175

**Fethi Benslama** is a psychoanalyst and professor of psychopathology at the University of Jussieu, Paris VII. He is the founding editor of *Intersignes*, a French-language journal of psychoanalysis and culture, and the author of many books on psychoanalysis and Islam, including *La nuit brisée* and *Une fiction troublante.*

**Robert Bononno** has translated more than a dozen books, including Albert Memmi's *Decolonization and the Decolonized* (Minnesota, 2006). He has taught translation at New York University and at the Graduate Center of the City University of New York.